I0102482

European Policy Analysis

Also from Westphalia Press

westphaliapress.org

European Policy Analysis

Volume 2, Number 2
Fall 2016

Edited by

Nils Bandelow, Peter Biegelbauer,
Fritz Sager & Klaus Schubert

WESTPHALIA PRESS
An imprint of Policy Studies Organization

European Policy Analysis 2.2, Fall 2016
All Rights Reserved © 2017 by Policy Studies Organization

Westphalia Press
An imprint of Policy Studies Organization
1527 New Hampshire Ave., NW
Washington, D.C. 20036
info@ipsonet.org

ISBN-13: 978-1-63391-524-4
ISBN-10: 1-63391-524-7

Cover design by Jeffrey Barnes:
jbarnesbook.design

Daniel Gutierrez-Sandoval, Executive Director
PSO and Westphalia Press

Updated material and comments on this edition
can be found at the Westphalia Press website:
www.westphaliapress.org

Table of Contents
EPA Vol. 2 No. 2 (Fall 2016)

SPECIAL FOCUS: DEMOGRAPHIC CHANGE AND HEALTH CARE IN EUROPE

WHY YOU SHOULD READ MY BOOK

Volume 2, Number 2 - Winter 2016

European Policy Analysis (EPA)
Editorial Board & Editors

Editorial Board

Jolanta Aidukaite, Lithuanian Social Research Centre, Lithuania
Andreas Balthasar, University of Lucerne, Switzerland
Sonja Blum, Vienna University of Economics and Business, Austria
Nissim Cohen, University of Haifa, School of Political Sciences, Israel
Claire Dunlop, University of Exeter, United Kingdom
Jakob Edler, University of Manchester, Manchester Business School, United Kingdom
Iris Geva-May, Baruch College, City University of New York, USA
Hanne Foss Hansen, University of Copenhagen, Denmark
Patrick Hassenteufel, University of Versailles St. Quentin-en-Yveline, France
Simon Hegelich, Technical University of Munich, Bavarian School of Public Policy, Germany
Karin Ingold, University of Bern, Switzerland
Nicole Kerschen, Luxemburg Institute for Socio-Economic Research, Luxemburg
Tanja Klenk, University of Kassel, Germany
Martino Maggetti, University of Lausanne, Switzerland
Miroslav Mareš, Masaryk University, Brno, Czech Republic
Ive Marx, University of Antwerp, Belgium
David Natali, University of Bologna, Italy
Daniel Nohrstedt, University of Uppsala, Sweden
Jose António Correira Pereirinha, University of Lisbon, Portugal
Claudio Radaelli, University of Exeter, United Kingdom
Friedbert Rüb, Humboldt University, Berlin, Germany
James Sloam, Royal Holloway, University of London, United Kingdom
Rumiana Stoilova, Academy of Sciences, Sofia, Bulgaria
Minna van Gerven, University of Twente, The Netherlands
Frans van Nispen tot Pannerden, Erasmus University Rotterdam, The Netherlands
Josef Schmid, University of Tübingen, Germany
Frédéric Varone, University of Geneva, Switzerland
Hubert Zimmermann, Philipps University of Marburg, Germany

Editors

Nils Bandelow, University of Braunschweig, Germany; nils.bandelow@tu-braunschweig.de
Peter Biegelbauer, Austrian Institute of Technology, Austria; peter.biegelbauer@ait.ac
Fritz Sager, University of Bern, Switzerland; fritz.sager@kpm.unibe.ch
Klaus Schubert, University of Muenster, Germany; klaus.schubert@uni-muenster.de

Editorial Assistants

Kate Backhaus, University of Muenster, Germany; kateback@uni-muenster.de
Johanna Hornung, University of Braunschweig, Germany; j.hornung@tu-braunschweig.de

European Policy Analysis - Volume 2, Number 2 - Winter 2016

Understanding Brexit

Kurt Hübner[A]

They did it, and now the UK and its current, as well as future, European partners have to deal with a situation only a few observers were actually expecting to happen. All had to learn the hard way, that neither traditional political pollsters nor the London bookies were correctly anticipating the outcome of the referendum of June 23rd, and it seems that even the "Brexiteers" were surprised by the choice of the voters (Sapir 2016). The business of vote forecasting in times of political polarization is a difficult one, and has become even more difficult with the change of people from analogue to digital technologies. The outcome of the referendum indicates that the leave camp was extremely successful in dissipating an overwhelmingly converging expert view of negative economic effects, medium term as well as long-term, of a Brexit. Moreover, giving the then PM Cameron and his treasurer Osborne the opportunity to be 'the' stay proponents was not helping the stay camp at all, as voters were well aware of the negativism of both politicians toward the EU. Nor was the weak and very undecided position of the Labour leaders that left traditional Labour voters in the unknown about the preferences of their party. The pro-leave majority may have not been an overwhelming victory but a result of close to 52% of all votes still handed the Brexit faction a strong mandate to bid farewell to the EU.

A strong mandate, though, does not mean that Brexit will happen soon. As a matter of fact, the newly configured British government may wait for quite a while until it is ready and willing to trigger article 50 of the TFEU (Treaty on the Functioning of the European Union). This postponement reflects, on the one side, the enormous complexity of the task at hand and, on the other side, the strategic consideration on the side of the British government that hopes for some EU-tiredness of old and—after the next election round—potentially new governments in core EU countries. Given the political mood in countries like Germany, France, and Italy—to name a few—such a Brexit-approach actually may be a realistic way to get as many concessions as possible from the side of the European Council. More so, the delay in triggering article 50 also reflects the fact that the main proponents seem not have had a convincing and operative plan how to actually leave the EU and what kind of relations should be put in place with its European partners. In this regard, it was a strategically wise decision by PM May to hand responsibilities for the operation Brexit into the hands of three main "Brexiteers". If they will not succeed in coming up with at least a cost-neutral hard Brexit, then she always can make the case for a soft Brexit. To keep this

[A] Institute for European Studies, University of British Columbia, Canada

doi: 10.18278/epa.2.2.1

option open, Theresa May, of course, needs first to exploit all pathways for a successful hard Brexit. This seems to imply that a debate in the Parliament about Brexit and the modalities for leaving the EU will not take place.

Brexit: The Who and The Why

The UK was a latecomer to the EU, not least due to the political-ideological heritage of its imperial past that dominated thinking in the early 1950s. The main reason for its early skepticism toward European integration can be seen in the British liberal economic narrative where it needs simple trade arrangement in order to achieve economic growth and prosperity. Given that the EU, with the Treaty of Rome, more or less began already as a customs union rather than as a free trade area, it was thus no real surprise that the British political class did not opt to join this newly created club at the very start. In this sense, the UK's decision for a strong EFTA rather than for a customs union was nothing other than an early indication that the UK was not interested in giving up parts of its sovereignty in exchange for an open trade area. Skepticism toward the project of European integration was not a monopoly of one political party but for a while widely shared across the party spectrum. Unlike in the cases of Labour and the Liberals, though, skepticism and open rejection of European integration found a comfortable home in the Conservative Party. The strong, very vocal, and for the government indispensable critical minority of Conservative MPs never hesitated to utter their hostile views, thus fostering a line of British nativism that eventually

could successfully be picked up by UKIP. What was for a long time a rumbling concern about the too big bureaucracy in Brussels, which intruded on British sovereignty, quickly centered on a radical anti-migration stance that saw the influx of foreigners as the ultimate cause of unemployment, welfare state failures and an overall feeling of a loss of social and cultural security. And yet, immigration may have topped the public debates but it was not highly relevant for the actual voting decisions: The connection between the number of immigrants in the overall 380 local authorities and the number of leave-votes is rather loose and not at all significant in a statistically meaningful way (Johnston, Jones, and Manley 2016). As a matter of fact, immigrants tend to be attracted to relatively dynamic regions, and those regions/cities overall tended to have high remain-vote shares.

According to Google Trends the second most searched question in the UK following the results of the vote was "What is the EU?", followed closely by "Which countries are in the EU?". This flashlight is as funny as it is disturbing, and nourishes the interpretation that voters used the referendum as a welcome opportunity to express their frustration and rage about a loss of faith in their future. That the EU is a well-known object of rejection and even hatred is not unique to the UK; as a matter of fact, the EU's own Eurobarometer only recently published data that show that only a third of Europeans have trust in the institutions of the European Union (33%). Meanwhile, trust in the national political institutions is even lower; only 28% of Europeans tend to trust their national parliament. Interestingly enough, the share of UK citizens who trust the EU institutions is close to the EU average, and actually has improved between fall 2015 and spring 2016 before the referendum. What such data insinuates is a strong loss of output legitimacy of political institutions, abroad and at home. Distrust does not imply that citizens across the EU would want to leave the EU. This is only a necessary condition. It needed the steep rise of an extreme EU-hating party like UKIP and a strong contingent of parliamentarians within the ruling party to encourage PM Cameron to make an internal party conflict to a national issue (Jennings and Stoker 2016). It helped his case that the EU Commission, due to unfortunate policy decisions taken in the course of the Eurozone crises, became more and more the preferred scapegoat across the EU, in the UK as well as in other corners of the EU. Given the policy approaches of the Commission and even more so of the Council, there are plenty of good reasons to take a critical stance toward the whole project of European integration. And yet, the referendum was not so much about the real policies of the EU than about perceptions of EU policies as well as about economic situations that were mainly the result of domestic policy actions since the global financial crisis in 2008.

The leave votes came from those with quite distinct socio-economic features. First, the older the voter, the more he/she opted to leave. Second, this feature goes hand in hand with the level of education, where data shows that younger voters who have higher educational qualifications tended to opt to stay. This implies that older people with relatively lower education levels opted to leave. Third, leave votes are significantly related to the level of the poverty rate, i.e. the higher the poverty rate in a local authority, the higher the share of leave votes. A similar statistical significance holds true for the impact of income inequality in the region, i.e. the higher the level of income inequality, the higher the share of leave votes. Fourth, disposable household income was no driving variable for a leave vote but then the level of employment in a given local authority was a factor: When those units were controlled for student numbers then data show that the higher the employment rate the lower the leave share was. Fifth, political geography has been critical, given that London, Scotland, and Northern Ireland came out with a clear majority of remain votes. Provincial backwaters on average tended to opt for leave; while more globally integrated parts of England and distinct political entities (Scotland, Northern Ireland) opted for stay (Darvas 2016).

It may be an exaggeration to argue that the leave camp consists of only the "left behind" voters. Post-referendum voter data and voter questionnaires indicate that political–cultural factors also played a role for voting behavior. In other words, being in favor of a stand-alone Britain goes beyond pure economic reasons. The leave campaigners may have used all the tricks of the trade, and never hesitated to bend facts and to operate with open lies, but then all this would have been of no avail if there had not have been a sentiment on the side of critical voters who acted as a proper sounding board for the spin doctors of the leave camp. It is well known that it does not take a large number of foreigners in a region or a city for the majority to support and express strong anti-foreigner policies. In the same way, it does not need bad-intended EU policies to make the EU to be the bad boy that is responsible for everything that goes wrong in a political jurisdiction. In this sense, it is quite a paradox that a country like the UK has, on the one hand, the most unregulated economy of all OECD countries and acted on all levels as a strong supporter of hyper-globalization and, on the other hand, has not engaged in a meaningful way to deal with the fallout of such an open door approach. Already textbooks of international economics make clear that a truly liberalized economy that allows for free trade in goods and services generates winners as well as losers—that is actually the whole principle of a liberalized international division of labor (O'Rourke 2016). It is then the job of the nation-state to adequately deal with the losers. The Hicks–Kaldor criterion tells us exactly that: The gains of the winners must be sufficiently large to install a compensation scheme that would make no one worse off and at least some people better off. In other words, winners may still keep some of their gains but will cover the whole losses of the losers. This argument very much is supported by the empirical insight that, for a long time, greater international openness came with bigger governments (Rodrik 1998). Neoliberalism has cut off this connection, and this cut-off is increasingly becoming a problem for the social–political stability of open economies. The same idea holds when it comes to the free mobility of labor. Economic mainstream tells us that labor mobility generally is welfare-enhancing but usually comes with negative distributional effects (Özden and Parsons 2015). When the UK, jointly with Ireland, opted in the event of the eastern enlargement of the EU in 2004 for the immediate free movement of people, it was a decision that was very much in line with the comparative advantage principle of open economies. Brexit then is a reversal of this decision, as the UK opted for a policy that wants to combine openness for goods and services with restriction and control of labor mobility, thus violating the core principle of the common market and also rejecting basic insights of traditional trade models of mainstream economics. Worker migrants from Eastern Europe contributed to a relatively stronger labor market competition, particularly in those segments where they could benefit from the combination of good skills and low pay, but also made a critical contribution to British GDP. Rather than leaving the losers behind, an adequate policy would have been to actively improve the fate of the losers—a policy requirement that fell victim to the strong austerity policy of the Conservative government. The outcome of the referendum created the political puzzle how to keep optimum access to the critical EU market and at the same time to be in total control of the outer border. In the words of Theresa May: "Make a success of Brexit".

What Now?

Brexit means Brexit means Brexit—according to the mantra of the new British PM. And yet, the newly formed government so far neither triggered article 50 nor is it really clear what relations the UK wants to develop with the EU (Grant 2016). At this point, the UK continues to be a paying member of the EU with all its rights and duties. This situation contributed to quite some uncertainty but so far has not generated a huge economic fallout—this will only happen when eventually Brexit is under way. The outcome of the referendum caused a sharp fall in the exchange rate of the British Pound, and thus created the kind of exchange rate shield that countries with their own currencies can enjoy. It is doubtful, though, that the current exchange rate already reflects all the concerns of economic actors. A further fall is to be expected when the negotiations with the EU start. The fall of the exchange rate indicates worries of economic actors, and this is becoming relevant when it comes

inferior productivity performances over the last couple of years, but then the UK did worst, if we take deflationary Japan out of the picture. This loss of international competitiveness reflects deep-seated changes in the modalities of British capitalism and its version of financialization. Moreover, the current account deficit is not a one-time event but a structural feature of the British economy. There are quite a number of countries that can live easily with current account deficits, most prominently the US that enjoys the advantages of the dollar being the leading global currency. The British

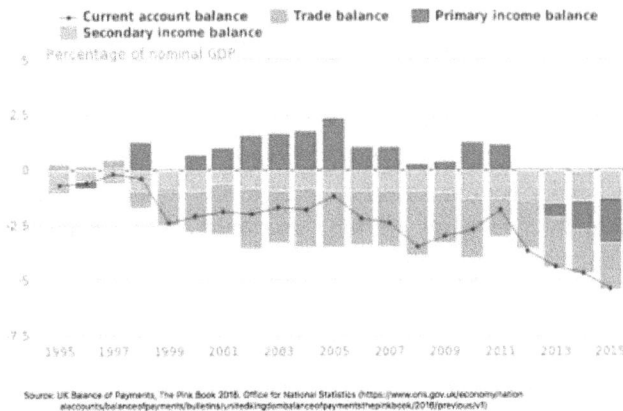

Source: UK Balance of Payments, The Pink Book 2016. Office for National Statistics (https://www.ons.gov.uk/economy/nation alaccounts/balanceofpayments/bulletins/unitedkingdombalanceofpaymentsthepinkbook/2016/previous/v1)

to the British current account.

In 2015 the UK came up with the largest current account deficit share among all G-7 economies, and as the graph shows this deficit is not only due to deficits in the primary income balance but mainly due to deficits in the trade balance. The latter can be seen as the outcome of a deteriorating international competitiveness that has its roots in the stagnation of labor productivity. As a matter of fact, all G-7 economies showed

pound, on the other hand, is a second-tier currency, and as a result it is up to the economic promises of British capitalism that international investors see the UK as a profitable regime that is worthy of receiving capital inflows. Arguably, leaving the common market may question future profitability of British capitalism.

Against this background the simplistic optimism of the leave camp that the UK will become a blooming and prospering economy when it is freed from

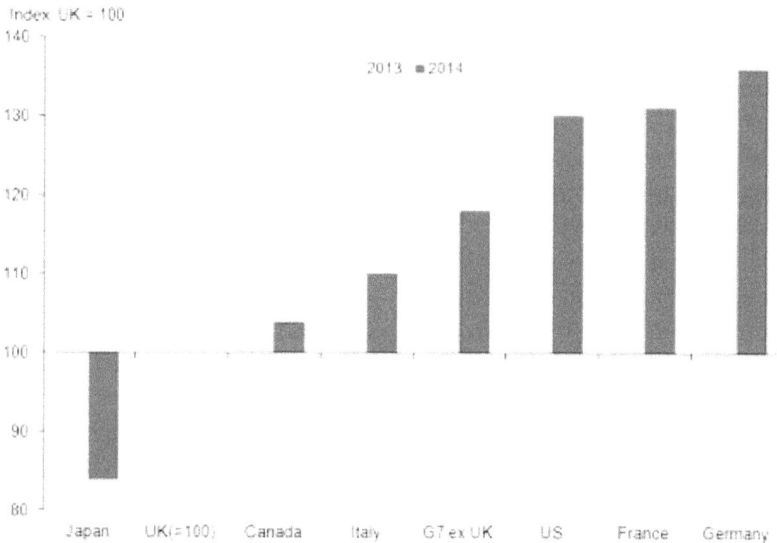

Index: UK = 100

2013 ■ 2014

Japan UK(=100) Canada Italy G7 ex UK US France Germany

Source: International Comparisons of UK Productivity (ICP), First Estimates 2015. Office for National Statistics. https://www.ons.gov.uk/econo
my/economicoutputandproductivity/productivitymeasures/bulletins/internationalcomparisonsofproductivityfirstestimates/2015

the red tape of Brussels seems more like a cry in the dark woods than a promise based on economic fundamentals. The UK for now is in a situation to deal with a further deterioration of its current account deficit that either asks for more depreciation of the British pound and/or a courageous productivity policy that eventually turns the UK into a competitive economic space. In any case, the deficit needs to be financed and this requires a steady and sufficient inflow of foreign direct investment. And this again depends on a minimum level of certainty on the side of investors, backed not least by working trade agreements that allows in particular the strong British service industries to succeed abroad.

As things stand, the UK has no chance of achieving an optimum market access to the EU without violating the core of the Brexit referendum, namely the mobility of labor. The most debated model for an EU–UK agreement is the case of Norway (De Grauwe 2016). Together with such heavy weights as Iceland, Switzerland, and Liechtenstein, Norway forms the group that makes the European Free Trade Association (EFTA); at the same time, Norway is a member of the European Economic Area (EEA), and it is through this that Norway has access to the EU. As such, Norway has to fully subscribe to the four freedoms of the EU, and this includes of course the free movement of people. Moreover, Norway has to adhere to EU laws and regulations and also to pay into the budget of the EU. Unlike the UK, Norway is not a member of the customs union and thus has the right to negotiate and sign trade agreements with any other country. Obviously, all those factors are either not covered by the Brexit vote or were not part of the pre-referendum considerations. If outer borders want to be controlled, the UK needs to take the WTO path and start to negotiate an agreement with the EU which happens to be a WTO member. Of course, such negotiations can only start after article 50 has been triggered. The UK may be able to get a CETA-like agreement that may even cover parts of the service sector, but definitely not "passporting rights" for its financial industry. However, such an agreement would still require for the UK to fulfill EU rules in terms of standards, safety, and health regulations, i.e. most of what has been labeled as "red tape" by the proponents of the leave camp. This may become even more of an issue if the EU moves along more quickly with its banking union and financial market regulations. The potential loss of the EU "passport" for financial institutions will not be the end of the City of London but would for sure generate far-reaching changes in the set-up of financial businesses, including partial re-locations. Taking the WTO path, of course, not only demands negotiations with the EU; the UK needs to apply for full membership with the WTO at the same time. Then it needs to start negotiations with the 53 countries with whom the EU currently has free trade agreements, as all those agreements will no longer apply to the UK when the country leaves the EU. It seems fair to expect that most of those potential trade partners of the UK want to know a bit more about the modalities of the future EU–UK relations.

Brexiteers may make the case that neither the Norway model nor the WTO model actually are realistic paths forwards. Rather, they are optimistic that the EU will treat the UK as a special case and will be much more willing to compromise. A hard-case special deal would be to allow the UK unlimited access to the common market and, at the same time, exempt the country from free movement of people. Of course, such a special deal is in the interest of UK but would be the self-abandonment of the EU, and thus will not happen. Given the worrisome state of the union and given national preferences of some member countries, it may well be the case that the European Council with the support of the Parliament eventually offers the UK a deal that would give the UK the right to control free movement from within the EU not only for a brief period and under certain conditions, as offered to the country pre-referendum, but for a longer period without a precise criteria catalogue. Such an offer would simulate the exemption countries like Germany and France negotiated at the time of the Eastern enlargement. Such a deal would present a bad equilibrium, though, that, on the one hand, is not reflecting the initial Brexit intentions and, on the other hand, would make the EU an even more fragile entity that is easy game of national politics. In the EU, where German Chancellor Merkel very much sets the course of the ship, such a deal should not be discarded easily, yet it would be a deal that turns the EU into an increasingly useless entity.

References

Darvas, Z. 2016. http://bruegel.org/2016/07/brexit-vote-boosts-case-for-inclusive-growth/.

De Grauwe, P. 2016. "How to Prevent Brexit from Damaging the EU." www.socialeurope.eu/2016/08/prevent-brexit-damaging-eu/. Grant, Ch. 2016. "Theresa May and Her Six-pack of Difficult Deals." www.cer.org.uk/insights.

Jennings, W., and G. Stoker. 2016. "The Bifurcation of Politics: Two Englands." *The Political Quarterly*, Vol 87, No 3, July-September, pp. 337-341

Johnston, R., K. Jones, and D. Manley. 2016. "Predicting the Brexit Vote: Getting the Geography Right (more or less)." http://blogs.lse.ac.uk/politicsandpolicy/the-brexit-vote-getting-the-geography-more-or-less-right/.

O'Rourke, K. 2016. "Brexit: This backlash has been a long time coming." http://voxeu.org/article/brexit-backlash-has-been-long-time-coming.

Özden, C., and C. Parsons. 2015. "On the Economic Geography of International Migration." *The World Economy* 39 (4): 478–95.

Rodrik, D. 1998. "Why Do More Open Economies Have Bigger Governments?." *Journal of Political Economy* 106 (5): 997–1032.

Sapir, A. 2016. http://bruegel.org/2016/08/should-the-uk-pull-out-of-the-eu-customs-union/http://bruegel.org/2016/10/beyond-hard-soft-and-no-brexit/

Facts or Feelings, Facts and Feelings? The Post-Democracy Narrative in the Brexit Debate

Karin Forss[A] and Linnea Magro[B]

Abstract

This article begins with the widely asked question, which arose after the European Union (EU) Referendum in the UK; how do we explain that people's views and opinions so drastically diverge from experts? We consider the recurring narrative that the outcome of the Referendum portrays a post-factual democracy in which people who voted for the UK to leave the EU no longer trust the facts-based arguments of experts, but rather vote for politicians who represent an outcome which they feel is more desirable to them. We propose that this narrative is simplistic and that we must seek to explore the way both sides of the debate used, and failed to use, facts and feelings to support their arguments.

In late spring 2016 the Brexit campaign was heating up, the leading Conservative party was divided—not in terms of the traditional right-wing or moderate conservative spectrum, but regarding the question of the role of experts. On the one hand, Prime Minister David Cameron, the leader for the Remain campaign, said, "It's not just the 'Remain' side, you've got expert after expert, the OECD, the IMF, the Bank of England, the Institute for Fiscal Studies" (Witte, The Washington Post), with warnings of a disaster to come if Britain votes to leave, and on the other hand, Member of Parliament Michael Gove, one of the leaders of the Leave campaign, said, "People in this country have had enough of experts" (Mance, Financial Times). A recurring narrative of the Brexit debate was that the European Union (EU) Referendum became, to a great extent, a Referendum between the facts of experts and the feelings of people. Thus, after June 23, 2016 when Britain voted to leave the EU by 52% to 48%, some claimed that we have entered a post-factual democracy, where the feelings of the people have more political weight than the facts that experts present.

In order to answer the question why people's views and opinions diverged from the experts', we suggest that we must broaden our understanding of how facts and feelings operate in liberal democracies and how politicians actively played on both these components of political engagement and electoral behavior in the debate on the Referendum.

[A] MSc Gender, 2014-15, London School of Economics, United Kingdom

[B] MSc Social Policy (European and Comparative Social Policy), 2014-15, London School of Economics, United Kingdom

doi: 10.18278/epa.2.2.2

Three Perspectives to Analyze the Outcome of the EU Referendum

The EU Referendum has been the subject of much debate both domestically and internationally since its inception. When analyzing European integration, a common method is to use statistical measurements to depict the voting pattern in combination with structural, political sociology, or institutional perspectives. Different theoretical perspectives offer different explanations to make sense of the Referendum. The structural argument focuses on the role of inequality, immigration, and the role of winners and losers of globalization. In contrast, the institutional perspective regards the democratic deficit debate within the EU, the second-order national contest syndrome and the new media landscape as the most important factors. The political sociology perspective discusses the role of identity, values, nationalism, and populism.

These schools of thought each offer valuable perspectives on the EU Referendum, but they also reveal the very complex nature of understanding what the Referendum was actually about, or rather, what aspects of the Referendum mattered most to voters. There is no doubt that the Referendum is one of the most important political events in our times; hence, we need to understand it well to draw the right lessons for the future.

Is the UK a Post-Democracy Now?

Unfortunately, the debate concerning the Referendum has not been able to forge a complete and comprehensive understanding of the results with the help of an interdisciplinary synthesis. As a result, important issues have been discussed in a simplistic way. A common explanation of the EU Referendum is that the election was a display of how people, and here the people should be understood as the groups that voted Leave, were tired of and mistrusted experts. The rhetoric of experts versus peoples' feeling that was coined in the debate before the referendum took place continues to be a dominant narrative. Political scientist Colin Crouch (2000) coined the term post-democracy to describe a state in which the pillars of a democracy, such as advisory expertise, are not functioning. In a post-democracy all democratic institutions are in place and elections are held, but the electoral debate is, as Crouch puts it, "a tightly controlled spectacle, managed by rival teams of professional experts in the techniques of persuasion, and considering a small range of issues selected by those teams" (2000, 1). In a post-democracy, facts and expertise thus no longer play a central role in the political scene, as they are produced in a context that does not give most voters enough incentives or information to participate in elections.

In the debate surrounding the EU Referendum, a common claim is that this was exactly the state in the UK prior to the Referendum. Blogger Vincent F. Hendricks writes that today, politicians win elections by getting the feelings right, even if the facts are wrong. As an illustration, he refers to the way the leave-side politician Nigel Farage promised that if the UK left the Union they could take the £350 million a week that the country sent to the Union and instead spend it on the National Health Service. After the election, Farage admitted that this was a mistake, but his argument was powerful in making voters feel that leaving the Union would result in increased financial resources for British people in need, rather than disappear in the "EU machine". The £350 million a week "mistake" has thus been presented as a proof that Leave voters disregarded facts in favor of a narrative that made them feel like they would benefit more from being outside the Union than in it. Nevertheless, this is an excessively simplified argument. Mr. Farage was obviously wrong, but the argument as such is factual. He presents a quantitative estimate of savings as a consequence of leaving. To argue that voters were swept away by a convincing narrative is thus only a part of the truth, the other aspect being the framework in which facts and expert advice figure in the political discourse.

Expertise in the Context of the EU

Politics, and especially policy, has a strong commitment to facts and so-called evidence-based decisions (Dahler-Larsson 2011; Lindgren 2006). Thus, the consequences of a new era where people support politicians that make them feel good, rather than the ones that present the most accurate facts, would be problematic—if it were true. But can it really be that simple? The post EU-referendum discourse has scapegoated the Leave voters for not being rational and to trust feelings rather than obey facts—and for putting their trust in the wrong hands. However, trust might work in more complex ways than simply

following facts or feelings.

The phenomenon of expertise plays a dubious role in the public discourse (Beck 1992). In today's evidence-based policy movement, the expert is ubiquitous (Culpitt 1999). There is an inherent inequality of power between the one that possesses the role of the expert and the people. The problem with this inequality of power between experts and the people in a democracy is, as Jürgen Habermas among others have argued, that it makes an equal debate impossible. The role of experts puts the state's "neutrality" into question as governments depend on, subsidize, and give status to the opinions of experts and the facts they present.

However, facts are not free of ideology. They are produced from a certain viewpoint and often with a certain motive. They are, hopefully, better researched than opinions, and they are usually grounded in experience, theoretical knowledge, and logic, but they are not neutral. This does not mean that people cannot trust facts, but it means that facts should always be understood in the context that produced them (Boswell 2009). Obviously, not all experts are united in their opinion of the benefits of the EU and why the UK should remain in the Union—criticism of the European project has been widespread. This criticism has ranged from that toward the decision group formed by the European Commission, the IMF, and the ECB, commonly called the Troika, to the Transatlantic Trade and Investment Partnership (TTIP), which have mobilized huge protests across Europe against the EU's policymaking. Referring to Michael Gove's statement that people are 'fed up with experts', perhaps it is not only that people are tired of experts, but rather how people lack trust in *these* experts' policymaking. Jean Pisani-Ferry (2016) has highlighted two interesting reasons why voters resisted the advice of experts and voted to leave; the lack of trust of experts and how people felt "left behind". Consequently, he argues that the lack of trust of expertise had its starting point with the financial and economic crises that hit the UK very hard; the real wages in the UK fell by about 10.4% between 2007 and 2015 (Trades Union Congress report). The geographical areas that suffered the largest reductions in average wages turned out to be the ones where most people were likely to vote for Brexit. A question raised by Queen Elizabeth, and many others, during a visit to the London School of Economics when the financial crises had just started was: "why did no one see it coming"? The economic crisis and its aftermath was an important breeding ground for criticism of experts according to Pisani-Ferry. Secondly, he highlights that the economic arguments put forward by the Remain side mainly spoke about positive net contributions to the UK's financial system, but forgot to mention the policy effects distributed over time and among social classes. Thus, the arguments failed to pay attention to, for example, the experience of workers who had been affected by downward pressure on wages. The combination of negative experiences of free movement and the lack of trust of the experts and their knowledge production, we argue, are important factors to understanding why some people did not trust or follow the experts' advice to remain in the Union. Nor should one underestimate the impact of some 50 years of negative publicity for the European project. The experts in Brussels and in European institutions have been blamed for many of the ills in British society—often by the very same political

establishment that now argued to Remain. Hypocrisy—just the suspicion of it—is not a winning feature in political debates.

Concluding Remarks

The ancient Greek philosopher Aristotle already made a distinction between the role of facts and feelings in politics, or as he called it pathos—emotion—and logos—reason. Rather than choosing one or the other, Aristotle claimed that a winning politician needs both (as well as ethos—ethics). In order for politicians to be considered trustworthy, Aristotle claimed that they needed to engage both emotionally with voters and present well-grounded facts that appeal to voters' reason. In spite of Aristotle's appeal to a holistic understanding of arguments and comprehensive view of rationality that encompasses pathos, logos, and ethos, the distinction between pathos and logos, in particular, is a very powerful figure of speech. It is thus not surprising that it plays a major role in social and political analysis more than 2000 years later. It is a figure of thought that has been, and is, persistent in Western philosophy. From there it influences all the social sciences. In recent years, political scientists Amartya Sen (2002) and Martha Nussbaum (1986, 2001) have written on the need to integrate rational, intellectual logic, and feeling, and have convincingly shown that a distinction between the two is false. And thus is not suitable for a comprehensive analysis of important social issues to frame facts and feelings as competing narratives.

What stands out in the debate surrounding the EU Referendum is how facts, reason, feelings, and emotions have been pitted against each other—as if a winning political argument either rests on one or the other. Leave voters have been portrayed as voting with their feelings, disregarding facts, while the Remain side voters have been portrayed as making an informed, fact-based vote. In tandem, Remain campaign politicians have based many of their arguments on expert advice from economists and academics, but have emphasized the feeling of unity within the Union much less. Instead, their arguments were mainly focused on the economic incentives for remaining in the Union. The Leave campaign focused more on feelings of independence, nationalism, and pride in the British way of life, in contrast to more liberal European values. Reflecting on the dichotomy facts and feelings, we put forward some hypotheses that might be fruitful for future research on the Referendum:

• Neither of the two opposing sides in the Referendum articulated a narrative that integrated fact-based and feelings-based arguments convincingly, and the Remain side, in particular, failed to connect to other arguments than those of economic benefits.

• Even before the Referendum results were known, while the debates were on-going, the dichotomy of facts and feelings played a part in the unfolding narrative, and as the dichotomy is false—but powerful—it contributed to a simplistic understanding of the choices to be made and their consequences.

• The debate has put blame on the experts, rather than on the particular context in which experts advice were given and formed within. The knowledge and experience experts have is certainly vital for the forthcoming debates on the EU Referendum, but it must be presented in a context facilitating for people to understand, trust, and assess the ideological reasoning behind expert advice.

• Seeing the EU Referendum as a question of facts versus feelings is simplistic, as does claiming that the outcome puts us in a post-factual democracy. It would be a more fruitful analysis to see the two as competing narratives—and analyze how facts and feelings are interwoven in the political deliberation. The role of media, and its ability to handle both, as well as expert's arguments to reflect them fully are dimensions that need to be considered and call for further research for exploration.

Our analysis of the EU Referendum presents a reflection on parts of the debate and analysis. Our aim was to address what we perceived as a simplified discussion of the election outcome, to outline the elements of a critical discourse, and to generate some hypotheses for future research. With this framework, the debate following the EU Referendum could focus on how well both sides presented facts, how well grounded they were, and how well both sides addressed the feelings that move voters to a certain political decision; that is, how facts and feelings are integrated and complementary.

References

Beck, U. 1992. *Risk Society: Towards a New Modernity*. London: Sage.

Boswell, C. 2009. *The Political Uses of Expert Knowledge.* Cambridge: Cambridge University Press.

Crouch, C. 2000. *Coping with Post-Democracy*. London: Fabian Society.

Culpitt, I. 1999. *Social Policy and Risk.* London: Sage.

Dahler-Larsson, P. 2011. *The Evaluation Society.* Stanford: Stanford University Press.

Hendricks, F, V. 2016. *In the post-factual democracy, politicians win by getting feelings right and facts wrong.* http://qz.com/723537/in-the-post-factual-democracy-politicians-win-by-getting-feelings-right-and-facts-wrong/ Published 2016-07-05

Lindgren, L. 2006. *Utvärderingsmonstret. Kvalitets- och resultatmätning i den offentliga sektorn*. Lund: Studentlitteratur.

Mance, H. "Britain has had enough of experts, says Gove" *Financial Times*, https://www.ft.com/content/3be49734-29cb-11e6-83e4-abc22d5d108c , Published 2016-06-13

Nussbaum, M. 1986. *The Fragility of Goodness: Luck and Ethics in Greek Tragedy and Philosophy.* Cambridge: Cambridge University Press.

Nussbaum, M. 2001. *Upheavals of Thought: The Intelligence of Emotions.* Cambridge: Cambridge University Press

Pisani-Ferry, J. 2016. *"Why are Voters Ignoring Experts?"* Project Syndicate—The world's opinion page, Published 2016-07-01 https://www.project-syndicate.org/commentary/brexit-voters-ignoring-experts-by-jean-pisani-ferry-2016-07?barrier=true

Sen, A. 2002. *Rationality and Freedom.* Belknap: Harvard.

TUC "UK workers experienced sharpest wage fall of any leading economy" https://www.tuc.org.uk/economic-issues/labour-market/uk-workers-experienced-sharpest-wage-fall-any-leading-economy-tuc Published 2016-07-27

Witte, G. "9 out of 10 experts agree: Britain doesn't trust the experts on Brexit", *The Washington Post*, https://www.washingtonpost.com/world/europe/9-out-of-10-experts-agree-britain-doesnt-trust-the-experts-on-brexit/2016/06/21/2ccc134a-34a6-11e6-ab9d-1da2b0f24f93_story.html, Published 2016-06-21

European Policy Analysis - Volume 2, Number 2 - Winter 2016

A Review of Applications of the Advocacy Coalition Framework in Swedish Policy Processes

Daniel Nohrstedt[A] & Kristin Olofsson[B]

In recent decades, there has been a growing interest among public policy scholars to explore the applicability of policy process frameworks across political systems. One popular framework simplifying the complexity of public policy is the Advocacy Coalition Framework (ACF). Prior research suggests that the ACF is useful for identifying variables and relationships influencing the policy process but also that questions remain regarding its applicability in different political systems. This paper addresses some of these questions by conducting a review of empirical ACF applications in Sweden—a country where the ACF has received growing attention. We code 25 of the most complete applications across themes associated with advocacy coalitions, learning, and policy change. We also examine what research methods are employed, what comparisons are made between the ACF and other frameworks, and what modifications are suggested by scholars. The conclusion identifies strengths and limitations of the ACF in the context of the Swedish policy process and suggests directions for future research in Sweden and beyond.

Keywords*: Advocacy coalition framework; policy process; policy analysis; corporatism; Sweden*

Introduction

A central objective for the policy sciences is to advance the understanding of how political systems develop and change public policy in the context of complex interactions between actors, events, and institutions. This is a long-standing challenge, which has resulted in the development and refinement of multiple frameworks and theories that seek to simplify the complexity of the policy process. Theory development is thus an ongoing and constantly evolving task for the policy sciences research community and a source of scientific debate. Textbooks and journal articles offer a wide range of candidate approaches and a whole repertoire of methodological tools for scholars to develop, test, and refine hypotheses about what drives public policies in different countries and different levels of policymaking from the local to the international. One of the key challenges to this field is to critically assess the applicability, both in terms of descriptive accuracy and explanatory validity, of theories and frameworks across political systems.

[A] Department of Government, Uppsala University, Sweden

[B] School of Public Affairs, University of Colorado, USA

doi: 10.18278/epa.2.2.3

One increasingly popular theoretical framework that seeks to simplify the complexity of public policy is the Advocacy Coalition Framework (ACF). Prior work suggests that the ACF is useful as an organizing framework for identifying variables and relationships related to learning and policy change in different political systems (Sabatier 1998; Weible, Sabatier, and McQueen 2009; Weible et al. 2011). However, critics have argued that the ACF, rooted in American pluralism, has limited applicability in countries with democratic corporatist traditions (Carter 2001; Eberg 1997; John 1998; Parsons 1995). These competing claims call for comparative work to identify strengths and weaknesses in the framework, particularly in neo-corporatist settings. This study makes a contribution to this ongoing effort by reporting on an analysis of empirical ACF applications in Sweden.

The goal of the ACF is "to provide a coherent understanding of the major factors and processes affecting the overall policy process—including problem definition, policy formulation, implementation, and revision in a specific policy domain—over periods of a decade or more" (Sabatier 1998, 1350). The ACF has gradually evolved into an international research program in which cases from around the world have been examined using the same concepts and assumptions. As such, the ACF provides a common theoretical lens to guide and standardize data collection, which supports structured comparison across cases and countries (Jenkins-Smith et al. 2014; Weible and Nohrstedt 2012). Internationally, the ACF is one of the most widely applied policy process frameworks. In a recent

count of empirical applications from 1987 to 2013, Jenkins-Smith et al. (2014) found 224 applications worldwide out of which 94 (42 percent) involved European cases. In fact, this number is on par with applications in the United States (n = 95, 42 percent), suggesting that European cases have been an important empirical base for theory testing and development within the ACF. In this study, we identify 25 case studies of policy processes in Sweden spanning a range of substantive topics. These numbers place Sweden at the top in Europe, together with the United Kingdom and Switzerland, in terms of the number of empirical applications per country. We seek to explore what these studies actually tell us about policy processes in Sweden and the validity of the ACF in this context.

Sweden, like other corporatist countries in Europe, has gone through major change regarding the terms for participation, influence, and policy change. Scholars suggest that Swedish policymaking has gradually become more open and conflictual but note that the country still retains important corporatist elements, including coordinated wage agreements, local-level interest mediation, and the key role of labor market organizations in policymaking (Lindvall and Sebring 2005). While researchers debate the nature and scope of these changes (see, e.g., Pierre 2015; Svallfors 2016), the trend brings questions about how the Swedish policy process can be depicted and understood.

The objective of this review is twofold: we explore (i) how the ACF may contribute to knowledge about Swedish policy processes and (ii) if and how application of the ACF in Sweden might suggest refinement and specification of the ACF. Although the study is focused on Swedish applications, we discuss avenues for future research that may apply in other countries as well. In this regard, the study adds to existing reviews of ACF applications in different cases and settings. Except for one comparative examination of applications in South Korea (Jang, Weible, and Park 2016), previous reviews of the ACF cover larger samples of applications across policy issues and countries (Jenkins-Smith et al. 2014; Sotirov and Memmler 2012; Weible, Sabatier, and McQueen 2009; Weible et al. 2011). While both strategies are needed to support further development and specification of the ACF, there is a shortage of comparative work that examines the strengths and weaknesses of the framework across policy issues within the same country. Such contributions are needed to better understand how policy subsystems are influenced by broader governing system attributes (Jenkins-Smith et al. 2014).

We proceed in four steps. The paper begins with a brief overview of the ACF, including its key assumptions and theoretical revisions. The next section presents a summary of recent developments of public policymaking in Sweden along with a discussion about the terms for applying the ACF in this context. In the third step, we present our methodology for the review of empirical applications of the ACF in Sweden. In the final sections, we summarize and discuss the main findings from the review and draw lessons regarding the Swedish policy process and about the ACF, ending with a brief agenda for future research.

The Advocacy Coalition Framework—Assumptions and Revisions

Figure 1 summarizes the 2007 version of the ACF flow diagram, including the role of advocacy coalitions within a policy subsystem and the role of exogenous factors in shaping the constraints and opportunities of subsystem actors over time. The framework assumes that policy subsystem actors are influenced by relatively stable parameters (such as sociocultural values and basic constitutional structure). These parameters are seldom the target for coalition strategies but shape the long-term opportunity structures of subsystem actors. Subsystem actors are also influenced by external system events, which include changes in socioeconomic conditions, public opinion, governing coalition, and other subsystems. These are developments that are outside the control of subsystem actors and that are likely to change over time (a decade or more). A policy subsystem is depicted as adversarial competition among actors who form coalitions, engage in analytical debates, and exploit political strategies, resources, and venues to advocate for their preferred policy problems and solutions. Coalition interactions result in one or more governmental programs, generating policy outputs and impacts, which in turn might prompt advocacy coalition actors to revise their beliefs and/or strategies (Sabatier and Weible 2007; Sabatier and Jenkins-Smith 1999).

The ACF is a framework supporting several areas of theoretical emphasis that narrow the scope of inquiry, link concepts in the form of expectations, propositions, or observable implications, and establish causal mechanisms that explain how concepts interrelate (Jenkins-Smith et al. 2014; Weible and Nohrstedt 2012). Theoretical emphases include advocacy coalitions, policy-oriented learning, and policy change.

political behavior is conditioned by subsystem institutions and events outside the control of subsystem participants. The most important institutional factors that constrain subsystem actors are the openness of the political system and norms of consensus, which affect the level of inclusiveness of coalitions, exchange of information across coalition boundaries,

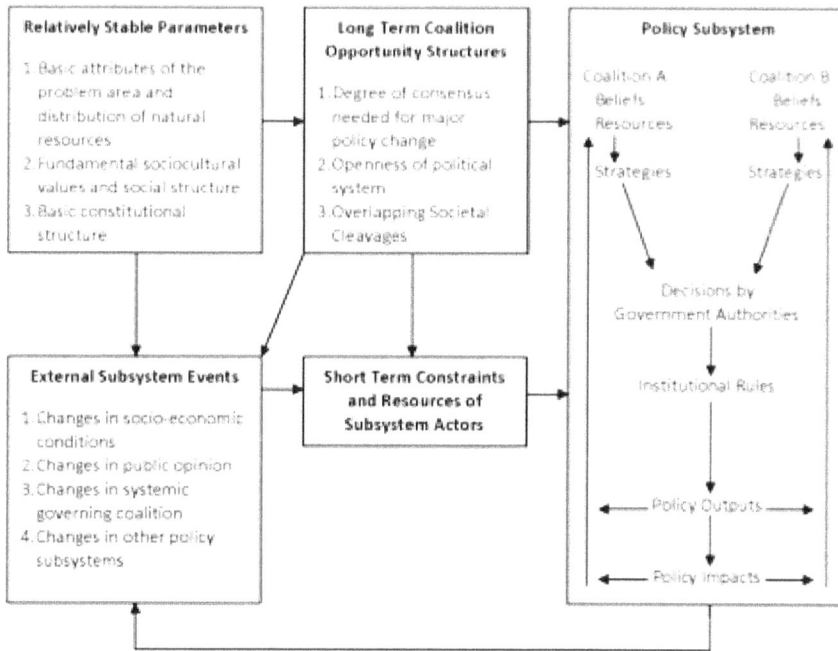

Figure 1. Flow Diagram of the Advocacy Coalition Framework; Source: Adapted from Sabatier and Weible (2007, 202).

Advocacy coalitions are defined as groups of actors sharing policy core beliefs and coordinating their behavior in a nontrivial manner. Advocacy coalitions emerge because actors vary in their belief systems (e.g., normative values regarding a particular policy topic) and seek to form alliances to translate their beliefs into actual policies before actors with different belief systems can do the same. The formation and stability of advocacy coalitions over time and their

and access to policy venues (Sabatier and Weible, 2007). Events are likely to affect coalition behavior, particularly by providing opportunities for exploitation of new resources (including mobilization of new coalition members) and strategy in terms of venue exploitation.

• *Policy-oriented learning* is defined as "enduring alterations of thought or behavioral intentions that result from experience and which are concerned with the attainment or revision of the precepts of the belief system of individuals or of collectives" (Sabatier and Jenkins-Smith 1993, 42). Policy-oriented learning may entail better understanding of political goals, the causal relationship among key factors in the subsystem, and effective strategic behaviors, especially as used in analytic debates. The ACF seeks to understand and explain what constitutes learning and why learning occurs within coalitions and between coalitions. Four general factors are important for explaining policy-oriented learning: the openness of participation rules; level of conflict between coalitions; level of analytical tractability of the phenomenon; and attributes of individuals, including belief systems, resources, and network contacts.

• *Policy change* is the third theoretical emphasis within the ACF. The ACF assumes that policies are translations of beliefs and can be conceptualized and measured hierarchically like belief systems. A change in policy core aspects (components that span a policy subsystem) indicates a major change in the direction of the subsystem and is defined as major policy change. A change in secondary aspects (components that deal with only a part of a subsystem or technical components of a policy) indicates a minor change in the subsystem and is defined as minor policy change (Sabatier and Jenkins-Smith 1999). The ACF specifies four pathways to policy change (Sabatier and Weible 2007; Nohrstedt and Weible 2010). First, external events occur outside the territorial boundaries of the subsystem and/or the topical policy boundaries of the subsystem and are, hence, largely outside the control of subsystem actors. Second, internal events

occur inside the territorial and/or the topical area of the policy subsystem and are more likely affected by subsystem actors. Third, policy-oriented learning is assumed to lead to policy change by altering the beliefs of coalition members. Policies may change after a dominant coalition learns or after learning occurs between adversarial coalitions. Fourth, policy might change as the result of negotiated agreements fostered by, for instance, a hurting stalemate or a lack of alternative venues.

The ACF supports empirical research into policy processes within and across countries. While the framework provides a set of general questions about the policy process, each area of theoretical emphasis lays out a number of testable hypotheses. The level of attention devoted to these hypotheses varies and some have attracted more attention than others (Weible, Sabatier, and McQueen 2009). Also, some of the hypotheses have been revised or modified following empirical application, while others have remained the same (Jenkins-Smith et al. 2014).[c]

Based on empirical applications, the framework has been reviewed regularly (Jenkins-Smith et al. 2014; Sabatier and Weible 2007; Sabatier and Jenkins-Smith 1993; 1999). These reviews have suggested revisions of some of the framework's assumptions

---

[c] See Jenkins-Smith et al. (2014) for the most recent list of hypotheses within the ACF.

[D] Revisions in the ACF have been consistent with the basic principles of the ACF, which have not changed. These principles include the model of the individual, the focus on the policy subsystem, advocacy coalitions as the key political actor, and concern with the role of science in policy (Sabatier and Weible 2007).

and concepts.[D] The 2007 version of the ACF contains four major revisions compared to the original version. The first two—including the degree of consensus needed for policy change and the degree of openness of political systems—were added as long-term opportunity structures. These attributes are assumed to affect coalition membership and strategy in reaching agreements and were added to "ease application outside of the pluralist system of the United States to corporatist regimes" (Weible, Sabatier, and McQueen 2009, 123–24). The other two revisions included addition of internal subsystem events (occur within the subsystem and are expected to highlight failures in subsystem practices) and negotiated agreements as two alternative paths to policy change in a subsystem.

Assessment of the applicability of the ACF in cases of Swedish policymaking—or any other political system—involves issues related to descriptive and explanatory validity (Weible et al. 2011; Weible and Nohrstedt 2012). We are interested in both of these dimensions. Regarding descriptive validity, we examine if studies find that the concepts and assumptions of the ACF are useful as a basis for describing policy processes in Sweden. Examples include the notions of policy subsystems and advocacy coalitions but also learning and policy change. When assessing the explanatory validity of the framework, we are interested whether the causal logic suggested by the framework holds in the face of empirical evidence. Specifically, do cases confirm the ACF's predictions regarding relationships between independent and dependent variables? Do cases provide evidence of causal

mechanisms suggested by the ACF?

Application of the ACF in a Shifting Political Landscape

Two decades ago, Sabatier and Jenkins-Smith (1993, 225) argued that the ACF applies "in at least modern industrial polyarchies". Critics remained skeptical, however, and suggested that the framework would be less valid in democratic corporatist systems due to their centralized political and administrative arrangements and long-term consultative processes, which narrow the scope of participation and influence (Carter 2001; John 1998; Parsons 1995). Yet, assessment of the applicability of the ACF in corporatist systems is complicated by conceptual confusion over the notion of corporatism and recent changes in Swedish policymaking.

Corporatism and pluralism are theoretical ideal types on a continuum and most policymaking "styles" fall somewhere in between. In practice, the level of openness of a political system and access to venues for debate and influence are subject to some variation over policy subsystems and across time. Corporatist interest representation may be common in some policy subsystems, while pluralism prevails in other areas (Wilson 1983). These variations are crucial in explaining policy change, especially since the relative openness of policy areas have an impact upon knowledge exchange and the introduction of new actors and interests in policymaking (Howlett and Ramesh 1998). Variations also occur across different phases of the policy process. For instance, Blom-

Hansen (2000) notes that, in Denmark, corporatism has generally declined in the policy formulation stage, while it is still evident in the implementation stage. Also, the corporatist–pluralist distinction is usually a basis for documenting patterns of democracy at the "macro-level" (Lijphart 1999), while the ACF is concerned with policymaking within policy subsystems. Democratic polities include a variety of policy subsystems presenting different mixes of state and societal relationships and so the corporatist–pluralist continuum may not be the ideal nor exclusive way in which to describe these relationships (Atkinson and Coleman 1989).

Research indicates that policy processes in traditionally corporatist countries have become more open, informal, and conflictual. Lewin (1994), Lindvall and Sebring (2005), Lindvall and Rothstein (2006), and others point to a gradual decline of corporatist arrangements in Sweden. In Sweden, policymaking has traditionally been based on institutionalized contact, negotiation, and joint decision-making between the state and organized interests. Öberg et al. (2011) depict these corporatist arrangements as a game in institutionalized arenas in which selected organizations are granted the status of group representatives in the policy process. However, over time, interest organizations in Sweden have increasingly turned to lobbying and advocacy for political influence. Also, as more and new actors (e.g., policy professionals, large companies, think tanks, and other organized producers of policy ideas) have become engaged in policymaking, competition for politicians' attention increased and professionalized opinion formation and media contacts as well as personal contacts and networks became increasingly important as means of influence (Svallfors 2016).

Corporatism has not been completely abandoned in Sweden, however. Svallfors (2016) suggests that policymaking in Sweden remains a highly elite-driven process, yet it has become less clear-cut and visible. The country still retains important corporatist elements, such as coordinated wage agreements, local-level interest mediation, and the key role of labor market organizations in policymaking (Lindvall and Sebring 2005). In this setting, Lindvall and Sebring (2005) warn of the risk of exaggerating or underestimating the scope and nature of changes in Swedish policymaking, which can lead to erroneous conclusions regarding changes in institutions and policy. Rather, they "propose that institutions and organisations are best studied indirectly, by identifying important decisions in core policy areas and then analysing the political process that brought them about" (2005, 1058). Against this background, we agree with Parson (1995, 200) that "we need to see a good deal more use of the [advocacy coalition] framework outside America and with case studies from other polyarchies if we are to come to any conclusions as to its general applicability". Since Parson made this statement 20 years ago, we have witnessed a steady increase in the number of empirical applications of the ACF in Sweden. These applications are the unit of analysis for this review.

Methods and Data

To compile a list of empirical applications of the ACF in Sweden, we searched three databases: Web of Science, Google Scholar, and Diva Portal (a repository of research publications written at 37 universities and research institutions in Sweden). Multiple databases were used to account for the limitations of the search capacity in each database as well as regional specificity. Each database was searched systematically using a combination of "advocacy coalition framework", "advocacy coalitions", and "Sweden" as key words in both Swedish and English. Explicit use of any of these keywords constituted the first criterion for inclusion in the dataset. Peer-reviewed journal articles, book chapters, and doctoral dissertations were included. Unpublished manuscripts, conference papers, and undergraduate- and master's-level theses were all excluded. We included all applicable publications regardless of the date of publication. After the initial database search, we had identified 50 potential applications for coding. The final sample contains 25 publications in the period from 1998 (first publication found) to 2015 (final search conducted in August, 2015).[E] Rules for inclusion in the final sample were (i) the title and/ or abstract should explicitly mention "advocacy", "coalition", or "learning" and (ii) at least two foundational ACF works should be cited.[F] All applications that met this criterion were manually reviewed by authors to confirm inclusion. The majority of applications were published in peer-reviewed journals (n = 18); five were published doctoral dissertations, with one book chapter and one report comprising the remainder of the sample.

Informed by prior efforts to review the state of the field of ACF scholarly work (Jang, Weible, and Park 2016; Weible, Sabatier, and McQueen 2009), we applied a coding framework containing a total of 60 elements divided into eight main parts: (1) application attributes (publication descriptives, e.g. author(s), year of publication), (2) application scope (e.g. purpose of using the ACF, empirical domain, level of analysis), (3) research objective (main areas of theoretical emphasis, e.g. coalitions, policy change, learning), (4) methods (data collection and analysis), (5) coalitions (number of coalitions, belief system, membership, strategies used), (6) learning (among or between coalitions, brokers), (7) policy change (minor or major change, role of learning, and/or external events), and (8) overall evaluation (generalizability and/or modifications discussed). Based on these parts, we report results below focusing on substantive topic, application methods, level of government, and theoretical emphases. We also examine the extent to which the ACF has been used as the main framework or supplementary theory. Finally, we summarize scholars'

[E] Nine additional applications used "coalitions" as a description of groups of individuals or organizations sharing common beliefs or goals towards a particular issue or policy; however, these applications included no other mention of the ACF nor did they cite foundational works. Therefore, they were excluded from the sample. This approach to identifying applications has been used in previous reviews (see, e.g., Jones et al. 2015; Weible, Sabatier, and McQueen 2009).

[F] For this study and in accordance with previous meta reviews (Weible, Sabatier, and McQueen 2009), foundational ACF publications included the following: Sabatier (1986; 1988; 1998), Sabatier and Jenkins-Smith (1999), Sabatier and Weible (2007).

observations regarding the strengths and weaknesses of the ACF as a descriptive and explanatory lens in Sweden.

Results

Substantive Topic

The first application of the ACF in Sweden was a research report published by the Finnish Forest Institute in 1998 (Berggren 1998). This was about ten years after the inception of the framework and just as European applications were starting to emerge (Weible, Sabatier, and McQueen 2009). Figure 2 displays the count of publications over time by the substantive topic area.

forestry, and carnivore management. Cases involving issues related to energy policy, such as nuclear energy and hydraulic fracturing, followed closely at seven applications. The six social policy applications display a wide diversity, from e-government initiatives to alcohol and drug treatment policy. Finally, there have been three applications related to environmental policy, which would seem to represent somewhat of a departure for the ACF, as it is most often applied in the area of environmental policy (Weible, Sabatier, and McQueen 2009). However, we see this pattern as resulting from our coding procedure, which defined natural resource management as a stand-alone category separate from environmental

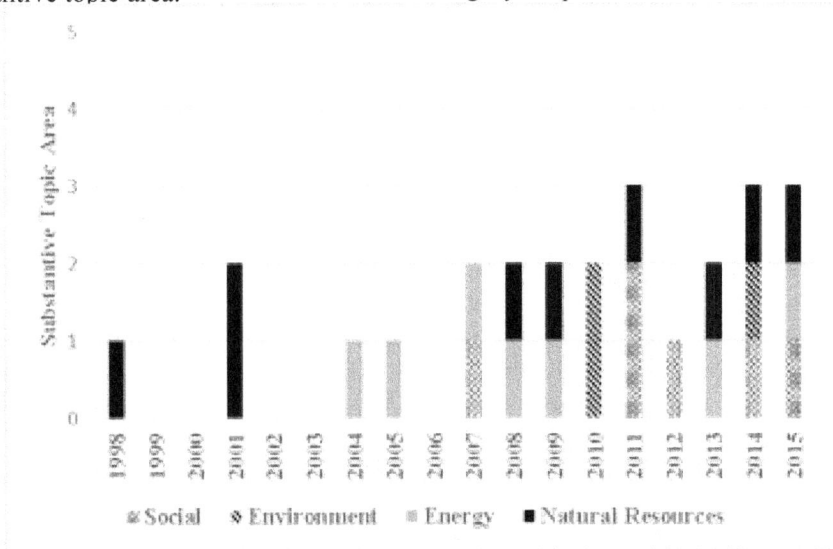

Figure 2: Applications by Substantive Topic Area Over Time (1998–2015)

After the first application in 1998, there were only four applications until 2007. Since that time, the number of applications has increased markedly with a steady stream of publications in recent years. Nine of the 25 applications involve cases of natural resource management, primarily

policy. By contrast, other ACF reviews (Jang, Weible, and Park 2016; Jenkins-Smith et al. 2014; Weible, Sabatier, and McQueen 2009) have incorporated natural resource management into environmental policy. If defining natural resource management as environmental policy, the empirical basis for Swedish

ACF work is dominated by environmental and energy policy issues (76 percent), followed by smaller group of studies addressing social issues (24 percent). In summary, the distribution of substantive topics among Swedish applications is consistent with the distribution of ACF applications globally, which are dominated by environmental and energy policy issues but with a growing number of social policy issues (Jenkins-Smith et al. 2014).

While the ACF applies broadly in cases involving contentious and technically complex policy issues, it also hypothesizes that certain issue-specific attributes will influence the dynamics of learning across belief systems. Specifically, it asserts that issues involving natural systems are more conducive to learning compared to issues involving social or political systems. It also suggests that learning is affected by the quantity and subjective nature of scientific information (Jenkins-Smith et al. 2014). However, results regarding these hypotheses are somewhat ambiguous, which calls for more comparative work across policy issues. The growing number of social issues covered is one step toward this goal, but—as we will demonstrate below—studies addressing the characteristics of learning remain limited.

Application Methods

The increasing number of applications has also displayed a variety of research methods. The ACF has been marked by methodological pluralism (Weible et al. 2011), which is reflected in Table 1. Note that multiple data collections and analysis are possible within the same application.

Document analysis has been the most common method of data collection, used in about half of all applications. This might be a reflection of the principle of public access in Sweden, which ensures access to various public documents and a high level of tractability in the study of the policy process. Although a diversity of methods have been applied with the ACF, interviews and surveys are generally among the most common methods (Weible, Sabatier, and McQueen 2009). Of the Swedish applications, three rely on interviews and eight use surveys. Content analysis has typically been used as an ancillary to another form of data collection.

In their review of ACF applications in 2009, Weible, Sabatier, and McQueen (2009, 126) found that nearly half of the applications used unspecified methods and drew upon "unsystematic collection and analysis of existing documents and reports". Unspecified methods also remain common in Swedish applications (n = 9). In keeping with the prevalence of content analysis as a method of data collection in Swedish applications, analysis through interpretive or mixed methods was relatively common and represented 64 percent of the authors' choice of method of analysis (n = 18). Interpretive analysis through process tracing was used in nine applications, usually in conjunction with content analysis. Mixed methods often drew upon interviews and surveys. There was only one quantitative study (Storbjörk 2014), which utilized content analysis of more than 200 written comments on a proposal

DATA COLLECTION	Number of Applications	Composition of Total
Survey	3	9%
Interview	7	22%
Content Analysis	12	38%
Observation	1	3%
Unspecified	9	28%
ANALYSIS		
Quantitative	2	7%
Qualitative	5	18%
Mixed Methods	9	32%
Interpretive	9	32%
Unspecified	2	7%

Table 1: Methods of Data Collection and Analysis

submitted to a government ministry.

Owing to the focus of the ACF on connections between individuals that coordinate activities within advocacy coalitions, social network analysis has become an increasingly popular tool (see Ingold 2011). In the 25 Swedish applications, social network analysis has been used in three applications since 2011 (Matti and Sandström 2011; 2013; Nohrstedt and Olofsson 2016). These studies explore relationships between actors in the policy subsystem and how those relationships may explain coalition activity and policy change. As is typical with ACF network studies, two of the applications derived network information from surveys and one application (Nohrstedt and Olofsson 2016) applied a web-sphere content analysis procedure to map the public representations of individual connections.

Level of Government

The ACF can be used to explore the policy process at all levels of government. As shown in Figure 3, applications in Sweden have primarily focused on the local and national levels of government. Note again that analysis of multiple levels of government is possible within one application. All but five of the applications focused on the policy process at both the local (n = 21) and the national level (n = 21).

There have been a limited number of applications that considered subsystems in which policy issues span a regional area, and only four applications studied the transnational level of government (Elliot and Schlaepfer 2001a; Eriksson, Karlsson, and Reuter 2010; Hysing and Olsson 2008; Valman 2014). Although the international policy process is notoriously difficult to map, it could be expected that there would be more reflection regarding the transnational level of government

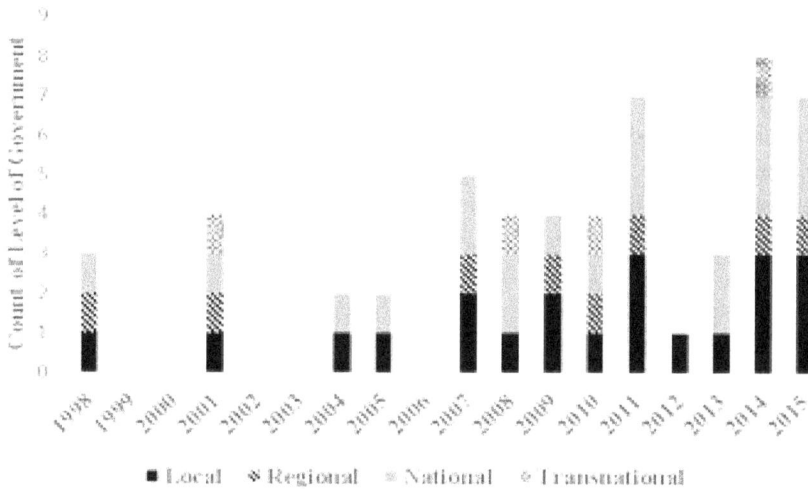

Figure 3: Applications by Level of Government Over Time (1998–2015)

in Sweden, given its membership in the European Union. However, none of the ACF applications included in this sample explore transnational processes. Thus, processes related to Europeanization have so far been a blind spot in Swedish ACF research. The role and impact of Europeanization has been a recurrent theme in other European ACF studies (Hogl 2000; Irondelle 2003; Princen 2007) and should be seen as an avenue for research in future ACF applications in Sweden and beyond.

Theoretical Emphases

Of the 25 applications, 16 focused on identifying coalitions and understanding their associated beliefs and positions on the policy issue at hand. The same number of applications (n = 16) focused on explaining policy change, often through coalition structure and occasionally through learning. Only seven applications addressed policy-oriented learning and its impact on the

policy process (n = 7).

Advocacy Coalitions

The vast majority of applications in Sweden (n = 19) identified coalitions.[G] Of these applications, two-thirds described a subsystem with two coalitions and the remainder identified more than two coalitions within the subsystem. Out of the 19 applications that identified coalitions, only 13 specified who the coalition members were. The organizational affiliation of coalition members varied across nine categories determined inductively after coding all applications. On average, the coalition members represented five different organization types, with a minimum of four and a maximum of seven organization types identified within the same application. Figure 4 shows the number of applications in which a coalition member was identified, aggregated to the organizational level.

The most often identified coalition member organization type was interest groups, followed closely by government agencies. Both national- and local-level politicians were identified with moderate regularity; members of unions or the media were rarely identified as members of coalitions. The ACF assumes that "most coalitions will involve not only interest group leaders, but also agency officials, legislators from multiple levels of government, applied researchers, and perhaps even a few journalists" (Sabatier and Jenkins-Smith 1999, 120). However, with regard to corporatist systems, coalition membership is assumed to be less inclusive (Sabatier and Weible 2007). Although we did not code the number of members of coalitions, our findings suggest that, in most cases, coalition membership is relatively restricted. Most studies coded here document interest

groups and government agencies, which would be expected given Swedish corporatism. This insight also seems to corroborate expectations within the ACF literature concerning the composition of advocacy coalitions in corporatist systems (Sabatier and Weible 2007). By contrast, this finding appears to be at odds with the overall trend toward greater openness in the Swedish policy process. Nevertheless, our sense is that the studies included here are insufficient as a basis for drawing general conclusions about coalition membership. Primarily, we suspect that patterns of coalition membership might be an artefact stemming from different sampling procedures and approaches to determine advocacy coalition boundaries.

The stability of coalitions over time is also a fundamental component of the ACF. However, few applications

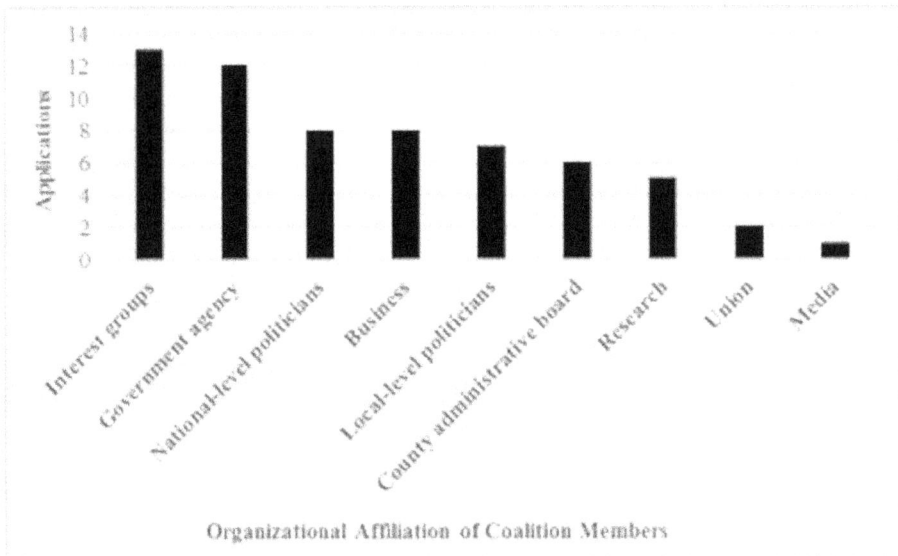

Figure 4: Applications by Organizational Affiliation of Coalition Members

---

[G] Note that among the 19 applications that identified coalitions, 16 focused on advocacy coalitions as the main area of theoretical emphasis.

in the Swedish context address this idea. Coalition stability and/or defections from the coalition were explicitly addressed in only six applications. One application (Elliot and Schlaepfer 2001a; 2001b) proposed a new hypothesis related to determinants of membership defection between coalitions.

In the 16 applications that focused on coalition identification, only ten directly discussed the belief systems of the coalitions. Eight of these identified deep core beliefs, nine identified policy core beliefs, and seven identified secondary beliefs. Out of these applications, seven identified policy-oriented beliefs at all three levels. It should be noted, however, that the majority of Swedish applications (n = 16, 64 percent) did not empirically document belief systems. Six applications tested hypotheses related to the structure of advocacy coalitions and their associated belief systems. Strong support was found for the assumption that shared beliefs are a driving force in coalition structure (Matti and Sandström 2011; 2013; Nohrstedt 2007; 2009). However, questions still remain regarding the nuances of the belief system, particularly which tier of the three-tiered structure is more influential in stimulating coalition formation and behavior. The ACF also hypothesizes that coalitions will be stable over a period of a decade or more (Sabatier and Jenkins-Smith 1993). Through empirical testing of this hypothesis, Elliot and Schlaepfer (2001a; 2001b) found that there may be changes in the membership of coalitions but that these rare changes are often preceded by policy-oriented learning and/or significant external perturbations to the subsystem.

Beliefs are not the only unifying force within advocacy coalitions; coordination and cooperation are also important mechanisms by which groups of like-minded actors work toward a common goal (Schlager 1995). However, very few applications in Sweden explicitly discussed coordination or cooperation among policy subsystem actors. Only two applications identified strategies of collaboration (Matti and Sandström 2011; Nohrstedt and Olofsson 2016). These same applications plus one additional application (Matti and Sandström 2013) also identified cooperation strategies among advocacy coalitions. As was concluded by Weible, Sabatier, and McQueen (2009) and demonstrated again in this review, the role and influence of coordination and cooperation are areas in which the ACF has unexploited potential, particularly given the growth of networks as a form of political organization in Sweden.

Policy Change

In our sample of Swedish ACF applications, we found 16 applications that focused solely on policy change, with an additional three applications that addressed policy change tangentially. Eleven of those 19 applications identified instances of major policy change, defined in the ACF as a change that is related to the policy core aspects of a government program (Sabatier and Jenkins-Smith 1999). The remaining applications described policy change as minor, which refers to changes in the secondary aspects of a government program. The explanations for the policy change, whether major or minor, were largely attributed to external shocks (n = 14), sometimes to learning (n = 11), and seldom to internal shocks (n = 2). The relatively small number of applications examining internal shocks is expected, given that this notion was first introduced in the 2007 version of the framework.

ACF hypotheses regarding policy change were tested empirically in five applications. Moderately strong support was found relating external events as a driver of policy change (Elliot and Schlaepfer 2001b; Nohrstedt 2007; 2009; 2011; Ulmanen, Swartling, and Wallgren 2015); however, disagreement remains more broadly over the specific mechanisms by which external events or shocks may impact the policy process. Three applications also tested the impact of policy-oriented learning as a mechanism for policy change, with results indicating moderate support for this hypothesis (Elliot and Schlaepfer 2001a; 2001b; Ullmanen et al. 2015).

Policy-Oriented Learning

The ACF's hypotheses related to policy-oriented learning have received varying levels of attention and empirical support. For example, some studies on the connection between learning and policy change find a strong connection; others describe a weak connection, while some studies question if there is a connection at all (Weible, Sabatier, and McQueen 2009). Thus, learning remains an area that needs further testing and development in the ACF (Jenkins-Smith et al. 2014). In this study, we asked first if learning was the focus of the application and, second, if learning was identified among or between coalitions. Seven applications focused on learning as the main theoretical emphasis within the research; an additional eight applications explored learning among or between coalitions as a mechanism for policy change. There was agreement among the applications that learning was important in the policy process but that work remains to be done regarding the more specific characteristics and determinants of learning within and between coalitions, and what impact that might have on subsystem dynamics.

Main Framework or Supplemental Theory?

Other reviews demonstrate that the ACF has frequently been applied in conjunction with other frameworks and theories (e.g., Weible, Sabatier, and McQueen 2009; Weible et al. 2011). We considered whether the ACF was the main framework used, and if so, how was it used in applications involving Swedish cases. The results show that the ACF was the only framework used in nine of the 25 applications. It was the main framework in an additional nine applications and was used as a supplementary, largely descriptive framework in the remaining seven applications. The extent to which an application utilized the framework was coded to reflect (i) descriptive usage, such as actor constellations described as coalitions with shared beliefs, (ii) conceptual analysis, for example borrowing key terms such as learning or policy change, and (iii) hypothesis testing. Note again that multiple uses are possible. The results show that 20 percent of the applications drew only descriptive analysis from the ACF (n = 5). Half of the applications (n = 12) went one step beyond, directly applying ACF terms such as "learning" or "advocacy coalition". The remaining eight applications directly explored and tested ACF hypotheses. This pattern corroborates findings reported elsewhere—that more than half of the applications generally do not explicitly test any of the hypotheses (Weible, Sabatier, and McQueen 2009).

The ACF was the only framework used in nine of the 25 applications. In an additional nine applications, the ACF was the main application used in conjunction with other frameworks or theories. In total, the ACF was the primary theoretical framework in 18 of the 25 applications. There was a wide spread of supplementary frameworks; policy network theory was the most common but it was referenced in only four applications (Elliot and Schlaepfer 2001a; 2001b; Olsson 2009; Olsson and Hysing 2012). Many supplementary frameworks appeared to be utilized based on their theory regarding actor behavior— such as resource dependency theory, public choice theory, and institutionalism— while other policy process theories— such as multiple streams, stages heuristic, punctuated equilibrium, and bottom-up implementation—were relatively common choices to complement the ACF.

Generalizability and Revisions

Our results show that eight applications explicitly discussed the generalizability of the ACF in Sweden. All of these eight applications addressed issues concerning descriptive validity, discussing whether the notion of advocacy coalitions is useful to describe actor constellations in the Swedish policy process and whether the ACF demonstrates an accurate description of the reality of the policy process. However, most applications addressed generalizability at a fairly broad level with reference to

fundamental differences between politics in Sweden compared to, for example, the United States. These studies did not present empirical observations confirming or disconfirming applicability of the ACF's assumptions in Sweden. Other case studies were more specific in identifying examples where the ACF has limited applicability. One recurrent observation concerned the prevalence of party politics, particularly the role of party discipline, in contested policy subsystems. As issues pose a threat to partisan interests, the importance of advocacy coalitions and their interactions becomes more limited as an explanation for policy change (Nohrstedt 2005; 2009; Rossegger and Ramin 2013).

To address some of the shortcomings of the ACF in Sweden, authors suggested possible modifications. Overall, the modifications focused on developing a more specified model of the policy process. For example, Berggren (1998) recommended refining the concept of policy-oriented learning by co-opting insights from Heclo's model. Elliot and Schlaepfer (2001b) advocated developing the concept of coalitions by taking insights from policy networks and epistemic communities. Matti and Sandström (2013) and Olsson (2009) argued that the framework would be enhanced with more empirical work and theoretical distinction on the tripartite belief system. Finally, several authors offered suggestions for incorporating contextual factors, including a stronger emphasis on socioeconomic and historical developments (Hysing and Olsson 2008) and partisan cleavages and political elite responsiveness to subsystem politics (Nohrstedt 2005; 2009).

[H] As noted earlier, nine additional applications described groups of individuals as "coalitions"; however, these applications were excluded from the final sample as they did not acknowledge coalitions as a concept attributable to the ACF by referring to any of the foundational ACF works (second inclusion criterion).

Discussion—Patterns of Swedish Policy Processes Through the Lens of the ACF

This analysis sets out from the observation that the terms for policymaking in Sweden have gone through some substantial changes in the past decades. While some core properties of corporatism remain, key changes in Swedish policymaking include a movement toward a more open, informal, and conflictual policy process. Scholars suggest that these changes have opened up possibilities for new actors to participate and influence policymaking. In addition, actors increasingly exploit alternative strategies for political influence, including lobbying, networking, and advocacy. Grasping the nature and scope of these changes as well as how they affect policy processes, including terms for policy change and stability, is essential to our understanding of public policymaking. We argue that the ACF is one candidate theoretical framework that can structure research into these questions.

So how can the ACF contribute to knowledge about Swedish policy processes? Results reported in this review of Swedish ACF applications point to several specific patterns and observations.

First, the studies reviewed here *confirm the importance of advocacy coalitions as a form of political organization in the policy process.* The majority of the studies reviewed here (n = 19, 76 percent) identified two coalitions or more, including participants from up to nine different types of organizations. This insight applies across substantive issues and suggests that advocacy coalitions are a potentially important form of political organization in Sweden. However, in previous Swedish ACF applications, advocacy coalitions have been al-most exclusively identified based on shared beliefs, while empirical evidence on coordination remains sparse. This pattern is at odds with our observation that some studies observing coalitions did not actually empirically identify the elements of actors' belief systems, which speaks to a tendency among applications to identify coalitions in a fairly superficial or ad hoc manner. This limitation is understandable, however, given the research challenges and costs involved with disentangling the belief systems and coordination of policy actors. This is nevertheless an important step toward developing the understanding of policy actors' behavior. In addition, many of the studies that focused on advocacy coalitions did not identify the coalition members. More empirical research is therefore warranted to assess the structure and internal dynamics of coalitions in terms of the structure of belief systems and coordination strategies. This begins with efforts to empirically document coalition membership. In addition, studying coordination is critical as a basis for examining the role of advocacy coalitions as a form of political organization vis-à-vis traditional corporatist networks involving horizontal interconnections between organized labor, business, and government and vertical ideologically based alliances between parties and organized interests (see Lembruch 1984).

Second, our review provides *mixed evidence of participation by new organized participants in Swedish policymaking*, such as policy professionals, large companies, and think tanks (cf. Öberg et al. 2011; Svallfors 2016). Our review suggests that many policy subsystems are still dominated by representatives of interest groups, public administrators, and elected politicians. When looking at the organizational affi-

-liation of advocacy coalition members (in those studies in which members are identified), we found that interest groups and government agencies are the dominating actor types in Swedish policy subsystems.

We found no empirical evidence of policy professionals or think tanks in any of the 25 cases. However, we also found that many coalition members are business representatives who participate regularly in the policy process. In summary, our findings provide tentative evidence that policy actors increasingly engage in networking as a strategy for coordinating and obtaining influence in the policy process. At the same time, our findings regarding the organizational affiliation of coalition members would seem to be at odds with a trend toward more open policy process.

Third, our results suggest that *many policy subsystems contain interactions between national and local levels of government,* which speaks to the notion that policy subsystems are nested across actors operating at different levels of government—yet, they show less evidence of Europeanization. We interpret this finding primarily as a result from the bias in the sample toward issues related to environmental and energy policy and natural resource management, which tend to feed tensions between national regulations and local interests. While this might explain regular participation by local-level politicians in many cases, the lack of focus on Europeanization is noteworthy and something that calls for more research.

In addition to these country-specific patterns, we also ask if and how applications of the ACF in Sweden might suggest refinement and specification of the ACF? We found that approximately one-third of the applications explicitly acknowledge

limitations to the ACF, primarily related to the framework's descriptive validity. Some applications question whether the notion of advocacy coalition is useful to describe actor constellations in the policy process and some offer concrete suggestions for modification of the ACF. It can be noted though that most suggestions for modification involve specifications of ACF's core concepts (learning, advocacy coalitions, and belief systems), while no study addresses the utility of the notion of "coalition opportunity structure" as a means to support the application of the ACF in corporatist settings. In fact, we found only three studies dealing superficially with opportunity structures but these studies did not empirically examine the role of opportunity structures—including the level of openness and consensus needed for policy change—in shaping advocacy coalition formation, strategies, or policy change. Thus, while the notion of coalition opportunity structures was introduced by ACF theorists to ease application of the framework outside the United States, this specification has received virtually no empirical attention in Swedish applications.

About one-third of the applications reviewed here test hypotheses derived from the ACF. These studies largely support the explanatory validity of the framework when applied in Sweden. Specifically, studies confirm the importance of policy core beliefs as an explanation of advocacy coalition formation, the role of learning in the policy process, and external shocks as a driver of major policy change. Nevertheless, our review suggests that the compilation of prior applications of the ACF in Swedish policymaking is insufficient as a basis for thoroughly assessing the applicability of the framework in Swe-

-den. Primarily, as long as studies do not clearly operationalize the core elements of the framework, including coordination within coalitions and coalition opportunity structures, it is difficult to assess the framework's bounds of applicability.

In summary, empirical applications of the ACF in cases of Swedish policy processes give a somewhat mixed picture regarding the "portability" of the ACF to Swedish policy processes. On the one hand, many studies apply the ACF's concepts and assumptions to structure analyses of different aspects of policy processes in Sweden, including advocacy coalition formation, learning, and policy change. These studies provide evidence confirming the usefulness of the ACF as a theoretical lens for simplifying and understanding how policy actors organize themselves to gain influence, what factors and events shape policy change, and the role of learning in the policy process. On the other hand, the fact that about one-third of the applications reviewed here propose suggestions for revision and specification is an important reminder that there are areas where scholars question the validity of the framework, or at least struggle to translate some of its key concepts and assumptions into the realm of Swedish policymaking. In our view, these strengths and weaknesses encourage more conceptual and empirical work on the ACF in Sweden, possibly in conjunction with supplementary or competing theories and frameworks, to advance our understanding of the policy process. Such studies will be important to assess in what issues or aspects the ACF may fall short as a theoretical lens and to help identify viable theoretical alternatives.

Conclusion

This review of applications of the advocacy coalition framework (ACF) in Sweden explores (i) how the ACF may contribute to knowledge about Swedish policy processes and (ii) if and how application of the ACF in Sweden might suggest refinement and specification of the ACF. We compiled a dataset of case studies in Sweden, which we coded to assess the frequency of ACF applications, their substantive focus, areas of theoretical emphasis, research methods, and recommendations for theoretical revision. The results confirm that the ACF has received growing attention in Sweden. We identified an initial sample of 50 case studies from which we determined 25 complete applications for coding. Most studies included cases of energy and environmental policy, while cases involving social policies were less common. The most commonly tested set of assumptions involved advocacy coalitions and policy change, while learning attracted less attention. We conclude this study by identifying four areas for which future research is particularly warranted to support theory testing and development within the ACF. Although these areas are derived specifically from our review of policy processes in Sweden, they could apply in any coutry.

First, in order to examine the role of advocacy coalitions as a form of political organization in policymaking—including what importance actors attribute to coalition membership as a means to gain influence and what role coalitions have in influencing policy processes—future studies are needed to empirically explore how coalition members overcome threats to collective action and engage in coordination. Here, scholars can draw on prior ACF work offering theoretical as well as methodological guidance to analyze coordination (Henry 2011; Ingold 2011; Schlager 1995).

Second, studies are needed to explore alternative ways to simplify how subsystems are influenced by political institutions and other external factors. In ACF terms, this is partially a question about how policy actors are enabled and constrained by relatively stable parameters and how their behavior is affected by internal and external events (see Figure 1). As we have demonstrated in this study, there is a shortage of studies in Sweden examining the role of coalition opportunity structures. In addition, examination of other country-specific factors such as size and system of government might generate new insights regarding coalition membership and behavior. Policy subsystems are also constrained by more specific rules and practices guiding participation, influence, and conflict resolution in individual subsystems. What these institutions are and what role they play in shaping policy subsystem politics remain open empirical questions.

To guide inquiry into these questions, we encourage scholars to think broadly about what institutional properties might shape subsystem affairs in the context of Sweden's political system. Which specific institutions are important depends in part on theoretical emphases—whether the objective is to explain or describe advocacy coalition formation and behavior, learning, or policy change. For example, if the objective is to explain policy change, we need to consider constitutional rules that determine the capacity of government to legislate and implement public policy, including, e.g. scope for unilateral action (i.e. the probability that executive decisions will be confirmed at subsequent points). The relative stability of parliamentary majority is another factor that determines policymaking since it affects whether executive decisions will be overturned by Parliament (Immergut 1992). However, our analysis shows that these institutional properties have been given limited analytical attention in Swedish ACF applications. In return, this is an area of future inquiry focusing on how institutions shape political situations by influencing, for example, the capacity of governments to carry out policy change, what actors are included in policy subsystems, what political strategies they chose, and how power is distributed between actors (see Pontusson 1995).

A third avenue of research involves longitudinal studies of policy processes over time to document changes in the scope of participation. Longitudinal studies are important to examine to what extent advocacy coalition membership is susceptible to institutional change (Sabatier and Jenkins-Smith 1993). In Sweden, for example, we have witnessed changes in the formal framework of administrative corporatism and in the norms and practices of corporatism. In addition, there have been a number of other fundamental institutional changes in Sweden, including the gradual dismantling of socialist policies and disintegration of the highly centralized Swedish labor market. Lindvall and Rothstein (2006) suggest that the political and administrative processes in Sweden have moved away from a "strong state" characterized by consensus-oriented policymaking involving politicians and interest groups, toward a weakening of central administrative institutions. These changes, in turn, have paved the way for major policy change, primarily in the social sector. Whether and how these changes have impacted advocacy coalition membership and behavior within and across policy subsystems are questions that demand comparative work over time.

Finally, studies should employ clearly specified research methods to foster transparency and collective learning among scholars. We found that one-third of the studies in Sweden relied upon unspecified methods of data collection—a pattern noted elsewhere as well (Weible, Sabatier, and McQueen 2009).

Given the increasing number of Swedish ACF applications, we expect that the trend will continue into the future. We hope that this trend will be accompanied by the development and application of inter-subjectively reliable methods based on best practices. Of course, this is not an effort that is limited to Sweden but a joint responsibility for the international community of ACF scholars to share experiences and insights.

Although our study is limited to ACF applications in Sweden, one may speculate as to whether there any recurrent patterns that characterize changing corporatist systems in Europe in terms of the structure of advocacy coalitions and processes of learning and policy change. Our findings are largely consistent with applications in other countries and settings that find relatively heterogeneous coalitions populated by representatives of different organizations seeking to influence public policy. In this regard, results reported here do not reveal any observations unique to neo-corporatist governing systems. However, other studies indicate that there are aspects of the policy process where more particular effects might be evident. For instance, Rommetvedt et al. (2013) show that in Denmark and Norway the gradual dismantling of corporatist representation has pushed interest groups to resort increasingly to political lobbyism directed at elected representatives in Parliament and the government. Also in a study of Denmark, Larsen, Vrangbaek, and Traulsen (2006) demonstrate that policy actors may be affiliated with several advocacy coalitions simultaneously, which paves the way for negotiation and compromise rather than conflict among competing coalitions. In our view, these findings encourage future analysis of how changing corporatist structures and practices might feed certain unique patterns of behavior and strategies of policy actors.

We find it necessary to conclude this study with a caveat. This review focuses exclusively on empirical applications of the ACF in Swedish policy processes, which is deliberately a narrow theoretical and empirical contribution. We do not claim that the ACF is the only approach available or that it provides better descriptions or explanations compared to other alternative frameworks offered by the vast public policy literature. However, as indicated by the number of applications in the recent years, the ACF clearly constitutes one useful theoretical starting point for scholars interested in Swedish policy processes. Also, we stress that the ACF does not make any aspirations to be a complete framework capturing all the aspects and nuances of the policy process. The policy process is simply too complex, which calls for comparative research using different and partially complementary theoretical perspectives. By demonstrating how the ACF has been applied in Sweden, including the most important contributions and limitations, we hope to contribute to the cumulative effort by policy scholars to advance the understanding of policy processes across systems and settings.

Acknowledgment

This work was supported by the Swedish research council Formas under Grant 211-2012-627. A previous version of this manuscript was presented at the 2015 Swedish Political Science Association (SWEPSA) annual meeting in Stockholm. The authors are thankful to the participants at the SWEPSA working-group Public Administration and Policy Analysis for their insightful comments. A special thanks also to Chris Weible and Jonathan Pierce for their advice on previous versions of this article.

References

Atkinson, M. and W. Coleman. 1989. "Strong States and Weak States: Sectoral Policy Networks in Advanced Capitalist Economies." *British Journal of Political Science* 19 (1): 47–67.

Berggren, R. 1998. "The Advocacy Coalition Framework: Its Applicability to a Swedish Land-Use Conflict." In S*ocial Sustainability of Forestry in the Baltic Sea Region*, ed. M. Hytönen. Helsinki: The Finnish Forest Research Institute.

Blom-Hansen, J. 2000. "Still Corporatism in Scandinavia? A Survey of Recent Empirical Findings." *Scandinavian Political Studies* 23 (2): 157–81.

Carter, N. 2001. *The Politics of the Environment: Ideas, Activism, Policy.* Cambridge: Cambridge University Press.

Eberg, J. 1997. *Waste Policy and Learning. Policy Dynamics of Waste Management and Waste Incineration in the Netherlands and Bavaria.* Delft: Eburon.

Elliot, C., and R. Schlaepfer. 2001a. "The Advocacy Coalition Framework: Application to the Policy Process for the Development of Forest Certification in Sweden." *Journal of European Public Policy* 8 (4): 642–61.

Elliot, C., and R. Schlaepfer. 2001b. "Understanding Forest Certification Using the Advocacy Coalition Framework." *Forest Policy and Economics* 2: 257–66.

Eriksson, J., M. Karlsson, and M. Reuter. 2010. "Technocracy, Politicization, and Noninvolvement: Politics of Expertise in the European Regulation of Chemicals." *Review of Policy Research* 27 (2): 167–85.

Henry, A. 2011. "Ideology, Power, and the Structure of Policy Networks." *Policy Studies Journal* 39 (3): 361–83.

Hogl, K. 2000. "The Austrian Domestic Forest Policy Community in Change? Impacts of the Globalisation and Europeanisation of Forest Politics." *Forest Policy and Economics* 1 (1): 3–13.

Howlett, M., and M. Ramesh. 1998. "Policy Subsystem Configurations and Policy Change: Operationalizing the Postpositivist Analysis of the Politics of the Policy Process." *Policy Studies Journal* 26 (3): 466–81.

Hysing, E., and J. Olsson. 2008. "Contextualising the Advocacy Coalition Framework: Theorising Change in Swedish Forest Policy." *Environmental Politics* 17 (5): 730–48.

Immergut, E. 1992. "The Rules of the Game: The Logic of Health Policy-Making in France, Switzerland, and Sweden." In *Structuring Politics: Historical Institutionalism in Comparative Perspective*, eds. K. Thelen and S. Steinmo. New York: Cambridge University Press.

Ingold, K. 2011. "Network Structures Within Policy Processes: Coalitions, Power, and Brokerages in Swiss Climate Policy." *Policy Studies Journal* 39 (3): 435–59.

Irondelle, B. 2003. "Europeanization Without the European Union? French Military Reforms 1991–96." *Journal of European Public Policy* 10 (2): 208–26.

Jang, S., C. Weible, and K. Park. 2016. "Policy Processes in South Korea Through the Lens of the Advocacy Coalition Framework." *Journal of Asian Public Policy* 9 (3): 274–90.

Jenkins-Smith, H., D. Nohrstedt, C. Weible, and P. Sabatier. 2014. "The Advocacy Coalition Framework." In Theories of the Policy Process. 3rd ed., eds. P. Sabatier and C. Weible. Boulder, CO: Westview Press.

John, P. 1998. *Analysing Public Policy*. London: Pinter.

Jones, M., H. Peterson, J. Pierce, N. Herweg, A. Bernal, H. Raney, and N. Zahariadis. 2015. "A River Runs Through It: A Multiple Streams Meta-Review." *Policy Studies Journal* 44 (1): 13–36.

Larsen, J., K. Vrangbaek, and J. Traulsen. 2006. "Advocacy Coalitions and Pharmacy Policy in Denmark: Solid Cores with Fuzzy Edges." *Social Science and Medicine* 63 (1): 212–24.

Lehmbruch, G. 1984. "Concertation and the Structure of Corporatist Networks." In *Order and Conflict in Contemporary Capitalism*, ed. J. Goldthorpe. Oxford: Clarendon Press, 60–80.

Lewin, L. 1994. "The Rise and Decline of Corporatism: The Case of Sweden." *European Journal of Political Research* 26 (1): 59–79.

Lijphart, A. 1999. *Patterns of Democracy: Government Form and Performance in Thirty-Six Countries.* New Haven, CT: Yale University Press.

Lindvall, J., and B. Rothstein. 2006. "Sweden: The Fall of the Strong State." *Scandinavian Political Studies* 29 (1): 47–63.

Matti, S., and A. Sandström. 2011. "The Rationale Determining Advocacy Coalitions: Examining Coordination Networks and Corresponding Beliefs." *Policy Studies Journal* 39 (3): 385–410.

Matti, S., and A. Sandström. 2013. "The Defining Elements of Advocacy Coalitions: Continuing the Search for Explanations for Coordination and Coalition Structures." *Review of Policy Research* 30 (2): 240–57. *European Public Policy* 12 (6): 1041-1059.

Matti, S., and A. Sandström. 2013. "The Defining Elements of Advocacy Coalitions: Continuing the Search for Explanations for Coordination and Coalition Structures." *Review of Policy Research* 30 (2): 240–57.

Nohrstedt, D. 2005. External Shocks and policy Change: Three Mile Island and Swedish Nuclear Energy Policy'. Journal of European Public Policy 12 (6): 1041-1059.

Nohrstedt, D. 2007. *Crisis and Policy Reformcraft: Advocacy Coalitions and Crisis-induced Change in Swedish Nuclear Energy Policy*. Uppsala: Uppsala University.

Nohrstedt, D. 2009. "Do Advocacy Coalitions Matter? Crisis and Change in Swedish Nuclear Energy Policy." *Journal of Public Administration Research and Theory* 20: 309–33.

Nohrstedt, D. 2011. "Shifting Resources and Venues Producing Policy Change in Contested Subsystems: A Case Study of Swedish Signals Intelligence Policy." *Policy Studies Journal* 39 (3): 461–84.

Nohrstedt, D. and K. Olofsson. 2016. "Advocacy Coalition Politics and Strategies on Hydraulic Fracturing in Sweden." In *Policy Debates on Hydraulic Fracturing: Comparing Coalition Politics in North America and Europe*, eds. C. Weible, T. Heikkila, K. Ingold and M. Fischer. New York: Palgrave.

Nohrstedt, D. and C. Weible. 2010. "The Logic of Policy Change After Crisis: Proximity and Subsystem Interaction." *Risks, Hazards and Crisis in Public Policy* 1 (2): 1-23.

Öberg, P., T. Svensson, T. Christiansen, A. Nørgaard, H. Rommetvedt, and G. Thesen. 2011. "Disrupted Exchange and Declining Corporatism: Government Authority and Interest Group Capability in Scandinavia." *Government & Opposition* 46 (3): 365–91.

Olsson, J. 2009. "The Power of the Inside Activist: Understanding Policy Change by Empowering the Advocacy Coalition Framework (ACF)." *Planning Theory & Practice* 10 (2): 167–87.

Olsson, J., and E. Hysing. 2012. "Theorizing Inside Activism: Understanding Policymaking and Policy Change from Below." *Planning Theory & Practice* 13 (2): 257–73.

Parsons, W. 1995. *Public Policy: An Introduction to the Theory and Practice of Policy Analysis*. Cheltenham: Edward Elgar.

Pontusson, J. 1995. "From Comparative Public Policy to Political Economy: Putting Institutions in Their Place and Taking Interests Seriously." *Comparative Political Studies* 28 (1): 117–47.

Princen, S. 2007. "Advocacy Coalitions and the Internationalization of Public Health Policies." *Journal of Public Policy* 27 (1): 13–33.

Rommetvedt, H., G. Thesen, P. Christiansen, and A. Norgaard. 2013. "Coping with Corporatism in Decline and the Revival of Parliament: Interest Group Lobbyism in Denmark and Norway, 1980–2005." *Comparative Political Studies* 46 (4): 457–85.

Rossegger, U. and R. Ramin. 2013. "Explaining the Ending of Sweden's Nuclear Phase-out Policy: A New Approach by Referring to the Advocacy Coalition Framework Theory." *Innovation: The European Journal of Social Science Research* 26 (4): 323-343.

Sabatier, P. 1986. "Top-Down and Bottom-Up Approaches to Implementation Research: A Critical Analysis and Suggested Synthesis." *Journal of Public Policy* 6 (1): 21–48.

Sabatier, P. 1988. "An Advocacy Coalition Framework of Policy Change and the Role of Policy-Oriented Learning Therein." *Policy Sciences* 21 (2-3): 129–68.

Sabatier, P. 1998. "The Advocacy Coalition Framework: Revisions and Relevance for Europe." *Journal of European Public Policy* 5 (1): 98–130.

Sabatier, P., and H. Jenkins-Smith. 1993. *Policy Change and Learning: An Advocacy Coalition Approach.* Boulder, CO: Westview Press.

Sabatier, P., and H. Jenkins-Smith. 1999. "The Advocacy Coalition Framework: An Assessment." In *Theories of the Policy Process*, ed. P. Sabatier. Boulder, CO: Westview Press.

Sabatier, P., and C. Weible. 2007. "The Advocacy Coalition Framework: Innovations and Classifications." In *Theories of the Policy Process*. 2nd ed., ed. P. Sabatier. Boulder, CO: Westview Press.

Schlager, E. 1995. "Policy Making and Collective Action: Defining Coalitions Within the Advocacy Coalition Framework." *Policy Sciences* 28 (3): 243–70.
Sotirov, M., and M. Memmler. 2012. "The Advocacy Coalition Framework in Natural Resource Policy Studies – Recent Experiences and Future Prospects." *Forest Politics and Economics* 16: 51–64.

Storbjörk, J. 2014. "Stakeholders' Arguments for and Against Moving Swedish Substance Abuse Treatment to the Health Care System: How a Fat Reform Proposal Became a Thin Government Bill." *Nordic Studies on Alcohol and Drugs* 31: 81–110.

Svallfors, S. 2016. "Politics as Organized Combat: New Players and New Rules of the Game in Sweden." *New Political Economy* 21 (6): 505–19.

Ullmanen, J., Å. Swartling, and O. Wallgren. 2015. "Climate Adaptation in Swedish Forestry: Exploring the Debate and Policy Process, 1990–2012." *Forests* 6: 708–33.

Valman, M. 2014. *Three Faces of HELCOM – Institution, Organization, Policy Producer.* Stockholm: Stockholm University.

Weible, C., and D. Nohrstedt. 2012. "Coalitions, Learning, and Policy Change." In *Routledge Handbook of Public Policy*, eds. E. Araral, Jr., S. Fritzen, M. Howlett, M. Ramesh, and X. Wu. New York City, NY: Taylor & Francis.

Weible, C., P. Sabatier, H. Jenkins-Smith, D. Nohrstedt, A. Henry, and P. DeLeon. 2011. "A Quarter Century of the Advocacy Coalition Framework: An Introduction to the Special Issue." *Policy Studies Journal* 39 (3): 349–60.

Weible, C., P. Sabatier, and K. McQueen. 2009. "Themes and Variations: Taking Stock of the Advocacy Coalition Framework." *Policy Studies Journal* 37 (1): 121–40.

Wilson, F. 1983. "Interest Groups and Politics in Western Europe: The Neo-Corporatist Approach." *Comparative Politics* 16 (1): 105–23.

Bricolage or Entrepreneurship? Lessons from the Creation of the European Centre for Disease Prevention and Control

Thibaud Deruelle[A]

This paper belongs to the field of theories of the Policy process and contributes to the literature on the multiple streams approach (MSA), by investigating bricolage as an alternative type of agency in agenda-setting and policy formulation. The bricoleur frames conditions as a problem that can and must be fixed and emerges as the one who looks for a solution. For the bricoleur outcome goals, or rather, the choice of a particular outcome is less important than the process goal. Therefore, the bricoleur selects policy ideas depending on the properties they display and combines them to create the best "fit" to couple the streams. Bricolage relates to the organizational properties of certain actors, in this case the European Commission. Evidence comes from the case of the European Centre for Disease Prevention and Control (ECDC) and its origins, created in the aftermath of the severe acute respiratory syndrome crisis. I will demonstrate that the crisis did not trigger the creation of the ECDC but rather was framed as a salient issue to be resolved by the Commission. The process of policy formulation that followed resulted in a bespoke solution. As such, this paper contributes to the development of the MSA but also to the literature on ideational politics and European agencies.

Keywords*: European Agencies, Multiple Streams, Bricolage, Crisis, Health Policy*

[A] University of Exeter, United Kingdom

doi: 10.18278/epa.2.2.4

Introduction

Cross-border health crises have attracted a lot of attention among the general public in the last few years, most recently with the Ebola virus. The European Union (EU) has a long history of health crises (such as the Bovine spongiform encephalopathy or "mad cow" disease). Most pertinently perhaps, the creation of the European Centre for Disease Prevention and Control (ECDC) is often portrayed as the functional response to the severe acute respiratory syndrome (SARS) crisis that occurred between November 2002 and July 2003 (Greer 2012; Greer and Löblová 2016; McKee, Atun, and Coker 2008). This perspective on the importance of the crisis in the creation of the agency is often used to explain why such a short period was spent between the European Commission drafting a proposal to create the ECDC in July 2003 and the creation *in situ* of the agency in May 2005. The ECDC hence looks like a mundane case of agency creation: a crisis triggered a response; this response was a new agency. This idea that the time "has come" for an agency to be created is a recurring theme in the official narratives of agency creation as well as in the literature on the emergence of agencies that regulate or distribute information used by regulators (Alam 2007; Maggetti 2013). The ECDC, in particular, is charged with bringing expertise to the table, thus reducing uncertainty and allowing an evidence-based regulation of risk.

The crisis-followed-by-agency-creation causal mechanism seems plausible. However, a minimum standard for causality is that the effect comes after the cause. But in the field of disease prevention and control in Europe, we can observe that some features of the ECDC were pre-existent to SARS; notably a network of epidemiological surveillance, now an integral part of the ECDC, existed since the early 1990s. Moreover, the creation of a European agency dedicated to disease control has been disputed among experts and has been a topic of disagreement between European institutions since the late 1990s. At a minimum, the creation of an agency as response to the crisis has to be put in its context of conflict and contestation of the various institutional choices aired at the time. In this paper, I challenge the conventional wisdom of agency creation as response to the crisis and open the black box of the organizational and political processes of creation dynamics. As shown by Moe (2005), institutional emergence is a political process where power is created, distributed, and re-arranged in the form of a precise set of organizational features.

To answer questions about the causes of institutional creation, it is necessary to go beyond the crisis as a single explanatory variable and open our *grand-angle* on the politics of agenda-setting and policy formulation. The multiple streams approach (MSA) seems a suitable, sophisticated theoretical lens to analyze how the agenda for the creation of the ECDC was set and how the policy idea of an agency emerged. In European Studies, the MSA has been fruitfully applied to the study of agenda-setting in the EU (Ackrill, Kay, and Zahariadis 2013; Herweg 2015; Zahariadis 2008)—adapting a model explaining agenda-setting in the United States (Kingdon [1984] 2003). But subsequent developments of the field have highlighted that the MSA can be applied to the entire policy formulation process (Blankenau 2001).

The model breaks down causality across three paths or streams: policy, politics, and problems. This is already more sophisticated than the crisis-response model. In addition, the model presents three necessary conditions for change (Herweg, Huß, and Zohlnhöfer 2015):

(1) Each stream must be "ripe", meaning that there is a perceived problem, that the policy stream comprises at least one viable alternative and that policymakers embrace a proposal.

(2) A policy window opens following a change in the politics or the problem stream.

(3) A policy entrepreneur couples politics, policy, and problem streams.

Using the MSA brings agency back into the study of institutional emergence: policy entrepreneurs have policy solutions which they try to link to changes in the preferences of policymakers or to the emergence of new problems. However, in the case of the ECDC, there is no figure that emerges as a policy entrepreneur. Some ideas were championed by different actors; however, rather than one idea emerging, bits and pieces of different ideas seem to have been recombined in a proposal of the European Commission. How can organizational change be explained without a policy entrepreneur? Can the MSA be refined to present coupling the

streams as something other than the result of policy-entrepreneurs? How can we explain that ideas, sometimes presented as contradictory, may be identified in the institutional features of the ECDC?

This paper makes two conceptual moves. First, this paper presents a critical approach to the MSA and looks for an alternative to the policy entrepreneur. I will define a new type of agency based on the search for solving a problem rather than the advancement of a solution. Second, this paper presents a different relationship between policy ideas and the agent; as such it contributes to the development of the MSA and to the literature on the creation of European agencies.

The recent literature on the MSA (Ackrill, Kay, and Zahariadis 2013; Cairney and Jones 2015) shows that there is an appetite for refinements of the model: "there is a need for a study to specify MSA's theoretical benchmarks and hypotheses to clearly identify the potential and limits of conceptual stretching" (Jones et al. 2015, 29). This paper contributes to refining our understanding of coupling the streams and suggests a critical approach to agency in the MSA.

Agency in the MSA is usually incarnated in the figure of the policy entrepreneur. Walker (1974, 113) defines policy entrepreneurship as the advancement of solutions that are tied closely with the maintenance of entrepreneurial needs and interests. Zahariadis (2008, 18) presents the policy entrepreneur as the proactive element of the MSA capable of developing strategies to promote her solutions. In the MSA, policy entrepreneurs are successful when their efforts for entrepreneurship lead to coupling the streams in accordance to their preferences. Policy entrepreneurship is thus defined as efforts made by the policy entrepreneur to promote solutions consistent with her needs and interest. From these definitions, I infer that the actions of the policy entrepreneur are a solution-driven process from softening-up to coupling the streams. Nevertheless, Zahariadis (2003, 73) identifies two types of coupling: "when windows open in the politics stream, coupling is likely to be doctrinal (finding a problem to a given solution)," and "when policy windows open the problem stream, coupling is likely to be consequential (finding a solution to a given problem)." While doctrinal coupling suits the traditional assumptions on the activities of the policy entrepreneur (a solution-driven process or an outcome process), consequential coupling underlines that coupling can be seen as a problem-driven process. Therefore, let us turn to the literature on the problem stream that is eloquent on the notion of focusing events and how they lead to policy windows. This notion, first introduced by Kingdon ([1984] 2003), was then adapted by Birkland (1998a; 1998b) to study the effect of accidents and natural disasters as drivers of change. In the literature, new research venues appeared recently, inspired by the financial and budgetary crisis, such as Saurugger and Terpan (2015), refining the MSA to demonstrate that the stronger the crisis, the more important the change. While the literature informs us on drivers and scope of change, there is room for studying a type of agency in the MSA that is defined as a problem-driven process rather than a solution-driven one.

I thus suggest the introduction of a new type of agency in the MSA. My argument is that coupling is not necessarily the result of the efforts of a policy entrepreneur, but rather arises out of a different type of agency: *bricolage*, in which the one who couples the streams combines different policy ideas to formulate a bespoke solution to a problem.

The *bricoleur* as a type of agent distinct from the policy entrepreneur does not have clear or fixed preferences for one solution over another. Her choice is thus dictated by a consequential search for fit (Zahariadis 2003, 73). Put bluntly, the *bricoleur* looks for policy ideas that would be useful in crafting a new solution: policy ideas as a resource to create solutions. Here enters the second theme: how does the *bricoleur* select these policy ideas? Why are *bricoleurs* drawn to some ideas rather than others? The emergence of ideas in the MSA is likened to a process of natural selection (Kingdon [1984] 2003) in which the "survival" of ideas is arbitrated by two criteria: value acceptability (compatibility with the values of the policy network) and technical feasibility (to what extent can the idea be translated into the real world?). These criteria are relevant to understand what ideas are at the disposal of the *bricoleur* and why they survived the natural selection process, but do not offer explanatory leverage on why the *bricoleur* selects some ideas rather than other ones. On what does the *bricoleur* base her judgement? I suggest two criteria that the *bricoleur* uses when she arbitrates different policy ideas.

• The first one is an important element of the MSA: the ripeness of the politics stream (Herweg, Huß, and

Zohlnhöfer 2015). The bricoleur selects policy ideas to which policymakers are ripe to; otherwise, the policy solution would not pass the decision-making stage.

• The second one is more innovative and suggests that the *bricoleur* builds on the initiatives developed by the policy community. This is the criterion of increasing returns: the *bricoleur* avoids the costs of exiting initiatives and even capitalizes on projects already developed by the policy community. Therefore, the bricoleur is likely to use ideas in which the policy community has invested time and efforts.

Following these criteria, the *bricoleur* creates a bespoke policy solution from different ideas presenting advantages in terms of ripeness of the politics stream and/or in terms of increasing returns.

This paper proceeds as follows: after entering *bricolage* and how it can contribute to the enrichment of the MSA, I first draw on process tracing to present the context in each stream, up to the SARS crisis. The first stream is the policy stream. Different ideas navigate in the policy stream: how do they stand the criterion of increasing returns? Evidence comes from the debate that animated the policy community by analyzing articles in different publications of practitioners. This paper then investigates the variations in the politics stream and analyze how the respective positions of the Council of the European Union and the European Parliament (EP) have shown appetite for different solutions, how the European Commission has evolved from opponent to promotor of the creation of the ECDC and how this has affected the

recombination of ideas. In order to do so, official positions of the institutions have been identified from the Official Journal of the European Union and the archives of the different institutions. The problem stream is eventually analyzed in terms of perception, also drawing from archives and speeches. The second methodological step is to demonstrate the lack of fit of the figure of the policy entrepreneur in a part that reflects on the window of opportunity and agency and on how the European Commission's framing of the SARS crisis led to coupling by *bricolage*. Eventually, building on the analysis of the three streams, this paper focuses on the policy formulation part of *bricolage*, as well as the decision-making process and delivers a review of the concept in conclusion.

The Relationship Between Bricolage and Change

Entering Bricolage

Bricolage is a concept that presents a mode of scientific thoughts. In his book *The Savage Mind*, first published in 1962, Levi-Strauss (1988, 12) introduced the *bricoleur* as one who "addresses himself to a collection of oddments left over from human endeavours". While Levi-Strauss looked at the concept from an anthropological point of view, the concept of *bricolage* resonated in different disciplines of social science. In public policy, the concept captures epistemological strategies and rationalities, under the name of *Epistemological Bricolage* (Freeman 2007). The concept is identified as a self-learning process, the act of piecing together knowledge, as one "acquires and assembles tools and material as he or she goes." (Freeman 2007, 486; see also Carstensen 2011). Freeman is interested in understanding how knowledge is formed and thus identified dynamics of learning. However, if the concept of policy change is questioned, identifying the type of "learning" only gives a partial answer. The concept of *bricolage* in public policy needs to be refined to unlock its potential in explaining policy change.

Levi-Strauss used the French word of *Bricolage* as an analogy to underline an oblique strategy. In his classic *bricolage* piece of 1962, the word is mainly used to describe some extraneous, oblique movements in ball games, as well as snooker or racing. The use of the word bricolage and bricoleur is nowadays very different. The bricoleur is one in a domestic environment such as a workshop, using whatever is at hand to perform a form of craftsmanship.

Now, imagine a bricoleur trying to fix a table, running out of screws. She is deprived of a solution to the problem and needs a new solution. However, she is bounded to what is available in the workshop; she looks for alternatives and decides to use a nail instead of screw. Let us now imagine that the nail is too short for the hole of the screw. The *bricoleur* looks again around her and finds a chip of wood. She has an idea: by sticking the chip of food at the bottom of the hole, she can use the nail. The *bricoleur* has thus fixed the table but rather than using "by the book" solutions, she combined different solutions to make it fit to the situation. The solution is not a type of modus operandi: the *bricoleur* will not start using nails and wood chips instead of screws. Rather, this solution is a devious mean used to keep the process of fixing the table on going.

Let us now return to Levi-Strauss to generate theoretical leverage on *bricolage* as a form of policy change. Applied to public policy, the *bricoleur* is one who cares about finding a solution rather than using a specific solution. *Bricolage* is thus a form of agency that is problem-solving oriented and characterized by:

1. Contextual conjectures: the *bricoleur* creates structures by means of events (Levi-Strauss 1988, 15). The *bricoleur* realizes there is a problem after an event occurs. The *bricoleur's* agency lays in the choice to ignore the problem or to solve it. Once the choice made to solve the problem, the *bricoleur* looks for the means to come up with a solution.

2. A process goal: the *bricoleur* uses devious means (Levi-Strauss 1988, 11) to create a bespoke solution to a specific problem. Outcome goals, or rather, the choice of a particular outcome, is less important than the process goal.

3. Bounded rationality and scarce resources that cannot be expanded: the elements used by the *bricoleur* are "pre-constrained" (Levi-Strauss 1988, 12), there is a finite amount of policy ideas at hand.

4. As a result, the *bricoleur* produces a policy solution created from the "new arrangement of elements" (Levi-Strauss 1988, 13).

These four characteristics of bricolage will be subsequently leveraged to understand the creation of the ECDC and more generally how the MSA can work when, instead of an entrepreneur, there is a *bricoleur*.

The Bricoleur inside the MSA

The *bricoleur* is a type of agent that is hybrid in the sense that she is active in both the problem and the policy stream. I develop below how the foundations of the MSA, contingency, and ambiguity are compatible with this type of agency.

Rüb (2016, 56) posits that two phenomena are contingent in the MSA: the political entrepreneur and the window of opportunity. This paper ought to add a third phenomenon, the *bricoleur*. Contingency is the assumption that everything that is could be different; I relate *bricolage* as background contingency (Rüb 2016) which predicates that agency is achieved in a context laced with coincidences and surprises. The *bricoleur* acts by means of events, but this explains only partially her agency; she makes the choice to focus on a problem and, therefore, is a contingent element following events.

The *bricoleur* borrows from the problem broker who promotes a particular problem, or "define(s) conditions as problems" (Knaggård 2015, 452). The bricoleur thus participates actively in opening a problem window, which in an ambiguous context "create(s) meaning for the policymakers" (Zahariadis 2008, 16). However, unlike the problem broker, the *bricoleur's* agency is not only a matter of creating meaning in the problem stream: she finds the imperative for policy change and consequentially engages on a search for solutions.

The *bricoleur* is not attached to one solution in particular, rather her attention is on the resolution of the problem and the means are secondary. This means that unlike the policy entrepreneur, the *bricoleur* does not look for a way of maintaining her needs and interests but rather defines her own role as one who takes responsibility for solving the problem. The *bricoleur* is the problem-solving driven agent that emerges to take responsibility for finding a solution.

I rely on the concept of consequential search for fit and problem windows to define *bricolage* as the process of finding a solution to a problem. The *bricoleur* is established as one who frames the problem and actively participates in opening a problem window. Zahariadis describes the consequences of a problem window as follows: "a problem window triggers a search with a problem already in mind, however vaguely it may be defined. […] Consequently, the process begins with a search for clues about appropriate solutions to an already existing problem" (Zahariadis 2003, 73). The search for an "appropriate" solution that "fits" is a theme that has been understudied in the MSA literature; nevertheless, Ackrill and Kay (2011) have developed a model of coupling that answers some of the interrogations raised by the consequential search for fit. However, this paper will suggest a departure from the direction taken by Ackrill and Kay.

Ackrill and Kay posit that changes in the political or problem streams may signal to policymakers to select from known proposals (Ackrill and Kay 2011, 77) and suggest that both selling an idea and selecting an idea are entrepreneurial.

The concept of policy entrepreneurship is thus stretched: policy entrepreneurs do not necessarily have a pet policy solution, they can pick-it up as a change in the politics or problem stream appears. I argue that the concept of policy entrepreneurs proves too limited when agents do not shape preferences for a solution but rather look for the best fit. Here then enters bricolage. The *bricoleur* has a process goal and as such cannot be likened to a form of policy entrepreneur that is inherently driven by an outcome goal. Rather than selecting ideas depending on preferences, the bricoleur creates by recombining ideas and formulating a bespoke solution. It is thus a type of agency that uses unexploited aspects of the full theoretical leverage of the consequential search for fit.

Inside the MSA the bricoleur is an agent who has an incidence on both content and content perception and who is active in two of the streams. In the problem stream, the bricoleur opens a window by framing conditions as a problem that she can and must be fix; the bricoleur thus sets her goal to engage on a path of consequential search for fit in the policy stream. Only then does the bricoleur modify the content to produce a "fit" solution. This *bricolage* leads to an oblique way of coupling the streams: rather than a solution being joined to a new problem, a bespoke solution is created to accommodate the definition of the problem.

Nevertheless, the search for "fit" does not only depend of the way the problem was framed but also of the ripeness of the politics stream and of the elements that the *bricoleur* finds in the policy stream. Hereby I address how the

bricoleur creates a bespoke solution.

Formulating Policy in an Oblique Way

Once the *bricoleur* has framed conditions as a problem, the search for fit depends on two variables: first, the ripeness of the politics stream and, second, increasing returns of policy ideas. These criteria determine how the bricoleur creates a bespoke solution. As for formulating policy, *bricolage* is an oblique way to create a new solution by selecting and recombining ideas depending on their properties, but also depending on how they are perceived by decision makers.

Ripeness of Policy-Makers

Building upon Kingdon's idea of receptivity ([1984] 2003), Herweg, Huß, and Zohlnhöfer (2015) contributed to the enrichment of the MSA by bringing the concept of "ripeness" of the stream which describes how the stream becomes ripe to new policy ideas. The *bricoleur* then pays attention to select elements of ideas which the policymakers are ripe to. With *bricolage*, it is even possible to piece together a solution that will comfort dissonant preferences among policymakers. This is a type of contingency defined by Rüb (2016) as action contingency in the sense that it arises from the interaction of individuals of groups competing for power.

Increasing Returns of Policy Ideas

Zahariadis in his definition of consequential search for fit posits that an "immediate action [such as *bricolage*] is motivated more by the need to avoid higher costs rather than the need to reap more benefits" (Zahariadis 2003, 72). This echoes Pierson's (2000, 252) conceptualization of increasing returns: "the relative benefits of the current activity compared with other possible options increase over time" (Pierson 2000, 252). The *bricoleur's* choice is to avoid the costs of exiting initiatives already developed in the field and, therefore, policy ideas with increasing returns are always bound to the case under consideration. The cost-efficiency analysis performed by the *bricoleur* is thus not only about the cost it represents for herself but also about the cost for the policy community.

Ideas represent a cost for the policy community when policies exist as initiatives. They thus do not bare any cost when ideas are "on the shelf": they have been simply exposed, most of the time in written form and bare virtually no cost but the time the author spent on shaping and communicating the idea. Ideas represent a cost and, therefore, produce increasing returns in two cases: The applicability of the idea has been successfully accepted within the policy community and developed as a turn-key solution. It involves efforts of research and policy design. These initiatives exist only on paper but the policy community has bared the cost of developing, designing, and preparing a policy solution directly exploitable by decision makers. The idea has been partially or fully translated into the real world and as such bares financial costs and/or mobilizes part of the policy community. It thus has a structuring value for the policy community, mobilizes resources and may be seen as a structure that inhibits organization members from seeing a need for change (Kelman 2005,

27);

The criterion of increasing returns tells us that the *bricoleur* avoids the costs of exiting initiatives and even capitalizes on projects that have been developed by the policy community. Therefore, the bricoleur is likely to use ideas in which the policy community has invested time and efforts. As such it is also a matter of *action contingency* (Rüb 2016) in the sense that it arises from the interaction of different individuals or groups within the policy community.

As developed in the Introduction section, the criteria for idea selection in bricolage are distinct from the criteria of survival of ideas. Nevertheless, I ought to contrast this distinction: while the two processes are a matter of emergence of policy ideas, the survival of ideas is an incremental process, whereas bricolage is an immediate selection. The two processes are not antithetic, rather the policy ideas that a *bricoleur* will take under consideration are at her disposal because these ideas survived in the primeval soup. The survival of ideas is a matter of contingency, while the two criteria of bricolage are a matter of agency and explains the judgement of the *bricoleur* when she considers different ideas.

Looking at each of the criteria, they add a new layer to the survival criteria.*Ripeness of policymakers* is about how much policymaker are receptive to the idea, while this receptiveness might depend on the value acceptability and technical feasibility of the idea, the focus remains on the relationship between an idea and the policymakers. *Increasing returns* is not a measure of how much an idea is accepted in the policy community or how much its technical feasibility has been proven, but a criterion based on the efforts made to make an idea acceptable, feasible or even to realize the idea.

Bricolage as a Mode of Coupling the Streams

Because of increasing returns, it can be assumed that the bricoleur tries to avoid the cost of exiting from initiatives developed by the policy community. I hypothesize that the bricoleur will incorporate elements of an idea with no increasing returns to the solution only because policymakers are ripe to it.

Coupling and formulating a policy are for the bricoleur simultaneous and intertwined processes. The *bricoleur* is thus an agent that couples the streams by formulating a bespoke solution. The bricoleur creates a policy solution that is wary of contextual elements in both the politics and the policy stream. She formulates a policy solution that "fits" and in doing so couples the streams.

The hypothesis underpinned by *bricolage* as a mode of coupling the streams is the following: after framing conditions as a problem, a bricoleur pieces together a solution in order to solve the problem. It is cost-effective for the bricoleur to use policy ideas demonstrating increasing returns; nevertheless, the bricoleur is also wary of the ripeness of policymakers. As such the *bricoleur* has the possibility to combine different policy ideas, selected because they present the advantage of increasing returns or because they resonate with policymakers' preferences. *Bricolage* results in a bespoke solution that, in a context framed as urgent, is then

swiftly adopted.

The Context: Streams of Disease Prevention and Control in Europe

The Policy Stream: Policy Ideas and Their Increasing Returns

The earliest traceable idea of organization of disease prevention and control in Europe is the "Charter Group." It has been briefly mentioned by Greer (2012, 1009), on the political science side and in public health publications by Krause (2008), MacLehose, McKee, and Weinberg (2002) and by Newton, Grimaud, and Weinberg (1999), in the latter cases as members of this "Charter group." The most precise academic source on the origins of the Charter Group is a 1998 lecture given in Washington by Chris Bartlett, the then-Director of the British Communicable Disease Surveillance Centre (CDSC) who shared paternity of the Charter group with Gijs Elzinga from the *Rijksinstituut voor Volksgezondheid en Milieuhygiene* (RIVM), the Dutch National Surveillance Centre. They convened experts from each of the then 12 EU member states, as well as the heads of institutions, with responsibility for national surveillance, to a meeting at CDSC London in December 1993. This was the first meeting of what would become the "Charter Group": a network of public health experts who would draw on national resources to achieve common surveillance in Europe (Bartlett 1998).

The *raison d'être* of the Charter Group was to actively flesh-out coordination of epidemiological surveillance between existing national centers of disease control. In the mid-1990s, the Charter Group had been developing jointly agreed standards for disease surveillance via the prioritization of infectious diseases (Newton, Grimaud, and Weinberg 1999); and, as soon as September 1995 they published a monthly peer-reviewed scientific journal of epidemiologic surveillance "Eurosurveillance" and developed a high-level program for Intervention Epidemic Training (EPIET), training public health doctors and epidemiologists to the same methods, standards and ethos (Bartlett 1998). At this point, the proposal was already producing increasing returns: it had been successfully accepted within the policy community and involved efforts of both research and policy design. The idea had then been translated into the real world and mobilized as part of the policy community. It thus had a structuring value for the policy community, mobilized resources and may, in the future, inhibit its members from seeing a need for change.

The Charter Group's network approach was politically endorsed in September 1998 with the creation of *A Network for the Epidemiological Surveillance and Control of Communicable Diseases in the Community* established by a decision of the EP and the Council of the European Union.[B] However, decisions are nonbinding instruments, here used in order to facilitate the work of the Charter group and provide limited funding rather than to create a new instrument. The decision lists epidemiological surveillance and prevention, two elements of the self-defined mission of the Charter group, and was first and foremost a list of guidelines on desirable developments of the networks. This decision underlines that increasing returns started to be more important because of the financial costs and because the network mobilized efforts from the experts of the policy community as well as European decision makers.

The primeval soup became thicker as another proposal emerged: in September 1998, the International Board of Scientific Advisors (a group mainly comprised of micro-biologists and researchers) met in Paris and manifested their support in favor of a European Centre for Infectious Disease (ECID) (Butler 1998). The idea was also supported by "several scientific organizations, including the European Society of Clinical Microbiology and Infectious Diseases" (Butler 1998). The proposal was championed by Michel Tibayrenc, Director of the *Centres d'Etudes sur le Polymorphisme des Mico-organismes* in Montpellier, France and suggested the creation of "scientific board" based on the existing US Center for Disease Control (CDC). In this perspective, the ECID would be created bearing in mind that "health policy remaining under the sovereignty of each nation and the ECID providing complementary overall coordination" (Tibayrenc 1998). Rather than cooperation based on surveillance of disease, the ECID would be a more ambitious idea, as its inspiration the

[B] Decision No 2119/98/EC of the European Parliament and of the Council of 24 September 1998 setting up a network for the epidemiological surveillance and control of communicable diseases in the Community, 1998).

US Center for Disease Control (CDC), being consequential in terms of training, surveillance, and research, areas in which the Charter group had demonstrated no ambition. The proposal enriched the primeval soup but never met a strong support within the policy community. As such it remained an idea "on the shelf": the only member of the policy community to put efforts and time in the idea was Michel Tibayrenc, but the idea never involved efforts from the community in designing a specific plan nor bared a cost. It is interesting to note that this policy idea is a cased for policy diffusion and as such cannot be considered to present increasing returns without the policy community making efforts to translate the US model to the European context.

The proposal for an EU agency triggered important debates among the members of the policy network and received thorough criticism from supporters and members of the Charter group. The journal for medical practitioners *The Lancet* featured an unsigned editorial titled "Not another European Institution" (Lancet 1998). The Editorial recalled the accomplishments of the Charter Group, in terms of trainings or surveillance. It was followed by a stream of back and forth open letters and articles dedicated to support one idea over the other one, in different public health journals (see Butler 1998; Dove 1998; Giesecke and Weinberg 1998; MacLehose, McKee, and Weinberg 2002; Newton, Grimaud, and Weinberg, 1999; Reichhardt 1998; Tibayrenc 1998; 1999).

This debate explains how these two policy ideas survived the primeval soup. The Charter Group seems to have won the battle: as a matter of technical feasibility, the Charter group was a "light structure" designed for the exchange of information not the funding and hosting of research facilities that is why a "bricks and mortar" solution was not deemed necessary. In terms of value acceptability, this was a clash between the creation of a European-wide institution and the reluctance of national institutionalized experts to cede sovereignty over public health policy. More importantly, the debate revolved around how each idea had the potential to be used by policymakers. However, I will demonstrate later on that the idea of an agency had limited receptivity in the politics stream.

Beyond the criteria of survival, this analysis of the policy streams ought to assess the increasing returns of the two different ideas. The initiative of the Charter Group is the only one of the two to demonstrate a cost for the policy community and the policymakers and as such fulfill the criteria. This being demonstrated, the next part ought to investigate how the evolving ripeness of the politics stream.

The Ripeness of the Politics Stream

The European Commission had a long history with the Charter group. It supported them throughout the 1990s. In 1993, the soon to be fathers of the Charter group put a proposal to the European Commission for a grant to draw up an inventory of all the international surveillance and training collaborations that were currently taking place in the EU, the grant was accepted (Bartlett 1998). Then, a representative of the Commission (DG V: Employment & Social Affairs) participated in the meeting of the Charter group. Eventually, the results of the prioritization of communicable diseases were communicated to the EU Commission as "expert advice" (Newton, Grimaud, and Weinberg, 1999). The support for this idea culminated in 1999 with the proposal for a decision creating a network for the epidemiological surveillance and control of communicable diseases in the European Communities, mentioned earlier.

The institutional bargaining that occurred during the decision-making on the proposal for a decision offers precise insights to map the institutions' preferences on the control and prevention of diseases. In the case of the EP, this happens in a context of growing hostility towards agencification where new agencies are seen as an "irresponsible" development of the European Executive that endangers the balance of power between elected bodies and technocratic institutions (Lord 2011, 912, quoting the Herman Report, European Parliament 1999). Nevertheless, the EP has demonstrated no suspicion toward the creation of an agency dedicated to the surveillance, control, and prevention of communicable diseases and even championed the creation of an institution from the beginning (Bowis 2004). What explains the role of the EP in championing the Agency approach rather than the Network approach? The agency idea presents technical characteristics that leave room for a greater oversight of the EP. While agencification is usually seen as a phenomenon that accentuates deparliamentarization (Lord 2011, 913), the case of the ECDC differs from policy sectors of exclusive competences. The EP's preferences were formulated in a

policy vacuum and it is then not surprising that an institution traditionally eager to secure oversight makes the choice of the most institutionalized option. Lord comes to this conclusion about the EP when the other option is a "voluntary pattern of co-operation" (2011, 915). Kelemen (2014) underlines that, where the EP has influence over agency design, it tends to weight on the creation of bureaucratic structures to enhance the transparency and accountability of agencies. The EP thus favors the Agency idea because it gives the Agency a stronger value acceptability than a network approach, based on oversight considerations. The amendments of the EP have been consistently suggesting creating a center rather than a network: "Having regard to the current shortcomings in the structures for the epidemiological surveillance of communicable diseases in the Member States and, therefore, the need to establish a permanent structure at Community level"; and suggests "collecting information relating to epidemiological surveillance and coordinating control measures in order then to forward them to a central body: the European Centre for the Surveillance of Communicable Diseases." (Cabrol 1997).

This approach was systematically countered by the EU Commission and the Council: "The situation is so diverse that one cannot talk about 'shortcomings in structures'. It would be wiser to refer to 'increasing needs'. The common position has largely taken over the text of the Commission's amended proposal"; "The term 'Eurocentres' does not properly describe these structures, whose activities are mainly geared towards national surveillance. […] On the contrary, it is likely to precipitate objections from the Council" (Commission 1998). The Council of Ministers was indeed favoring the network approach, with three prominent advocates: Spain, Sweden, and the UK showing clear concerns over the financing arrangements for the system, and clear preferences to leave the operational costs of the network to be financed by member states themselves (Council of the European Union 1997a; 1997b; 1997c; 1997d). This position was interpreted within the policy community as the reluctance of the EU's member states to cede sovereignty over public health policy (Butler 1998).

In the late 1990s the politics stream was thus more receptive to the idea of a network rather than the idea of an Agency. The role of increasing returns is probing: the decision to set up a network bares no additional costs economically and very little cost politically. However, the value acceptability argument shows that, at this moment, the politics stream was not fully "ripe" to the idea of a European agency. Nevertheless, this was subject to change in 2002, with the European Commissioner for Health and Consumer Protection mentioning in a speech the ambition of setting up an agency, "we have committed ourselves to creating a European Centre for Disease Control by 2005. This will bring together the expertise in Member States and will act as a reference and co-ordination point both in routine and in crisis situations." (European Commission 2002).

A classic explanation of this change in preferences in the MSA is the renewal of the members of the Commission between. In 1999 the Santer/Marin

Commission's mandate came to term and Pádraig Flynn was replaced by David Byrne as the European Commissioner for Health and Consumer Protection. The literature on the ECDC underlines the role of the severe acute respiratory syndrome (SARS) crisis in the Commission coming to terms with the idea of an Agency (Greer 2012; Greer and Löblová 2016). However, the dates do not exactly add-up. The SARS crisis began in November 2002 with an outbreak in southern China, while Commissioner Byrne mentioned the ECDC, for the first time, in September 2002. In the member states corner as well, some receptivity is observable before SARS happened. As early as June 2001, the possibility of a "European Centre" was mentioned in the conclusions of the European Council at Gothenburg (European Commission 2003b), where concerns about bioterrorism were specifically underlined.

The evolution of the politics stream ripeness shows that on the eve of the SARS crisis, policymakers were ripe to both ideas. This is due to the Commission and the Council are becoming ripe to the idea of a new agency, while, in the meantime, increasing returns of the network were consolidated and its proponents still vocal in the Council. The next part underlines the changing nature of the problem stream.

Ambiguity in the Problem Stream

The evolution of the problem stream, and the way problems have been perceived, can be used to understand how eventually conditions were framed in a way that opened a problem window.

The problem of disease prevention

and control in Europe in the 1990s differs from the general context of health policy in the EU. The development of a health policy in the EU has been described as an incremental development likened to a spillover dynamic: since most areas linked to health are progressively integrated, health will be eventually integrated (Greer 2006). If not relying on grand theories of integration, the assumptions have been that health policy was progressively Europeanized (Böhm and Landwehr 2013). However, the case of disease prevention is particular in the sense that the Maastricht Treaty (art. 129) gave, for the first time, legal competences to the European Commission to complement national policies, within the limits of disease prevention, health information, and education. The Maastricht Treaty paved the way for this opportunity for the fathers of the Charter group by asking the Commission to finance their initiative. This demonstrates that this policy idea emerged thanks to the realization of a problem that was recognized in the treaties, in line with the neo-functionalist or the Europeanization assumptions presented earlier. The problem is thus perceived as a consequence of the spillover of European integration: since borders are now open and microbes know no borders, transnational cooperation is needed to tackle potential transnational health problems.

Through the 1990s, there was a debate among experts and institutions on the possibility to create an agency. The problem was framed by the policy community and the institutions as follows: what kind of integration is desirable in the field of prevention and control of communicable diseases? The terms of the problem were never properly defined by the Charter group or the proponents of the ECID beyond spillover considerations; however, the institutional archives provide a clear understanding of how the problem was framed depending on the solution championed by the institutions. While the EP describes the problem of disease prevention and control as a matter of "shortcomings in structure" (Cabrol 1997), the Commission and the Council are more restrained and, respectively, underline "growing" (Draft Minutes of the 2131st meeting of the Council (Health) 1998) and "increasing needs" (European Commission 1998).

Problem perception changed radically in the 2000s due to the persistence of health crises at the end of the 1990s, whereas food-borne disease ("Mad Cow" disease) or bio-terrorism (the post 9/11 anthrax contamination) shifted the issue from a functional problem to the recognition of threats. This trend culminated in the early 2000 with the events of the SARS crisis.

The following part is dedicated to understanding how the Commission framed this focusing event in a way that led to bricolage. To draw a clear picture of the opening of the policy window and *bricolage* I first present reflections on the reasons why changes in the politics and the problem stream before the SARS crisis never led to coupling the streams.

Policy Windows, Failed Entrepreneurship, and Contingent Framing of the Problem

The process tracing of the three streams has let us to draw a precise image of the context. Before investigating the framing of the SARS, some of these contextual elements must be clarified in order to understand why some conditions that could be interpreted as windows of opportunity did not lead to change and why some agents who could be interpreted as policy entrepreneurs did not succeed in coupling the streams.

The first case would be to address the Charter Group. The Charter Group was arguably demonstrating some elements of policy entrepreneurship. Nevertheless, it is not a good fit for the MSA: the Charter Group was an experiment that happened outside of the traditional decision-making channels, its relationship with the decision makers was different from a policy entrepreneur seeking access to decision makers. The decision-making process of setting up a network for the epidemiological surveillance in 1998 could hardly be considered a coupling of the streams: the change is minimal and the result is a formalization of the EU's sponsorship of the initiative. Therefore, there is here a form of entrepreneurship with minimalist goals and fostering change at a modest level rather than by starting a complete policy cycle.

The second case is the policy entrepreneurship behind the ECID that fits the traditional definition. It is a case of failed entrepreneurship, probably due to the limited outreach of the proposal presented by Michel Tibayrenc and his lack of access to EU institutions. There was a change in the politics stream that happened just before, but the relative weakness of the EP did not allow a proper window to be opened. Eventually, the ECID remained a policy idea that was stifled by the debate in the policy community and efforts to make it emerged never met the right opportunity.

The final case before the SARS crisis is the opening of policy window where a change in the problem streams due to Mad Cow disease and the Anthrax attacks led the Member States to become ripe to the idea of an agency. Moreover, the new Commissioner for health who had taken office in 1999 seemed more receptive to the creation of an agency. Despite a window of opportunity being arguably opened, no agent emerged as a policy entrepreneur to set the agenda. The Commissioner for Health, Byrne, only mentions that he and his team had "committed to themselves" to creating a European Centre for Disease Control by 2005. There were no clear preferences stated on the precise organizational elements of this agency and the policy idea was exposed vaguely. Moreover, he was giving a speech for an audience of young specialists of public health in a forum dedicated to health issues in the EU (European Commission 2002) and there was no other evidence that there had been a concrete effort made to put the issue on the agenda. Perhaps the Commission could have exercised some entrepreneurship if the salience of SARS had not had an overwhelming impact on the problem stream only 2 months after Commissioner Byrne's announcement. Empirical evidences only show that Commissioner Byrne was ripe to the idea, not that he engaged in policy entrepreneurship.

The SARS crisis has been a focusing event in the sense used by Birkland (1998a) that it was sudden, rare, and potentially harmful. Nevertheless, the impact of SARS on the European continent was limited. According to the WHO (2015) in the month preceding the Commission's proposal (July 2003), 33 cases had been reported in the European continent—excluding Russia (31 in the EU). At the end of year 2003, the WHO concluded that 25 cases were confirmed in the EU, 27 in total for the continent (excluding Russia), with one case resulting in the death of the patient. All cases were imported; there was no domestic spread of the epidemic, no local transmission. At global level, however, 8096 cases were confirmed.

The crisis seemed a matter of global scale rather than a continental one. But the SARS crisis was framed by the European Commission as the example of a problem that *if* inflicted to the European continent would be devastating without a European Agency. First, the Commission framed SARS as a threat, even if the threat was limited "Communicable disease outbreaks can pose a significant threat to the health and well-being of the European Union's citizens, as shown during the recent spread of the SARS virus" (European Commission 2003a); but clarified that this was only one of the possible iterations of a systemic risk: "A major outbreak such an influenza pandemic could have catastrophic consequences" (European Commission 2003a). The risk of a similar outbreak

was thus what the proposal suggested to tackle: the Commission framed the SARS to show that competencies were lacking at the EU level, defining "public health matters as an area where Community competencies should be consolidated" (European Commission 2003a; 2003b). The solution the European Commission was looking for was not a tool to solve the threat of the SARS outbreak; rather it was the result of considerations that the EU could be at risk. Therefore, the Commission defined the problem as the recognition of new needs for the EU and emerged as an agent taking responsibility for finding a solution.

I identify the first step of bricolage done by the Commission which is to open a window by framing conditions as a problem that can and must be fixed. The next step is to engage on a path of consequential search for fit. Taking cues from bricolage, I reason that the Commission pieced together a good fit for the definition of the problem: fill the capacity building gaps at the EU level in the field of disease prevention and control. Therefore, I now investigate the policy formulation aspect of bricolage.

Coupling by Bricolage: Policy Formulation

The last parts of this paper gave us the picture of the streams, up to the opening of the policy window. After the presentation of the mechanisms that led to bricolage rather than the emergence of a policy entrepreneur, this part focuses on bricolage as policy formulation and the consequences on the decision-making process.

Bricolage, as an oblique way to formulate policy, will now guide our understanding of how different ideas were pieced together to create a solution that would go swiftly through the decision-making phase. The European Commission had two different policy ideas at hand. On the one hand, the network had strong, consolidated increasing returns and, on the other hand, the policymakers had been increasingly riper to the creation of a new agency.

The process tracing showed that the Commission was wary of the Communicable Disease Network created in 1999 and used it as the basis for the proposal "The basic formula for cooperation amongst Member States and the Commission in the framework of Decision 2119/98/EC is not being questioned" (European Commission 2003a). This shows the Commission paying attention to spare the cost of exiting organizational choices set up previously. Nevertheless, it presents the agency idea as the core concept, while the agency idea is actually superimposed on the existing network.

The proposal did not retain key features of the suggested ECID such as financing and hosting research labs. The ECDC is not a European "CDC" based on the US model but a "hub" (Greer and Matzke 2012), a center that coordinates a network, composed of different authorities in charge of epidemiological surveillance in the EU. It retains all the existing features (including, for instance, the publication of Eurosurveillance) and is still based on the coordination and "synergies between the existing national centres for disease control" (European Commission 2003a).

National information and expertise are still predominant in the functioning of the center, whereas for data exchange or for training purposes. The Commission pieced together a modest project "a large European Centre is not needed" (European Commission 2003a), which also prevents the most skeptical elements of the politics stream from opposing the proposal. The proposal also included the mention that the ECDC would be an agency without regulatory powers (European Commission 2003a), which echoed the concerns raised by two member states: the UK and Germany (Council of the European Union 2004).

This shows that *bricolage* was a process of creating a European Agency while incorporating many elements of the epidemiological network. By *bricolage*, the European Commission avoided the costs of exiting the initiative in which time and money had been invested while taking into account the changed ripeness of policymakers vis-à-vis the creation of agency.

Bricolage is thus seminal in understanding why a proposal is swiftly adopted, not the crisis itself. The Commission's proposal required only one reading facilitated by a conciliation meeting that was set up early on in the process, a practice that is relatively unusual in the inter-institutional bargaining at the EU level. Rather than a beacon of the consensual culture of decision-making in Brussels, the decision-making process was the result of the European Commission formulating a policy solution that "fit", which led to speeding-up policy formulation and decision-making.

Evidence that the European Commission did not act as a policy entrepreneur shows in the policy solution that was eventually formulated. Moreover, the proposal does not seem to serve the Commission's needs or interests. The literature on agencification would underline that the creation of an independent agency presents reputational elements for the Commission. While being a convincing explanation for agencification in general, it is limited in the case of the ECDC and not supported by evidence: the ECDC is a discreet agency. As demonstrated by the limit of its competences, the ECDC reflects the Member states' preferences more than the Commission's needs and interests in seeking reputational gains. The recombination of ideas is, however, in line with the assumption that the proposal was an "immediate action [is] motivated more by the need to avoid higher costs rather than the need to reap more benefits" as defined by Zahariadis in his definition of consequential coupling and search for fit (Zahariadis 2003, 72). The proposal of the Commission is thus the work of a bricoleur and not the pet solution of a policy entrepreneur who links her solution to the SARS crisis.

As a type of coupling in the MSA, *bricolage* shows that after framing the problem and with a process goal, the Commission acting as a bricoleur created a bespoke solution that was a new arrangement of elements. In creating a bespoke solution, the Commission made an arbitration between the different advantages of policy ideas and paid attention to the ripeness of policymakers, which led to a swift adoption and implementation of the Regulation.

Conclusion

The creation of the ECDC has been for long time interpreted in the light of the SARS crisis; however, our process tracing has shown that this crisis is a catalyst rather than the genesis of this agency. By showing that the ECDC is the result of a *bricolage*, this paper empirically proved that the traditional explanation found in the literature on the ECDC must be refined. Empirical elements such as the swiftness of the decision-making process and the hybrid features of the ECDC find stronger explanatory leverage in the process of policy formulation by *bricolage* than in the reaction to the crisis.

The creation of the ECDC was the contingent result of the Commission framing a problem due to events that had a limited impact on the European continent and looking for the solution that would fit this ambiguous context. No agent championing a solution could couple the streams. No policy entrepreneur emerged as the "hero" with a solution to a "crisis." This paper empirically confirmed an important property of bricolage: the bricoleur is an agent who frames the problem and sets her own goals: the consequential search for fit. This new take on agency in the MSA is a response to criticisms that underline that ambiguity of preferences clashes with the existence of a policy entrepreneur with a clear personal agenda (Zohlnhöfer and Rüb 2016). In *bricolage*, the agent does not have clear preferences on how to solve the problem. The micro-foundations of the *bricolage* are that preferences regarding solutions are secondary; the issue of problem solving is at the core of this type of agency.

The lack of preferences beyond looking forward to solving a problem explains why solutions are the result of an oblique mechanism. *Bricolage* produces a new arrangement of elements that are preconstrained because resources are scarce and cannot be expanded. In our case study, bricolage is performed by the European Commission who pieced together a policy solution that was based on previously consolidated organizational choices. Here the process tracing showed that the Commission's choice relates to the increasing returns of the network of epidemiological surveillance and the evolving ripeness of policymakers to the idea of an agency. Our *bricoleur* avoided the costs of exit from the network and combined elements of the agency idea to the solution because the member states were ripe to it.

Bringing *bricolage* into the MSA widens our understanding of agency in policy formulation. Unlike the policy entrepreneur who "softens-up" the policymakers to their ideas, the bricoleur makes use of the policy environment to piece a solution. *Bricolage* is a process of arbitration and recombination that creates bespoke solutions to fit a problem. This paper empirically proved that a bricoleur evaluates policy ideas by the yardstick of two criteria: the ripeness of decision-makers and the increasing returns of policy ideas.

Who can become a *bricoleur*? Is *bricolage* an individual property, or can a constellation of actors collectively engage in *bricolage*? The fact that the bricoleur is a process-oriented actor chimes with the organizational properties of the Commission, which is an actor that follows process goals to outcome goals. In the EU system, other institutions may be problem-minded rather solution-minded depending on the issues at stake – this is an open question for further empirical research. I suspect that the role of *bricoleur* would suit a single Member of the European Parliament (MEP) or a national delegate within a Council formation. Collectively the MEPs could become a bricoleur when the EP identifies problems that the Commission is reluctant to deal with. While the policy entrepreneur is defined by their activities rather than by means of their position, the *bricoleur* is a concept that rather suits policymakers until empirically proven wrong.

A distinction should be made between bricolage and other concepts with which it shares some features. Cram (1993) introduced the purposeful opportunist using a very similar empirical case: a policy field in which the EU has reduced competences but in which and there is still a form of European integration. The purposeful opportunist is different from the bricoleur, while both are empirically identified as the Commission, and both can be seen as process goal driven rather than solution goal driven. Important differences remain. Cram's purposeful opportunist is an agent that accumulates knowledge until the moment it can seize an opportunity. The *bricoleur* is less strategic in cumulating reservoirs of knowledge that can be mobilized when the right moment comes. *Bricolage* can also be put in relation to models of decision. Prima facie it may resemble muddling through (Lindblom 1959), especially considering the importance of the concept ripeness of the politics stream. *Bricolage* and muddling through are, nevertheless, different. Muddling through is a collective process of partisan mutual adjustment. *Bricolage* takes partisan adjustments as one of the elements of the equation along with increasing returns of ideas. Moreover, these adjustments are not mutual, rather the bricoleur should be seen as one who has a precise idea of the policymakers' preferences and who is able to come up with a solution in the function of these preferences.

In conclusion, this article shows that bricolage can assist in the development of the MSA. It also provides a lens to re-examine the relationship between framing problems and mobilizingideas, and provides a richer understanding of how exactly agency generates change. Finally, it allows us to scale down some claims made on crises as levers of change.

Acknowledgements

I would like to express my immense gratitude to Claudio Radaelli for his support during the process of writing this paper. I would like to thank the two reviewers with whom I engaged in a discussion with great pleasure and who provided excellent comments. Special thanks to attendees and discussants of the panel 'The Multiple Streams Framework: Empirical Applications and Theoretical Innovations' at the 2016 ECPR Conference in Prague for their comments, to Jonathan Kamkhaji for being my intellectual sparring partner and to Sophie Glaser for her inestimable support.

References

1998. "Decision No 2119/98/EC of the European Parliament and of the Council of 24 September 1998 setting up a network for the epidemiological surveillance and control of communicable diseases in the Community." *Official Journal of the European Union.* http://eur-lex.europa.eu/legal-content/EN/TXT/

Ackrill, Robert, and Adrian Kay. 2011. "Multiple Streams in EU Policy-Making: The Case of the 2005 Sugar Reform." *Journal of European Public Policy* 18 (1): 72–89.

Ackrill, Robert, Adrian Kay, and Nikolaos Zahariadis. 2013. "Ambiguity, Multiple Streams, and EU Policy." *Journal of European Public Policy* 20 (6): 871–87.

Alam, Thomas. 2007. "Quand la Vache Folle Retrouve son Champ. Une Comparaison Transnationale de la Remise en Ordre d'un Secteur d'Action Publique." PhD Thesis Universite du Droit et de la Sante - Lille II.Bartlett, Chris. 1998. "'Eurosurveillance': Monitoring disease in the European Union." http://depts.washington.edu/eminf/1998/Eurosurv/euro1.htm (accessed October 29, 2015).

Birkland, Thomas A. 1998a. "After Disaster: Agenda Setting, Public Policy, and Focusing Events." *Choice Reviews Online* 35 (8): 35–4778–35–4778.

Birkland, Thomas A. 1998b. "Focusing Events, Mobilization, and Agenda Setting." *Journal of Public Policy* 18 (1): 53–74.

Blankenau, Joe. 2001. "The Fate of National Health Insurance in Canada and the United States: A Multiple Streams

Explanation." *Policy Studies Journal* 29 (1): 38–55.

Böhm, Katharina, and Claudia Landwehr. 2013. "The Europeanization of Health Care Coverage Decisions: EU-Regulation, Policy Learning and Cooperation in Decision-Making." *Journal of European Integration* 36 (1):17–35.

Bowis, John. 2004. "Report on the pProposal for a European pParliament and Ccouncil Rregulation Eestablishing a European Ccentre for dDisease pPrevention and Ccontrol—A5-0038/2004." European Parliament.

Butler, Declan. 1998. "Call for Europe-Wide Public Health Agency." *Nature* 395 (6698): 106.

Cabrol, Christian. 1997. "Recommendation for Second Reading on the Common Position Adopted by the Council with a View to Adopting a European Parliament and Council Decision Setting up a Network for the Epidemiological Surveillance and Control of Communicable Diseases in the Europe." European Parliament.

Cairney, Paul, and Michael D. Jones. 2015. "Kingdon's Multiple Streams Approach: What is the Empirical Impact of this Universal Theory?" *Policy Studies Journal* 44 (1): 37–58.

Carstensen, Martin B. 2011. "Paradigm Man vs. The Bricoleur: Bricolage as an Alternative Vision of Agency in Ideational Change." *European Political Science Review* 3 (1): 147–67.

Council of the European Union. 1997a. Outcome of Proceedings 16 January

1997, Working party on Health.

Council of the European Union. 1997b. Outcome of Proceedings 14 February 1997, Working party on Health.

Council of the European Union. 1997c. Outcome of Proceedings 25 February 1997, Working party on Health.

Council of the European Union. 1997d. Outcome of Proceedings 13 March 1997, Working party on Health.

Council of the European Union. 1998. Draft Minutes of the 2131st meeting of the Council (HEALTH).

Council of the European Union. 2004. *Interinstitutional file Proposal for a Regulation of the European Parliament and of the Council establishing a European Centre [for Disease Prevention and Control]—Outcome of the European Parliament's first reading.* 2003/0174 COD.

Cram, Laura. 1993. "Calling the Tune Without Paying the Piper? Social Policy Regulation: The Role of the Commission in European Community Social Policy." *Policy & Politics* 21 (2): 135–46.

Dove, Alan. 1998. "'European CDC' Lobbies for Support." *Nature Medicine* 4 (11): 1214–15.

European Commission. 1998. "Opinion on the European Parliament's Amendments to the Council's Common Position Regarding the Proposal for a Decision Creating a Network for the Epidemiological Surveillance and Control of Communicable Diseases in the European Communities."

European Commission. 2002. "European Commission—PRESS RELEASES—Press Release—David BYRNE European Commissioner for Health and Consumer Protection Future Priorities in EU Health Policies European Health Forum on 'Common Challenges for Health and Car' Gastein, 26 September 2002." September 26. http://europa.eu/rapid/press-release_SPEECH-02-426_en.htm?locale=en (accessed March 30, 2016).

European Commission. 2003a. "Proposal for a Regulation of the European Parliament and of the Council Establishing a European Centre [for Disease Prevention and Control]/COM/2003/0441 final - COD 2003/0174."

European Commission. 2003b. "European Commission—PRESS RELEASES—Press Release—Extraordinary Council Meeting EMPLOYMENT, SOCIAL POLICY, HEALTH AND CONSUMER AFFAIRS Brussels, 6 May 2003." May 6. http://europa.eu/rapid/press-release_PRES-03-122_en.htm (accessed June 25, 2016).

European Parliament. 1999 "Report on Improvement in the Functioning of the Institutions without Modifications of the Treaties", The Herman Report, Brussels: European Parliament.

Freeman, Richard. 2007. "Epistemological Bricolage: How Practitioners Make Sense of Learning." *Administration & Society* 39 (4): 476–96.

Giesecke, Johan, and Julius Weinberg. 1998. "A European Centre for Infectious Disease?" *Lancet* 352 (9136): 1308.

Greer, Scott L. 2006. "Uninvited Europeanization: Neofunctionalism and the EU in Health Policy." *Journal of European Public Policy* 13 (1):134–152.

Greer, Scott L. 2012. "The European Centre for Disease Prevention and Control: Hub or Hollow Core?" *Journal of Health Politics, Policy and Law* 37 (6): 1001–30.

Greer, Scott L., and Margitta Mätzke. 2012. "Bacteria without Borders: Communicable Disease Politics in Europe." *Journal of Health Politics, Policy and Law* 37 (6):887–914.

Greer, Scott L., and Olga Löblová. 2016. "European Integration in the Era of Permissive Dissensus: Neofunctionalism and Agenda-Setting in European Health Technology Assessment and Communicable Disease Control." *Comparative European Politics* in print.

Herweg, Nicole. 2015. "Explaining European Agenda-Setting Using the Multiple Streams Framework: The Case of European Natural Gas Regulation." *Policy Sciences* 49 (13):13–33.

Herweg, Nicole, Christian Huß, and Reimut Zohlnhöfer. 2015. "Straightening the Three Streams: Theorising Extensions of the Multiple Streams Framework." *European Journal of Political Research* 54 (3): 435–49.

Jones, Michael D., Holly L. Peterson, Jonathan J. Pierce, Nicole Herweg, Amiel Bernal, Holly Lamberta Raney, and Nikolaos Zahariadis. 2015. "A River Runs Through It: A Multiple Streams

Meta-Review." *Policy Studies Journal* 44 (1): 13–36.

Krause, Gérard. 2008. "How Can Infectious Diseases be Prioritized in Public Health?" *EMBO reports* 9 (Suppl 1 Science and Society). http://www.ncbi.nlm.nih.gov/pmc/articles/PMC3327548/pdf/embor200876.pdf (Accessed October 27, 2015).

Kelemen, R. Daniel. 2014. "European Union Agencies." In *The Oxford Handbook of the European Union*, eds. Erik Jones, Anand Menon, and Stephen Weatherill. Oxford: Oxford University Press.

Kelman, Steven. 2005. *Unleashing Change: A Study of Organizational Renewal in Government*. Washington, DC: Brookings Institution Press.

Kingdon, John W. [1984] 2003. *Agendas, Alternatives, and Public Policies* (Longman classics edition) (2nd edition). 2nd ed. New York: Longman.

Knaggård, Åsa. 2015. "The Multiple Streams Framework and the Problem Broker." *European Journal of Political Research* 54 (3): 450–65.

Levi-Strauss, Claude. 1988. *The Savage Mind (Nature of Human Society)*. London, UK: Weidenfeld & Nicolson.

Lindblom, Charles E. 1959. "The science of "muddling through."" *Public Administration Review* 19 (2):79–88.

Lord, Christopher. 2011. "The European Parliament and the Legitimation of Agencification." *Journal of European Public Policy* 18 (6): 909–25.

MacLehose, Laura, Martin McKee, and Julius Weinberg. 2002. "Responding to the Challenge of Communicable Disease in Europe." *Science* (New York, N.Y.). 295 (5562): 2047–50.

Maggetti, Martino. 2013. "The Politics of Network Governance in Europe: The Case of Energy Regulation." *West European Politics* 37 (3): 497–514.

McKee, Martin, Rifat Atun, and Richard Coker, eds. 2008. *Health Systems and the Challenge of Communicable Diseases: Experiences from Latin America*. Oxford: Oxford University Press.

Moe, Terry M. 2005. "Power and Political Institutions." *Perspectives on Politics* 3 (2): 215–33.

Newton, Lisa, Olivier Grimaud, and Julius Weinberg. 1999. "Establishing Priorities for European Collaboration in Communicable Disease Surveillance." *European Journal of Public Health* 9 (3): 236–40.

Pierson, Paul. 2000. "Increasing Returns, Path Dependence, and the Study of Politics." *The American Political Science Review* 94 (2): 251–267.

Reichhardt, Declan Butler. 1998. "Call for Europe-Wide Public Health Agency." *Nature 395* (6698): 106.

Rüb, Friedbert W. 2016. "Agenda-Setting and Policy-Making in Time: What the Multiple Streams Approach Can Tell Us— and What It Cannot." In *Decision-Making Under Ambiguity and Time Constraints: Assessing the Multiple Streams*

Framework, eds. Reimut Zohlnhöfer and Friedbert Rüb. Colchester, UK: ECPR Press, 51–70.

Saurugger, Sabine, and Fabien Terpan. 2015. "Do Crises lead to Policy Change? The Multiple Streams Framework and the European Union's Economic Governance Instruments." *Policy Sciences* 49 (1):35–53.

The Lancet. 1998. "Editorial. Not Another European Institution." *The Lancet* 352 (9136): 1237.

Tibayrenc, Michel. 1998. "Coordinating European Public Health." *Nature* 396 (6707): 108.

Tibayrenc, Michel. 1999. "European Centre for Infectious Disease." *The Lancet* 353 (9149): 329.

Walker, Jack L. 1974. "Performance Gaps, Policy Research, and Political Entrepreneurs: Toward a Theory of Agenda Setting." *Policy Studies Journal* 3 (1): 112–16.

WHO. 2015. "Summary of Probable SARS Cases with Onset of Illness from 1 November 2002 to 31 July 2003." July 24. http://www.who.int/csr/sars/country/table2004_07_21/en/ (accessed September 28, 2016).

Zahariadis, Nikolaos. 2003. Ambiguity and Choice in Public Policy: Political *Decision Making in Modern Democracies (American Governance and Public Policy)*. Washington, DC: Georgetown University Press.

Zahariadis, Nikolaos. 2008. "Ambiguity and Choice in European Public Policy." *Journal of European Public Policy* 15 (4): 514–30.

Zohlnhöfer, Reimut, and Friedbert W. Rüb. 2016. "Introduction: Policy-Making Under Ambiguity and Time Constraints." In *Decision-Making under Ambiguity and Time Constraints—Assessing the Multiple Streams Framework,* eds. Reimut Zohlnhöfer and Friedbert Rüb. Colchester, UK: ECPR Press, 51–70. ds

Leaders' 'Green' Posts. The Environmental Issues Shared by Politicians on Facebook

Diego Ceccobelli[A] and Benedetta Cotta[B]

Is Facebook "green"? Do political leaders use this social medium to spread information on green policies? The aim of this paper is to investigate on whether and how Facebook is used by politicians as an arena to spread environmental policy proposals or simply information about the environment. The study covers 127 Facebook pages of political leaders in 31 different advanced industrial democracies. The 127 pages have been under observation for 26 months and 99,234 posts were scrutinized. 25,151 out of these 99,234 posts were manually coded and analyzed in order to measure how often contemporary leaders use Facebook to talk about environmental issues. We found that: (i) environmental issues do not represent a relevant concern for the main political leaders of contemporary advanced industrial democracies; (ii) left wing and younger leaders are the ones who used Facebook the most for spreading information about environmental issues; and (iii) relevant differences between leaders of countries with different levels of economic wealth and environmental pollution are noted in regard to Western countries.

Keywords: *comparative politics, environmental policy, green politics, social media, Facebook*

Introduction

The 1970s are also known as the "environmental decade" in which legislation, media coverage, and public opinion of many advanced industrial countries, primarily of North America and Europe, turned to environmental issues (Calvert 1989; Dunlap and Scarce 1991). These became salient with the publication of Rachel Carson's book "Silent Spring" (Carson 1962) and the first Club of Rome report (Meadows et al. 1972) as well as the organization of the first Earth Day in 1970 which became a milestone in increasing public awareness (Dunlap 1989; Dunlap and Gale 1972; Egri and Herman 2000; Erskine 1972; Ester, Halman and Seuren 1993) and overall relevance in political agendas and media exposure on environmental issues (Dunlap 1989; 1991; Dunlap and Allen 1976; Inglehart 1990a; 1990b; McEvoy 1972; Mitchell 1980; 1990; Schoenfeld, Meier, and Griffin 1979; Scichilone 2008; Trop and Roos 1971).

The 1970s environmental "peak" also had a strong impact on the scholarly works in the fields of public opinion

[A] Scuola Normale Superiore, Institute of Humanities and Social Sciences; Palazzo Strozzi, 50123 Florence, Italy.
[B] Gonzaga in Florence; Via Giorgio La Pira 11/13, 50121 Florence, Italy.

doi: 10.18278/epa.2.2.5

and agenda-setting. When analyzing environmental issues, research particularly covered the topic of public concern with the quality of the environment (Van Liere and Dunlap 1980), and addressed the role of media in influencing citizens' pro-environmental attitudes (Murch 1971; Shanahan, Morgan, and Stenbjerre 1997). Furthermore, studies analyzed political leaders' environmental policy preferences in party competition using party manifestos (Benoit and Michael 2006; Carter 2013; Dalton 2009; Neumayer 2004). However, despite the fact that the citizens' pro-environmental attitudes, the media attention to environmental problems and political parties' pro-environmental orientations are well developed topics of research, studies specifically focusing on political leaders' use of media to spread information on environmental issues appear to be far more scarce. In this article, we address the missing link between political leaders and the media in regard to environmental issues and we particularly look at the salience of environmental issues in the leaders' use of social media. We have chosen to focus on Facebook since it boasts the highest number of people using it on a daily basis, thus representing the natural starting point for comprehending how the advent of social media is affecting the communicative choices made by contemporary politicians in this particular media environment.

Social Media, Facebook, and Environmental Issues

The advent of the Internet and social media has significantly affected the political sphere (Bruns et al. 2016; Chadwick 2013; Chadwick and Howard 2010; Papacharissi 2002). Political actors can now build direct and immediate relationships with voters (Chadwick 2006; Golbeck, Grimes, and Rogers 2010; Karlsen 2009; Nielsen and Vaccari 2013; Vaccari and Valeriani 2013). With a simple Twitter account or a Facebook page they can constantly update citizens about each kind of issue, from sharing information about their policy preferences to commenting about non-political issues such as expressing their joy about the result of a soccer match. Among social media, Facebook is the one with the highest number of people using it on a monthly basis: around 1.65 billion[C] connect to Facebook at least once a month, and on August 27, 2015 there were more than 1 billion using this social medium during the same day. These numbers are even more significant if one considers that other social media with the highest numbers of monthly active users (e.g., QZone,[D] Instagram and Twitter) do not cross the 648 million threshold with regard to this indicator.[E] Furthermore, there are very few countries across the world where Facebook is not the social medium with the highest number of citizens using it on a daily basis. Thus, to conduct an analysis of how social media are affecting the contemporary political sphere one simply must first focus on Facebook.

[C] For details, see https://investor.fb.com/investor-news/press-release-details/2016/Facebook-Reports-First-Quarter-2016-Results-and-Announces-Proposal-for-New-Class-of-Stock/default.aspx.

[D] Zone is a Chinese social media.

[E] For details, see http://vincos.it/2016/06/21/social-media-nel-mondo-instagram-500-milioni-di-utenti-cresce-snapchat/

The communicative power of social media extends far beyond the Internet. What happens on Facebook does not remain on Facebook, but it reaches different kinds of audiences and media outlets thanks to the use that journalists make of the content published by political actors in their social media profiles (Burgess and Bruns 2012; Chadwick 2013; Deuze 2006; Mancini and Mazzoni 2014; Marchetti and Ceccobelli 2016; Van Dijck and Poell 2013). When politicians upload a picture on their Facebook profiles, they perfectly know that they are not communicating only with the citizens who follow their Facebook page. They are perfectly aware that the specific content they are sharing in their social media profiles represents a crucial tool to influence agenda building processes. If a politician posts a juicy policy proposal on their Facebook page, it is bound to get picked up by traditional media with the effect of providing a significant part of the electorate with in-depth information about that policy. Hence, social media and Facebook assume a pivotal role in political communication since the content posted by politicians in such media environments becomes a tool to measure what political actors think about specific policy areas.

Notwithstanding the potential role of Facebook in allowing political actors to communicate with a wide number of citizens, research on how politicians use this specific digital platform is still underdeveloped. The existing literature on Facebook is rich in terms of studies focusing on how key American politicians shape their presence in this social medium (for example, see Bond and Messing 2015; Bronstein 2013; Gulati and Williams 2013; Williams and Girish 2012) while there is a shortage of analyses that would go beyond the American case and adopt a comparative

perspective (Gerodimos and Justinussen 2015; Larsson and Kalsnes 2014; Parmeggiani 2015; Samuel-Azran, Yarchi, and Wolfsfeld 2015). This is even more evident when considering those analyses looking at how the main political leaders of contemporary democracies communicate on Facebook. What are the main differences between American and Western European leaders? And what about those cases lying outside the realm of Western democracies?

Political communication literature also lacks an in-depth and systematic analysis on how the advent of social media is affecting the salience that politicians attribute to environmental issues. No research has been designed so far with the aim of shedding light on how political actors of contemporary democracies use social media to inform on environmental issues. Moreover, no research has yet tested whether existing theories and hypotheses about political actors and environmental issues apply to the communicative choices of leaders on social media. Based on these considerations, the paper aims to answer the following research questions: (i) Do political leaders use Facebook to inform on environmental policies? (ii) And particularly, how often do political leaders talk about the environment on Facebook? (iii) Lastly, who are the leaders who talk the most about environmental issues on Facebook?

Environmental Issues and Political Leaders: A Review of the Hypotheses

Our work aims to investigate how much political leaders use Facebook to talk about environmental issues. Building upon existing research on pro-environmental attitudes and support, we propose 6 hypotheses related to features of countries,

,or of political leaders, that can explain environmental salience on Facebook. Borrowing from studies analyzing the relationship between the economy and the environment, we look at explanations related to the level of economic growth and environmental quality of a country. Alternative explanations are defined at the leaders' level and borrowed from research on public opinion polls and party competition; these hypotheses concern socio-demographic characteristics and party affiliations of the political leaders under consideration.

Economic Well-Being of a Country

The first studies pointing out the relationship between the economy and environmental issues date back to the eighteenth and early nineteenth century where classical economists called upon social and environmental limits to economic growth e.g., Malthus' Essay on the Principle of Population (1878), De Sismondi's New Principles of Political Economy (1991), and Mill's Principles of Political Economy (1882). A century later, Carson (1962) and Meadows et al. (1972) questioned the feasibility of a continued economic growth which could have had environmental and natural exhaustion consequences (Cole 2000). Nevertheless, other studies did not find evidence of environmental quality deterioration correlated with economic growth (Arrow et al. 1995; Cole, Rayner, and Bates 1997; Dasgupta et al. 2001; Fiorino 2011; Grossman and Krueger 1995; Selden and Song 1994).

The 1970s were also characterized by discussions on value changes and value prioritization in relation to economic growth and environmental attitudes. This debate was led by Ronald Inglehart who emphasized a shift from material well-being to (post-materialist) quality of life values during times of economic growth claiming that "countries with high levels of prosperity should have relatively high levels of post-materialist values" (Inglehart 1997, 143). In other words, after reaching a certain level of wealth, citizens preferred a better quality of life and thus were keener to support environmental issues (Arrow et al. 1995; Beckerman 1992; Fiorino 2011; Franzen and Vogl 2013). Additionally, as Fiorino (2011) pointed out, wealthier societies were also more inclined to invest in environmental protection. Therefore, with economic prosperity, citizens more often demanded their governments to invest in pollution control and conservation measures (Fiorino 2011, 32).

Whereas there has been some criticism on this hypothesis in explaining the rise of environmentalism in developing countries (for example, see Aoyagi-Usui, Vinken, and Kuribayashi 2003; Brechin and Kempton 1997; Dunlap and Mertig 1997; Kidd and Lee 1997), a large number of studies suggested a positive correlation between the economic wealth of a country and environmental salience. Hence, we hypothesize that:

H1 (a) *High levels of a country's economic well-being will positively affect the salience of environmental issues.*

Although scholars recognized an existing relationship between economic well-being and environmental protection (i.e., post-materialist values), studies emphasized how environmental issues can become less important in times of economic de-growth, e.g. during the economic and financial crisis that started in the United States in 2007 and spread to the rest of the world in 2008 (Cameron 2013; Cotta and Memoli 2015; O; Kallis 2011; Schneider, Kallis, and Martinez-Alier 2010). Considering that our analysis covers the years immediately following the 2007 crisis, we expect that its effects may still be ongoing in many advanced industrial countries, and hypothesize that:

H1 (b) *Shrinkage of a country's economic well-being will influence a decline in the salience attributed to environmental issues.*

Environmental Quality of a Country

Over the years, most research on the environment explored connections between environmental quality and economic growth or economic performance indicators (for a review, see Torras and Boyce 1998). However, researchers also considered the perception of environmental quality as an indicator for salience of the environment. In an article dating back to the early 1990s, Dunlap and Scarce reviewed the poll trends on environmental issues highlighting how, among different topics (e.g., environmental threats, government support, environment and business, economic growth), public support for environmental issues was generally linked to individuals' perception of environmental threats and the capacity of governments to protect the environment through regulations (Dunlap and Scarce 1991). In particular, this analysis indicated that public perception of environmental damages and threats in a country influenced not only the demand for stricter environmental regulation to be provided by the government, but also

increased public support for environmental protection. Additionally, studies taking into consideration measures for national environmental quality performance highlighted an existing correlation between low environmental quality levels and strong pro-environmental support measured with various environmental quality indexes (Arbuthnot and Lingg 1975; Dasgupta et al. 2006; Dillman and Christenson 1972; Esty 2008; Esty and Porter 2005; Fiorino 2011; Harris 1970; Tognacci et al. 1972).

The research on environmental quality measures and its relation with national environmental performance allows us to include this hypothesis in the study of environmental salience. Hence we hypothesize that:

H2. *Low levels of environmental quality in a country will increase the salience of environmental issues.*

Socio-demographic Characteristics of a Leader

Following the 1970s "environmental decade", many public opinion polls and academic surveys focused on citizens' environmental concern and quality of life (Dunlap 1989). Exploring the "social [basis] of environmental concern" (Jones and Dunlap 1992, 29), Van Liere and Dunlap (1980) emphasized that, "[b]ecause of the reliance on sample survey techniques, the largest body of data on correlates of environmental concern exists for the social and demographic variables that are routinely included in such surveys"

[F] Researchers emphasize that individuals with prestigious occupations (and good income) and living in cities (in comparison to those living in—less polluted—rural areas) are more supportive of environmental issues (Dunlap and Heffernan 1975; Harry, Gale, and Hendee 1969; Murdock and Schriner 1977; Tremblay and Dunlap 1978). However, considering that in our analysis we coded 127 Facebook pages of political leaders, we assume a similar occupational prestige and similar residence in cities for all the leaders under consideration. Additionally, researchers highlight a positive correlation between education and environmental concern suggesting that individuals with higher education were more inclined to support environmental issues (Arcury, Johnson, and Scollay 1986; Buttel and Flinn 1974, 1978; Carman

(Van Liere and Dunlap 1980, 168). In particular, they recognized a correlation between the preference for environmental issues and age, sex, income, education, occupational prestige and residence of citizens participating in these surveys (Van Liere and Dunlap 1980). A decade later, Jones and Dunlap (1992) emphasized that age had "remained stable over time" (Jones and Dunlap 1992, 29). More recently, studies by Elliott, Seldon, and Regens (1997), Konisky, Milyo, and Richardson (2008), and Franzen and Vogl (2013) identified age and gender as correlated to environmental salience.

When analyzing the socio-demographic variables, researchers found differences between age groups and cohorts (Malkis and Grasmick 1977) and that age was negatively correlated to environmental preference meaning that young people were more keen to support the adoption of environmental protection measures than old people (Arcury, Johnson and Scollay 1986; Buttel 1979; Carman 1998; Dunlap and Allen 1976; Egri and Herman 2000; Elliott, Seldon, and Regens 1997; Franzen and Vogl 2013; Jones and Dunlap 1992; Kanagy, Humphrey and Firebaugh 1994; Klineberg, McKeever, and Rothenbach 1998; Konisky, Milyo, and Richardson 2008; Mohai and Twight 1987; Van Liere and Dunlap 1980; Xiao and Dunlap 2007). Additionally, while a number of works found inconclusive results in the relationship between environmental preference and gender (Blocker and Eckberg 1989; Klineberg, McKeever, and Rothebach 1998), the majority of studies pointed out that women were more supportive of environmental issues in comparison to men (Bord and O'Connor 1997; Chen and Chai 2010; Davidson and Freudenburg 1996; Stern, Dietz and Kalog 1993; Elliott, Seldon, and Regens 1997; Fliegenschnee and Schelakovsky 1998; Franzen and Vogl 2013; Grossman and Potter 1977; Hamilton 1985; Hunter and Rinner 2004; Konisky, Milyo, and Richardson 2008; McCright 2010; Mohai 1992; Xiao and Dunlap 2007; Zelezny, Chua and Aldrich 2000).[G]

Considering the relevance that specific socio-demographic characteristics may play in influencing environmental salience, we hypothesize that:

H3. *Socio-demographic characteristics of political leaders influence environmental salience and particularly,*
(a)   environmental information will be more often shared by young leaders,
(b)   environmental information will be more often shared by women leaders.

Party Orientation of a Leader

It is recognized that literature dealing with aspects of policy orientation in party competition is "simply immense" (Laver and Hunt 1992, 4). Some studies explored the salience of environmental issues in public opinion and political discourse (Downs 1972; Dunlap 1989) while others analyzed how party affiliation influenced legislative choices in relation to environmental issues (Calvert 1979; Dunlap and Allen 1976; Dunlap and Gale 1974; Kamieniecki 1995;

1998; Converse 1964; Elliott, Seldon, and Regens 1997; Franzen and Vogl 2013; Howel and Laska 1992; Jones and Dunlap 1992; Kanagy, Humphrey and Firebaugh 1994; Klineberg, McKeever and Rothenbach 1998; Van Liere and Dunlap 1980; Xiao and Dunlap 2007). Only Kollmuss and Agyeman (2002) found that individuals' level of education was not necessarily correlated to environmental issues (Kollmuss and Agyeman 2010). Nevertheless, the 127 political leaders considered in our research have all graduated from college, therefore we assume a similar education level.

[G] Only McEvoy (1972), and Passino and Lounsbury (1976) found men more supportive of environmental issues (McEvoy 1972; Passino and Lounsbury 1976).

Kenski and Kenski 1980; Pierce and Lovrich 1980; Ritt and Ostheimer 1974) and the political orientation of public opinion on environmental issues (Buttel and Flinn 1974; Costantini and Hanf 1972; Dunlap and McCright 2008; Hamilton 2008; 2011; Hamilton and Keim 2009; Howell and Laska 1992; Jones and Dunlap 1992; Malka, Krosnick, and Langer 2009; McCright and Dunlap 2011; Tognacci et al. 1972; Tranter 2010; Uyeki and Holland 2000).

At the leaders' level, a broad number of works analyzed the environmental preference in the left-right party stream by looking at party platforms (Engelbert 1961; Sundquist 1968; Trop and Roos 1971). In some cases, they adopted the well-known Party Manifesto Project and Chapel Hill Expert Surveys (Bakker, Jolly, and Polk 2012; Budge, Robertson, and Hearl 1987; Carter 2013; Laver 2003; Laver and Hunt 1992; Neumayer 2004; Volkens et al. 2012). In other cases, they studied the policy orientation of parties in governments on environmental issues and presence of Green parties (Carter 2006; Dalton 2009; Jensen and Spoon 2011; Kitschelt 1998; Rohrschneider 1993; Rüdig 2012).

Despite the vast number of works that can be labelled as "party preference" on environmental issues, the majority of them recognized that left-wing politicians and party leaders attributed importance to environmental issues (Brulle, Carmichael, and Jenkins 2012; Calvert 1979; Carman 1998; Carter 2006; 2009; Dalton 2009; Dunlap and Allen 1976; Dunlap, Xiao, and McCright 2001; Elliott, Seldon, and Regens 1997; Franzen and Vogl 2013; Guber 2003; Jones and Dunlap 1992; Kenski and Kenski

1980; McCright and Dunlap 2011; Page and Jones 1979; Rohrschneider 1993; Tognacci et al. 1972; Uyeki and Holland 2000; Van Liere and Dunlap 1980).[H] Hence, we hypothesize that:

H4. *Left-wing political leaders will be more likely to attribute salience to environmental issues.*

Research Design

A comparative analysis has been designed to answer these research questions and to test the hypotheses listed in the theoretical section. Each hypothesis has been operationalized by adopting well-established measures. The two sub-hypotheses related to the levels of economic growth and well-being shrinkage have been tested against fluctuations of the gross domestic product (hereafter, GDP) which measures the monetary value of final goods and services produced in a country over a given period of time (Callen 2012). This measure was chosen because it is commonly used as a reference point for the health of national and global economies in the sense that, in countries where the GDP is growing, "workers and businesses are generally better off than when it is not" (Callen 2012). The environmental quality of each country was measured with the Environmental Performance Index (hereafter, EPI), a joint initiative of Yale and Columbia Universities to provide a data-driven assessment of environmental conditions which is recognized as "the most comprehensive and systematic effort [..] to assess environmental outcomes at a country level" (Fiorino 2011, 371).[I]

[H] Only a number of works found left-right party preference as inconsistent with environmental salience (Buttel and Flinn 1976; 1978; Carter 2013; Dunlap 1975; Springer and Costantini 1974). Moreover, researchers found that salience to environmental issues was attributed also by left-wing policy-makers (Costantini and Hanf 1972; Mazmanian and Sabatier 1981) and left-wing activists (Benton 1997; Edey 1970; Jahn 1998; King and Borchardt 1994; Lake 1983; Pierce 1977; Steger and Witt 1989; Tranter 2010; Weigel and Weigel 1978).

Table 1: Countries Under Examination

Western Europe	South America	North America	Oceania
Italy	Brazil	United States	Australia
Spain	Argentina	Canada	New Zealand
France	Venezuela	Mexico	
Portugal	Colombia		
Germany	Peru		
Austria	Bolivia		
Belgium	Chile		
Netherlands	Paraguay		
United Kingdom	Uruguay		
Ireland	Ecuador		
Sweden			
Finland			
Norway			
Denmark			
Switzerland			
Greece			
European Union*			

[1] In his article, Fiorino surveyed the existing variety of indexes to measure national environmental performances and recognized the Environmental Performance Index as the best national environmental performance measure, comparable to the GDP indicator in economic policy. Moreover, he emphasized that, unlike other environmental indexes, "[t]he EPI is distinctive in providing a comprehensive set of indicators" instead of focusing solely on "its specific components, such as pollution, land use, or energy consumption" (Fiorino 2011, 369). It "assessed environmental conditions in 163 countries, for 25 indicators, organized in 10 categories" (e.g., environmental health and ecosystem indicators such as climate change, forestry, fisheries, and habitat). Moreover, it "provides both a ranking and an assessment of each country and a 'proximity-to-target' analysis of how each compares to a widely accepted performance goal for a given indicator" (Fiorino 2011, 371).

The socio-demographic characteristics related to gender were dichotomized between male and female leaders while for age we considered the age of each leader as at 31 December, 2013. Finally, in relation to leaders' party orientations we simplified the political spectrum between left- and right-wing parties without distinguishing between central or more extreme positions on each side. Our choice was made for comparative purposes among the 31 countries under considerations. Moreover, we followed the typology developed by Van Liere and Dunlap (1980) who found that left-wing and liberal political positions attributed more importance to environmental issues in comparison to right-wing and conservative positions.

The presence of environmental issues has been analyzed using the Facebook pages of main political leaders of 31 contemporary democracies (plus the main political leaders of the European Union) from 01/09/2012 to 31/10/2014 (Table 1).

In this set of countries, 127 political leaders were analyzed (Table 2).[J] In order to decide which leaders to include in the data set, the following criteria were selected for the 26 months under consideration: (i) each head of government[K] of that period; (ii) at least one executive and one opposition leader for each country; (iii) for the countries with a parliamentary system, all leaders of those parties that, in the elections connected with

the period under examination, had crossed the 15% threshold (with respect to the lower house); and (iv) for countries with a presidential system, all the candidates that, in the presidential elections connected with the period under analysis, had crossed the 15% threshold.[L] Regarding the European Union, the leaders included in the data set have been: each president of the European Commission, each president of the European Council, each president of the European Parliament, and each candidate for the presidency of the European Commission (as the elections took place on 25/05/2014).

The Facebook pages were analyzed only in the actual period in which each single political actor included in the data set was *effectively*[M] the leader of her/his party. Therefore, not all pages of political leaders were analyzed for the 26 months under consideration.

[J] We have limited our analysis to Western and Latin-American countries for two different reasons: (i) for testing our hypotheses in a group of countries belonging to the same geo-political area, that is the Western countries; (ii) for comparing this first set with another group of countries with low in-group variation such as Latin-America. To include other countries beyond Western and Latin-American countries would have rendered our dataset overly heterogeneous.

[K] For the French case, all the heads of state and the prime ministers have been included. For the Swiss case, all the presidents of the federal council have been considered.

[L] When needed, exceptional criteria have been applied for some countries.

[M] A party leader can be replaced after a party meeting, following his/her resignation, etc. At the same time, a prime minister or a president can lose his/her executive position following his/her resignation or after having lost an election while he/she was in office. Consequently, some cases have been included into the data set only in a subset of the 26 months taken into consideration. This is the case, for example, of Mario Monti (Italian Prime Minister from 16 November 2011 to 28 April 2013) who has been included in the analysis from 1 September 2012 to 28 April 2013.

Table 2: Leaders Included in the Analysis

Leader	Time Period Under Consideration	Posts Published (Coded in Parenthesis)	Leader	Time Period Under Consideration	Posts Published (Coded in Parenthesis)
De Kirchner (Arg)	01/09/2012–31/10/2014	2.289 (395)	Samaras (Gre)	01/09/2012–31/10/2014	84 (84)
Massa (Arg)	01/09/2012–31/10/2014	1,030 (397)	Martin (Ire)	01/09/2012–31/10/2014	0 (0)
Abbott (Aus)	01/09/2012–31/10/2014	484 (313)	Kenny (Ire)	01/09/2012–31/10/2014	250 (161)
Gillard (Aus)	01/09/2012–26/06/2013	406 (331)	Gilmore (Ire)	01/09/2012–04/07/2014	116 (107)
Rudd (Aus)	26/06/2013–12/10/2013	244 (244)	Burton (Ire)	05/07/2014–31/10/2014	0 (0)
Shorten (Aus)	13/10/2013–31/10/2014	332 (167)	Renzi (Ita)	08/12/2013–31/10/2014	133 (100)
Mitterlehner (Au)	02/09/2014–31/10/2014	0 (0)	Berlusconi (Ita)	01/09/2012–31/10/2014	680 (454)
Spindelegger (Au)	01/09/2012–01/09/2014	Nc (0)	Grillo (Ita)	01/09/2012–31/10/2014	16,439 (465)
Strache (Au)	01/09/2012–31/10/2014	5,087 (465)	Bersani (Ita)	01/09/2012–23/04/2013	597 (381)
Faymann (Au)	01/09/2012–31/10/2014	1,465 (464)	Monti (Ita)	01/09/2012–28/04/2013	211 (211)
De Wever (Bel)	01/09/2012–31/10/2014	0 (0)	Letta (Ita)	28/04/2013–22/02/2014	279 (257)
Di Rupo (Bel)	01/09/2012–31/10/2014	698 (419)	Epifani (Ita)	11/05/2013–15/12/2013	254 (127)
Michel (Bel)	11/10/2014–31/10/2014	30 (0)	Nieto (Mex)	01/09/2012–31/10/2014	2,027 (395)
Morales (Bol)	01/09/2012–31/10/2014	0 (0)	Obrador (Mex)	01/09/2012–31/10/2014	500 (250)
Medina (Bol)	01/09/2012–31/10/2014	6,038 (467)	Madero (Mex)	01/09/2012–29/09/2014	2,336 (397)
Neves (Bra)	18/05/2013–31/10/2014	1,951 (414)	Anaya (Mex)	30/09/2014–31/10/2014	4 (0)
Silva (Bra)	01/09/2012–31/10/2014	2,523 (465)	Stoltenberg (Nor)	01/09/2012–14/06/2014	332 (281)
Rousseff (Bra)	01/09/2012–31/10/2014	4,890 (507)	Jensen (Nor)	01/09/2012–31/10/2014	502 (321)
Campos (Bra)	05/10/2013–13/08/2014	1,505 (156)	Store (Nor)	14/06/2014–31/10/2014	86 (86)
Guerra (Bra)	01/09/2012–17/05/2013	0 (0)	Solberg (Nor)	01/09/2012–31/10/2014	564 (352)
Rae (Can)	01/09/2012–14/04/2013	0 (0)	Key (NZ)	01/09/2012–31/10/2014	1,425 (465)
Trudeau (Can)	15/04/2013–31/10/2014	872 (419)	Cunliffe (NZ)	15/09/2013–30/09/2014	687 (260)
Harper (Can)	01/09/2012–31/10/2014	932 (488)	Shearer (NZ)	01/09/2012–15/09/2013	342 (171)
Mulcair (Can)	01/09/2012–31/10/2014	547 (338)	Parker (NZ)	01/10/2014–31/10/2014	24 (0)
Melero (Chi)	16/12/2013–09/05/2014	0 (0)	Wilders (Net)	01/09/2012–31/10/2014	Nc (0)
Walker (Chi)	01/09/2012–30/06/2013	0 (0)	Rutte (Net)	01/09/2012–31/10/2014	373 (187)
Bachelet (Chi)	01/07/2013–31/10/2014	980 (361)	Samsom (Net)	01/09/2012–31/10/2014	20 (0)
Ominami (Chi)	01/09/2012–17/11/2013	1,414 (291)	Saguier (Par)	07/08/2013–31/10/2014	0 (0)
Piñera (Chi)	01/09/2012–15/12/2013	10 (0)	Cartes (Par)	09//12/2012–31/10/2014	1,796 (416)
Matthei (Chi)	18/08/2013–15/12/2013	707 (234)	Alegre (Par)	17/12/2012–06/08/2013	611 (200)
Mendez (Chi)	10/05/2014–31/10/2014	148 (100)	Franco (Par)	01/09/2012–15/08/2013	426 (174)
Santos (Col)	01/09/2012–31/10/2014	853 (465)	Fujimori (Per)	01/09/2012–31/10/2014	183 (107)
Zuluaga (Col)	26/01/2014–31/10/2014	1,577 (269)	Kuczynski (Per)	01/09/2012–31/10/2014	1,449 (395)
Lopez (Col)	01/09/2012–31/10/2014	1,451 (313)	Toledo (Per)	01/09/2012–31/10/2014	207 (104)
Ramírez (Col)	26/01/2014–31/10/2014	939 (210)	Humala (Per)	01/09/2012–31/10/2014	172 (100)
Schmidt (Dan)	01/09/2012–31/10/2014	181 (100)	Seguro (Por)	01/09/2012–28/09/2014	Nc (0)
Rasmussen (Dan)	01/09/2012–31/10/2014	446 (223)	Coelho (Por)	01/09/2012–31/10/2014	2 (0)
Gutiérrez (Ecu)	01/09/2012–17/02/2013	892 (200)	Costa (Por)	29/09/2014–31/10/2014	1 (0)
Correa (Ecu)	01/09/2012–31/10/2014	2,571 (535)	Rajoy (Spa)	01/09/2012–31/10/2014	794 (427)
Lasso (Ecu)	01/09/2012–31/10/2014	2,352 (465)	Rubalcaba (Spa)	01/09/2012–12/07/2014	387 (253)
Barroso (EU)	01/09/2012–31/10/2014	0 (0)	Sanchez (Spa)	13/07/2014–31/10/2014	220 (100)
Juncker (EU)	12/03/2014–31/10/2014	72 (72)	Lofven (Swe)	01/09/2012–31/10/2014	459 (300)
Schulz (EU)	01/09/2012–31/10/2014	444 (292)	Reinfeldt (Swe)	01/09/2012–31/10/2014	27 (0)
Van Rompuy (EU)	01/09/2012–31/10/2014	371 (223)	Burkhalter (Swi)	01/01/2014–31/10/2014	0 (0)
Verhofstadt (EU)	12/03/2014–31/10/2014	311 (191)	Maurer (Swi)	01/01/2013–31/12/2013	0 (0)
Keller (EU)	12/03/2014–31/10/2014	228 (194)	Müller (Swi)	01/09/2012–31/10/2014	0 (0)
Sipilä (Fin)	01/09/2012–31/10/2014	0 (0)	Sommaruga (Swi)	01/09/2012–31/10/2014	0 (0)
Soini (Fin)	01/09/2012–31/10/2014	0 (0)	Brunner (Swi)	01/09/2012–31/10/2014	6 (0)
Katainen (Fin)	01/09/2012–23/06/2014	Nc (0)	Widmer (Swi)	01/09/2012–31/12/2012	36 (0)
Stubb (Fin)	24/06/2014–31/10/2014	27 (0)	Cameron (Uk)	01/09/2012–31/10/2014	644 (322)
Urpilainen (Fin)	01/09/2012–06/06/2014	357 (179)	Clegg (Uk)	01/09/2012–31/10/2014	214 (155)
Rinne (Fin)	07/06/2014–31/10/2014	93 (93)	Miliband (Uk)	01/09/2012–31/10/2014	541 (363)
Sarkozy (Fra)	01/09/2012–18/11/2012	1 (0)	Mujica (Uru)	01/09/2012–31/10/2014	0 (0)
Le Pen (Fra)	01/09/2012–31/10/2014	1,458 (422)	Vazquez (Uru)	01/06/2014–31/10/2014	0 (0)
Hollande (Fra)	01/09/2012–31/10/2014	18 (0)	Lacalle (Uru)	01/06/2014–31/10/2014	301 (200)
Fillon (Fra)	16/06/2014–31/10/2014	81 (81)	Bordaberry (Uru)	01/09/2012–31/10/2014	1,485 (463)
Copé (Fra)	19/11/2012–15/06/2014	308 (215)	Heber (Uru)	01/09/2012–22/04/2013	274 (117)
Valls (Fra)	01/04/2014–31/10/2014	16 (0)	Obama (Usa)	01/09/2012–31/10/2014	1,216 (465)
Ayrault (Fra)	01/09/2012–31/03/2014	168 (100)	Romney (Usa)	01/09/2012–06/11/2012	308 (108)
Merkel (Ger)	01/09/2012–31/10/2014	463 (370)	Boehner (Usa)	07/11/2012–31/10/2014	210 (105)
Steinbruck (Ger)	28/09/2012–27/09/2013	525 (346)	Capriles (Ven)	01/09/2012–31/10/2014	4,025 (540)
Gabriel (Ger)	01/09/2012–31/10/2014	1,662 (476)	Chavez (Ven)	01/09/2012–05/03/2013	1 (0)
Gysi (Ger)	17/12/2013–31/10/2014	350 (159)	Maduro (Ven)	14/02/2013–31/10/2014	1,076 (202)
Tsipras (Gre)	01/09/2012–31/10/2014	1,183 (395)			
Total					99,234 (25,151)

A Facebook application called Netvizz was used to conduct this analysis. Netvizz allows an automatic download of all posts published in the Facebook pages of the leaders under consideration. A total of 99,234 posts were discovered. Among these 99,234 posts, 25,151 posts were manually coded and analyzed.[N] The guiding criteria applied for the sampling process were the following: for each leader, we analyzed one post every 2 days and one post every day when the leader was involved in an election campaign.[O] The coding process concerned all leaders with a Facebook page that had published at least 50 posts. 89 out of 127 cases matched this criterion. Therefore, the content analysis concerns only a portion of the cases included in Table 2.

Our analysis focused on two main variables: the topic covered in the posts and the type of policy issue covered in the posts. The first variable examines if the leader has talked about a policy issue and differentiates between posts about policy issues and other posts where leaders do not mention at all a policy issue, such as those cases where they talk about their private life, a news story or campaigning issues. For the second variable, we looked at leaders' posts with an explicit reference to a policy issue. The type of policy issue has been coded in 10 different categories: (i) environmental policies; (ii) primary sector; (iii) secondary sector, energy and infrastructure; (iv) tertiary sector and public administration; (v) economy; (vi) social policies; (vii) security and immigration; (viii) foreign policy; (xi) human and civil rights; and (x) institutional reforms and justice. This second variable could have also been categorized by using the Party Manifesto Project (Volkens et al. 2012). However, the use of this typology has been confronted with some criticism over the years (for example, see Zulianello 2014). Therefore, we opted for a more parsimonious and autonomous categorization.

To ensure inter-coder reliability, a random selection of 523 posts was independently coded twice. Krippendorff's Alpha turned out to be 0.82 for the first dependent variable and 0.89 for the second one, indicating satisfactory results for the statistics.

We conducted the content analysis of Facebook pages of 89 leaders and the percentage of posts about environmental issues contained in these Facebook pages represents our dependent variable. After a descriptive outline of our data, we conducted bivariate analyses in order to test the research hypotheses from which we specified six independent variables such as: (i) gender; (ii) age; (iii) party orientation; (iv) economic well-being of country; (v) effect of an economic crisis; and (vi) environmental quality of a country. These variables were taken into consideration to identify the

---

[N] To tackle the different languages in our data set, we used online translation services to code posts in languages such as Finnish or Greek.

[O] Among the pool of coded posts, there can be the case of a hypothetical leader A who published 150 posts over a period of 400 days with no election campaigns in the period under consideration. In this case, all the 150 posts would have been coded. There can also be the case of a second hypothetical leader B who published 2000 posts over the period of 400 days with no election campaign. In this second case, 200 posts would have been coded by following a casual sampling process. There can also be the case of a third hypothetical leader C who published 2000 posts in 400 days and had been involved in an election campaign. In this case, we would have coded 230 posts. More precisely, 170 posts would have been coded during the 340 days when the leader was not involved in an election campaign, plus at least 60 further posts during the 60 days before the corresponding election day. The choice to double, if necessary, the number of posts coded during the 60 days before an election day, follows the empirical observation of the data. With the unique exception of Werner Faymann (Austria), all the leaders included in the dataset increased significantly the number of posts published in their Facebook pages during election campaigns.

Table 3: Typology for the Type of Policy Issues

Type of Policy Issue	Sub-Categories	Examples
Environmental policies	waste policies; water policies; global warming; etc.	https://www.facebook.com/216342268645/posts/10152727821168646
Primary sector	agriculture policies; fishing policies; raw materials; etc.	https://www.facebook.com/200178983466771/posts/261165600701442
Secondary sector, energy and infrastructures	manufacturing; energy and infrastructure policies; etc.	https://www.facebook.com/205395698264/posts/10152330648404913
Tertiary sector and public administration	services; telecommunications; public administration reforms; etc.	https://www.facebook.com/248984428464398/posts/679852542044249
Economy	taxation; government budget; monetary policies; etc.	https://www.facebook.com/7328265549/posts/10152303364560550
Social policies	health policies; education policies; social services policies; etc.	https://www.facebook.com/30876134768/posts/10152091093564769
Security and immigration	crime policies; prison policies; immigration policies; etc.	https://www.facebook.com/653092548048400/posts/812404315450555
Foreign policy	international relations; military policies; international security; etc.	https://www.facebook.com/104493292916735/posts/836450216387702
Human and civil rights	political rights; LGBT rights; religious rights etc.	https://www.facebook.com/329885883718979/posts/834243666616529
Institutional reforms and justice	electoral law; constitutional reforms; reforms of the judiciary system; etc.	https://www.facebook.com/401049006603015/posts/808530862521492

Table 4: Type of Policy Issue

Type of Policy Issue	N	% (Among All Posts)	% (Among Posts About Policy Issues)
Social policies	2,998	11.9	31.0
Economy	2,481	9.9	25.6
Security and immigration	795	3.2	8.2
Secondary sector, energy and infrastructures	636	2.5	6.6
Environmental policies	**559**	**2.2**	**5.8**
Institutional reforms and justice	517	2.1	5.3
Tertiary sector and PA	311	1.2	3.2
Foreign policy	260	1.0	2.7
Human and civil rights	194	0.8	2.0
Primary sector	180	0.7	1.9
Various policy issues together	635	2.5	6.6
Other	96	0.4	1.0
Nc	14	0.1	0.1
Total posts about policy issues	9,676	38.5	100.0

taken into consideration to identify which leaders focused most on environmental issues on Facebook and whether such a higher focus applied to communicative choices made by these political leaders.

We opted for bivariate analyses for three main reasons: (i) it represents the best analytical tool for answering our research questions; (ii) in this article we are not interested in determining the factors explaining a higher focus on environmental issues on Facebook, but we are interested in hypothesis testing tasks of relationship between two single variables; and (iii) the limited number of our cases (89) does not advice to run multivariate analyses, such as multivariate regressions. A possible choice could have been to conduct a QCA with our dependent variable as outcome and our six independent variables as six conditions in a fsQCA. However, since we did not find any theoretical reasoning for hypothesizing the presence of equifinality or conjunctural causation, we decided to not follow this possible analytical path.

Findings

9,676 out of 25,151 posts (38.5% of the total) included a reference to a policy issue. When leaders published a post about a policy issue they focused particularly on social (31.0%) and economic (25.6%) policies. On the Facebook pages of the leaders taken into consideration, environmental posts appeared only in 2.2% of the cases, while this percentage value would rise to 5.8% when considering the posts about policy issues only. This means that if a citizen hypothetically uses Facebook only to follow the main political leaders of contemporary democracies, he/she will find information about environmental issues only sporadically, and this is true even when looking at the

subset of cases in which leaders talk about policy issues.

Table 5 lists the percentages of posts about environmental issues per leader. The mean (5.1%) and the median (3.8%) values confirm the trend pointed out by Table 4, while the standard deviation (6.4) expresses the presence of a moderate level of variability: most of the leaders revolve around the mean and median values; 10 out of 89 leaders reach double digits values; 11 leaders published no posts at all about environmental issues; there is only an outlier, that is the Brazilian leader Marina Silva ($z = 7.5$), whose posts shared about environmental issues constituted 52.9% of the total number of posts she had shared on policy issues.

T tests analyses and bivariate correlations highlighted in Table 6 draw a complex scenario. First, gender and the effects of the crisis never reach statistically significant values. It does not make any difference on the propensity of publishing environmental posts whether the leader is a male or a female, or whether he/she acts in a country where the economic crisis of 2007 had a strong effect over economic well-being levels measured in terms of GDP. Second, only party affiliation and age are related to an environmental salience if considering all the leaders included into the data set: left-wing and younger leaders are the ones that publish the most posts about environmental issues. Third, Table 6 points out a clear divide when splitting up the analysis between Western and Latin-American leaders. While the independent variables show statistically significant values when conducting the analysis on Western leaders only, no independent variable affects the green agenda of the main political leaders when looking exclusively inside the Latin-American context. Regarding Western leaders,

Table 5: Posts About Environmental Issues per Leader

Leader	% of Posts About Environmental Issues (Among Posts About Policy Issues)	Leader	% of Posts About Environmental Issues (Among Posts About Policy Issues)
Silva	52.9	Rinne	3.8
Correa	16.7	Rutte	3.8
Store	16.7	Rajoy	3.8
Keller	14.7	Rasmussen	3.8
Mulcair	14.0	Schulz	3.5
Shorten	12.9	Heber	3.3
Nieto	12.9	Rousseff	3.3
Grillo	11.6	Gillard	3.2
Faymann	9.4	Strache	3.0
Obama	9.3	Trudeau	3.0
Schmidt	8.8	Capriles	2.8
Perez	8.0	Rubalcaba	2.7
Stoltenberg	7.9	Matthei	2.5
Massa	7.7	Obrador	2.4
Clegg	7.5	Di Rupo	2.3
Campos	7.1	Kenny	2.3
Bachelet	6.8	Le pen	2.1
Alegre	6.6	Gysi	2.0
Cunliffe	6.6	Neves	1.9
Gabriel	6.6	Gilmore	1.9
Bersani	6.5	Renzi	1.9
Lopez	6.5	Van Rompuy	1.9
Kuczynski	6.5	Verhofstadt	1.9
Medina	6.5	Bordaberry	1.8
Cameron	6.3	Shearer	1.7
Lofven	6.3	Lasso	1.6
Solberg	6.3	Urpilainen	1.2
Ramirez	6.1	Berlusconi	1.1
Franco	6.1	Letta	1.0
Maduro	6.0	Madero	0.9
Abbott	5.6	Miliband	0.7
Key	5.5	Jensen	0.6
Cartes	5.3	Harper	0.4
De Kirchner	5.3	Boehner	0.0
Lacalle	5.3	Cope	0.0
Tsipras	5.1	Fillon	0.0
Juncker	5.0	Gutierrez	0.0
Rudd	4.9	Merkel	0.0
Humala	4.8	Monti	0.0
Epifani	4.7	Romney	0.0
Mendez	4.7	Samaras	0.0
Santos	4.5	Steinbruck	0.0
Fujimori	4.3	Toledo	0.0
Ominami	4.0	Zualaga	0.0
Ayrault	3.8		
Mean			5.1
Median			3.8
SD			6.4

Table 6: Bivariate Analyses

	N	All Leaders		N	Western Leaders Only		N	Latin-American Leaders Only	
		t			t			T	
Latin-American	89	1,327							
Woman	89	1,028		66	0.138		33	1,021	
Left	89	2,651*		66	2,671*		33	1,485	
		R	rho		r	rho		r	rho
GDP	84	−0.039	−0.025	61	0.304*	0.227	33	0.043	−0.069
Crisis effect	84	0.123	0.148	61	0.269	0.183	33	0.017	0.020
EPI	84	0.110	−0.013	61	0.241	0.292*	33	−0.021	−0.198
Age	89	−0.141	−0.276*	66	−0.275*	−0.307*	33	−0.056	−0.221

Note: ***$p \leq .001$ **$p \leq .01$ *$p \leq .05$

in addition to gender and age, also higher levels of GDP and EPI are associated with statistically significant values. To be more specific, a higher propensity of focusing on environmental issues is correlated with higher levels of GDP and EPI.

Conclusions

The comparative analysis on the Facebook pages of the main political leaders carried out in this article returned some interesting findings with relevant theoretical implications. Our research indicated that environmental issues are not prioritized in the agendas of the 127 leaders taken into consideration. In line with the empirical analyses highlighting the role of media in shaping the salience of such issues among the general public (for example, see Cook et al. 1983; McCombs and Shaw 1972; Roberts, Wanta, and Dzwo 2002; Wanta, Golan, and Cheolhan 2004), our study showed that citizens following the main political leaders of contemporary democracies on Facebook would only find that 2 out of 100 posts touched upon environmental issues. Hence, our analysis points out that, despite its potential, Facebook is not used by political leaders as a tool to spread information on environmental issues.

Nevertheless, the question remains whether this is indeed unexpected. In line with studies focusing on the low salience of environmental policies in national campaigns (for example, see Dunlap 1987 and Dunlap 1991 on US electoral campaigns), our analysis identified a prioritization of social and economic policies in more than 50% of posts where leaders had included an explicit reference to these policy issues. We then found that the highest percentage of shared posts was associated with mes-

sages where leaders talked about health and school systems, or about the financial or labor sectors.

Analyzing the relationship between our theoretical framework and the Facebook data, the resulting findings show interesting patterns. While the Facebook posts under consideration confirm that left-wing and young leaders are more inclined to use Facebook to spread information about environmental issues, our hypothesis on the economic well-being of a country has been confirmed only in regard to Western countries. In particular, our findings show that high GDP levels are directly associated with the presence of environmental posts only when looking at the main leaders of Western Europe, USA, Canada, Australia, and New Zealand. Contrariwise, for Latin American countries, the presence of environmental posts is independent from the GDP levels. Moreover, rejecting our hypothesis on environmental quality, Facebook data reveal that leaders of countries with higher levels of environmental quality are showing a stronger focus on environmental issues. Furthermore, the findings do not support our hypothesis on the 2007 economic crisis. Data do not display a strong correlation between the effects of the crisis and the salience attached to environmental issues by political leaders

The most interesting consideration that can be drawn from our analysis concerns an existing distinction between leaders of Western and Latin American countries. As Table 5 pointed out, when jointly analyzing the 89 leaders included in our data set, there is no significant difference between Western and Latin American leaders ($t = 1.327$; $p = 0.188$). However, relevant differences arise when these two clusters are analyzed separately. As our data show, while a relationship between the hypotheses on economic well-being, environmental quality, socio-demographic characteristics, and leaders' party affiliation is clearly confirmed or rejected when analyzing the leaders of Western Europe, USA, Canada, Australia, and New Zealand, associations between these intervening variables and leaders' environmental salience are less distinct when we analyze Latin American leaders whose environmental focus appears more randomly influenced.

It goes without saying that considering the novelty of our analysis in the use of social media such as Facebook to understand policy orientations of political leaders, the study must inevitably be considered preliminary and there clearly is still room to further improve the explanations of our results. Nevertheless, by examining how specific variables relate to each other, this comparative analysis has had the strength of combining and testing together hypotheses from environmental policy and agenda-setting strands of literature. It did so by focusing on a media environment, Facebook, where no scholar had ever researched whether the main political leaders of contemporary advanced industrial democracies use social media for spreading information about environmental issues.

The relevance of Facebook in the contemporary media environment and all the dynamics resulting from the advent of a hybrid media system (Chadwick 2013) implicate an in-depth understanding on how this specific social medium is affecting agenda-setting developments. This comparative research did so in a rather indirect way by showing how important it is to talk about environmental issues for contemporary leaders. Further research should analyze whether, and to what extent, posting on Facebook one's own stance about water policies, waste policies, or the global warming issue is able to alter the environmental agendas of other media, political opponents, and citizens. More generally, it is also worth noting that this comparative study opens up new paths of research for the analysis of how political elites communicate after the digital revolution (Ceccobelli 2015). Since we live in a media environment where around 1.65 billion of users connect to Facebook at least once a month, the communicative choices made by politicians on this platform represent a relevant measure for decoding the salience of a given policy, far more reliably than party manifestos. These quickly become outdated in a political time characterized by rapid changes both at political, economic, social, and technological level; from this perspective, simply following political leaders' Facebook pages allows one to track the policy salience, developments, and dynamics with far greater accuracy; this is ever more true since we live in an era of personalized politics (Garzia 2014; Karvonen 2010; McAllister 2007).

Finally, it is worth mentioning that the focus on individual motivations of political leaders for environmental salience (such as an in-depth analysis of outlier cases such as Marina Silva, or two British right-wing leaders who published more Facebook posts about environmental issues than their left-wing counterparts) falls beyond the scope of this paper. Further research designed with the aim of establishing causality in the relationships highlighted in this analysis is in order and will mark the next step in better determining the role social media such as Facebook play in spreading information about the environment.

References

Aoyagi-Usui, M., H. Vinken, and A. Kuribayashi. 2003. "Pro-environmental Attitudes and Behaviors: An International Comparison." *Human Ecology Review* 10 (1): 23–31.

Arbuthnot, J., and S. Lingg. 1975. "A Comparison of French and American Environmental Behaviors, Knowledge, and Attitudes." *International Journal of Psychology* 10 (4): 275–81.

Arcury, T. A., T. P. Johnson, and S. J. Scollay. 1986. "Ecological Worldview and Environmental Knowledge: The 'New Environmental Paradigm'." *The Journal of Environmental Education* 17 (4): 35–40.

Arrow, K., B. Bolin, R. Costanza, P. Dasgupta, C. Folke, and C. S. Holling. 1995. "Economic Growth, Carrying Capacity, and the Environment." *Science* 268: 520–21.

Bakker, R., S. Jolly, and J. Polk. 2012 "Complexity in the European Party Space: Exploring Dimensionality With Experts." *European Union Politics* 13 (2): 219–45.

Beckerman, W. 1992. "Economic Growth and the Environment: Whose Growth? Whose Environment?" *World Development* 20 (4): 481–96.

Benoit, K., and L. Michael. 2006. *Party Policy in Modern Democracies*. London: Routledge.

Benton, T. 1997. "Beyond Left and Right? Ecological Politics, Capitalism and Modernity." In *Greening the Millennium? The New Politics of the Environment*, ed. M. Jacobs. London: Blackwell.

Blocker, T. J., and D. L. Eckberg. 1989. "Environmental Issues as Women's Issues: General Concerns and Local Hazards." *Social Science Quarterly* 70 (3): 58–93.

Bond, R., and S. Messing. 2015. "Quantifying Social Media's Political Space: Estimating Ideology from Publicly Revealed Preferences on Facebook." *American Political Science Review* 109 (1): 62–78.

Bord, R. J., and R. E. O'Connor. 1997. "The Gender Gap in Environmental Attitudes: The Case of Perceived Vulnerability to Risk." *Social Science Quarterly* 78 (4): 830–40.

Brechin, S. R., and W. Kempton. 1997. "Beyond Postmaterialist Values: National Versus Individual Explanations of Global Environmentalism." *Social Science Quarterly* 78 (1): 16–20.

Bronstein, J. 2013. "Like Me! Analyzing the 2012 Presidential Candidates' Facebook Pages." *Online Information Review* 37 (2): 173–92.

Brulle, R. J., J. Carmichael, and J. C. Jenkins. 2012. "Shifting Public Opinion on Climate Change: An Empirical Assessment of Factors Influencing Concern Over Climate Change in the US, 2002–2010." *Climatic Change* 114 (2): 169–88.

Bruns, A., G. Enli, E. Skogerbø, C. Christensen, and A. O. Larsson, eds. 2016.

Routledge Companion to Social Media and Politics. New York: Routledge.

Budge, I., D. Robertson, and D. Hearl. 1987. *Ideology, Strategy and Party Change: Spatial Analyses of Post-war Election Programmes in 19 Democracies.* Cambridge: Cambridge University Press.

Burgess, J., and A. Bruns. 2012. "(Not) the Twitter Election: The Dynamics of the #Ausvotes Conversation in Relation to the Australian Media Ecology." *Journalism Practice* 6 (3): 384–402.

Buttel, F. H. 1979. "Age and Environmental Concern: A Multivariate Analysis." *Youth and Society* 10 (3): 237–56.

Buttel, F. H., and W. L. Flinn. 1974. "The Structure of Support for the Environmental Movement, 1968–1970." *Rural Sociology* 39 (1): 56–69.

Buttel, F. H., and W. L. Flinn. 1976. "Sociopolitical Consequences of Agrarianism." *Rural Sociology* 40 (2): 134–51.

Buttel, F. H., and W. L. Flinn. 1978. "Social Class and Mass Environmental Beliefs a Reconsideration." *Environment and Behavior* 10 (3): 433–50.

Callen, T. 2012. "Gross Domestic Product: An Economy's All." *Finance and Development, International Monetary Fund* http://www.imf.org/external/pubs/ft/fandd/basics/gdp.htm

Calvert, J. W. 1979. "The Social and Ideological Bases of Support for Environmental Legislation: An Examination of Public Attitudes and Legislative Action." *The Western Political Quarterly* 32: 327–37.

Calvert, J. 1989. "Party Politics and Environmental Policy." In Environmental Politics and Policy. Theories and Evidence, ed. J. P. Lester. Durham and London: Duke University Press.

Cameron, S. M. 2013. "Postmaterialism in Times of Crisis." Presented at the European Consortium for Political Research General Conference 2013, Bordeaux.

Carman, C. J. 1998. "Dimensions of Environmental Policy Support in the United States." *Social Science Quarterly* 79 (4): 717–33.

Carson, R. 1962. *Silent Spring.* Boston: Houghton Mifflin.

Carter, N. 2006. "Party Politicization of the Environment in Britain." *Party Politics* 12 (6): 747–67.

Carter, N. 2009. "Vote Blue, Go Green? Cameron's Conservatives and the Environment." *The Political Quarterly* 80 (2): 233–42.

Carter, N. 2013. "Greening the Mainstream: Party Politics and the Environment." *Environmental Politics* 22 (1): 73–94.

Ceccobelli, D. 2015. "Political Leaders on Facebook: A Comparative Analysis of Popularization in Contemporary Liberal Democracies." Ph.D. diss. Florence, Scuola Normale Superiore.

Chadwick, A. 2006. *Internet Politics: States, Citizens, and New Communication Technologies.* New York: Oxford University Press.

Chadwick, A. 2013. *The Hybrid Media System: Politics and Power.* New York: Oxford University Press.

Chen, T. B., and L. T. Chai. 2010. "Attitude Towards the Environment and Green Products: Consumers' Perspective." *Management Science and Engineering* 4 (2): 27–39.

Cole, M. A. 2000. *Trade Liberalisation, Economic Growth and the Environment.* Celthelham (UK) and Northanpton (USA): Edward Elgar.

Cole, M. A., A. J. Rayner, and J. M. Bates. 1997. "The Environmental Kuznets Curve: An Empirical Analysis." *Environment and Development Economics* 2 (4): 401–16.

Cook, F. L., T. R. Tyler, E. G. Goetz, M. T. Gordon, D. Protess, D. R. Leff, and H. L. Molotch. 1983. "Media and Agenda Setting: Effects on the Public, Interest Group Leaders, Policy Makers, and Policy." *Public Opinion Quarterly* 47 (1): 16–35.

Costantini, E., and K. Hanf. 1972. "Environmental Concern and Lake Tahoe: A Study of Elite Perceptions, Backgrounds, and Attitudes." *Environment and Behavior* 4 (2): 209–42.

Cotta B., and V. Memoli. 2015. "Post-Materialism in Times of Crisis? The Perception of the Environmental Issue Among European Citizens." Paper presented at the European Consortium for Political Research General Conference 2015, Montreal.

Dalton, R. J. 2009. "Economics, Environmentalism and Party Alignments: A Note on Partisan Change in Advanced Industrial Democracies." *European Journal of Political Research* 48 (2): 161–75.

Dasgupta, S., K. Hamilton, K. D. Pand-

ey, and D. Wheeler. 2006. "Environment During Growth: Accounting for Governance and Vulnerability." *World Development* 34 (9): 1597–611.

Dasgupta, S., A. Mody, S. Roy, and D. Wheeler. 2001. "Environmental Regulation and Development: A Cross-country Empirical Analysis." *Oxford Development Studies* 29 (2): 173–87.

Davidson, D. J., and W. R. Freudenburg. 1996. "Gender and Environmental Risk Concerns a Review and Analysis of Available Research." *Environment and Behavior* 28 (3): 302–39.

De Sismondi, S. 1991. *New Principles of Political Economy: Of Wealth in Its Relation to Population.* New Brunswick (USA) and London (UK):Transaction Publishers.

Deuze, M. 2006. "Participation, Remediation, Bricolage: Considering Principal Components of a Digital Culture." *The Information Society* 22 (2): 63–75.

Dillman, D. A., and J. A. Christenson. 1972. "The Public Value for Pollution Control." In *Social Behavior, Natural Resources and the Environment*, eds. W. Burch, W. Creek, and L. Taylor. New York: Harper and Row.

Downs, A. 1972. "Up and Down with Ecology: The 'Issue-Attention-Cycle'." *Public Interest* 28: 38–50.

Dunlap, R. E. 1975. "The Impact of Political Orientation on Environmental Attitudes and Actions." *Environment and Behavior* 7 (4): 428–54.

Environment and Behavior 7 (4): 428–54.

Dunlap, R. E. 1987. "Polls, Pollution, and Politics Revisited Public Opinion on the Environment in the Reagan Era." *Environment: Science and Policy for Sustainable Development* 29 (6): 6–37.

Dunlap, R. E. 1989. "Public Opinion and Environmental Policy." In *Environmental Politics and Policy. Theories and Evidence*, ed. J. P. Lester. Durham and London: Duke University Press.

Dunlap, R. E. 1991. "Trends in Public Opinion Toward Environmental Issues: 1965–1990." *Society & Natural Resources* 4 (3): 285–312.

Dunlap, R. E., and M. P. Allen. 1976. "Partisan Differences on Environmental Issues: A Congressional Roll-Call Analysis." *The Western Political Quarterly* 29: 384–97.

Dunlap, R. E., and R. P. Gale. 1972. "Politics and Ecology: A Political Profile of Student Eco-Activists." *Youth and Society* 3 (4): 379–98.

Dunlap, R. E., and R. P. Gale. 1974. "Party Membership and Environmental Politics: A Legislative Roll-Call Analysis." *Social Science Quarterly* 55: 670–90.

Dunlap, R. E., and R. B. Heffernan. 1975. "Outdoor Recreation and Environmental Concern: An Empirical Examination." *Rural Sociology* 40 (1): 18–30.

Dunlap, R. E., and A. M. McCright. 2008. "A Widening Gap: Republican and Democratic Views on Climate Change." *Environment: Science and Policy for Sustainable Development* 50 (5): 26–35.

Dunlap, R. E., and A. G. Mertig. 1997. "Global Environmental Concern: An Anomaly for Postmaterialism." *Social Science Quarterly* 78 (1): 24–29.

Dunlap, R. E., and R. Scarce. 1991. "Poll Trends: Environmental Problems and Protection." *The Public Opinion Quarterly* 55 (4): 651–72.

Dunlap, R. E., C. Xiao, and A. M. McCright. 2001. "Politics and Environment in America: Partisan and Ideological Cleavages in Public Support for Environmentalism." *Environmental Politics* 10 (4): 23–48.

Edey, M. 1970. "Eco-Politics and the League of Conservation Voters," In *The Environmental Handbook*, ed. G. DeBell. New York: Ballantine/Friends of the Earth.

Egri, C. P., and S. Herman. 2000. "Leadership in the North American Environmental Sector: Values, Leadership Styles, and Contexts of Environmental Leaders and Their Organizations." *Academy of Management Journal* 43 (4): 571–604.

Elliott, E., B. J. Seldon, and J. L. Regens. 1997. "Political and Economic Derminants of Individuals' Support for Environmental Spending." *Journal of Environmental Management* 51 (1): 15–27.

Engelbert, E. A. 1961. "Political Parties and Natural Resources Policies: An Historical Evaluation, 1790–1950." *Natural Resources Journal* 1 (3): 224–56.

Erskine, H. 1972. "The Polls: Pollution and Its Costs." *The Public Opinion Quarterly* 36 (1): 120–35.

Ester, P., L. Halman, and B. Seuren. 1993. "Environmental Concern and Offering Willingness in Europe and North America." In *The Individualizing Society*, eds. P. Ester, L. Halman, and R. de Moor. The Netherlands: Tilburg University Press.

Esty, D. C. 2008. "Rethinking Global Environmental Governance to Deal with Climate Change: The Multiple Logics of Global Collective Action." *The American*

Economic Review 98 (2): 116–21.

Esty, D. C., and M. E. Porter. 2005. "National Environmental Performance: An Empirical Analysis of Policy Results and Determinants." *Environment and Development Economics* 10 (4): 391–434.

Fiorino, D. J. 2011. "Explaining National Environmental Performance: Approaches, Evidence, and Implications." *Policy Sciences* 44 (4): 367–89.

Fliegenschnee, M., and M. Schelakovsky. 1998. *Environmental Psychology and Environmental Education: An Introduction of Human Ecological Perspective.* Vienna: University Facultas Publisher.

Franzen, A., and D. Vogl. 2013. "Two Decades of Measuring Environmental Attitudes: A Comparative Analysis of 33 Countries." *Global Environmental Change* 23 (5): 1001–8.

Garzia, D. 2014. *Personalization of Politics and Electoral Change.* Houndmills, Basingstoke: Palgrave Macmillan.

Gerodimos, R., and J. Justinussen. 2015. "Obama's 2012 Facebook Campaign: Political Communication in the Age of the Like Button." *Journal of Information Technology & Politics* 12 (2): 113–32.

Golbeck, J., J. M. Grimes, and A. Rogers. 2010. "Twitter Use by the U.S. Congress." *Journal of the American Society for Information Science and Technology* 61 (8): 1612–21.

Grossman, G., and A. Krueger. 1995. "Economic Environment and the Economic Growth." *Quarterly Journal of Economics* 110 (2): 353–77.

Grossman, G. M., and H. R. Potter. 1977. *A Trend Analysis of Competing Models of Environmental Attitudes.* Working Paper# 127, Institute for the Study of Social Change, Dept. of Sociology and Anthropology, Purdue University.

Guber, D. L. 2003. The Grassroots of a Green Revolution: Polling America on the Environment. Cambridge MA: MIT Press.

Gulati, G. J., and C. B. Williams. 2013. "Social Media and Campaign 2012 Developments and Trends for Facebook Adoption." *Social Science Computer Review* 31 (5): 577–88.

Hamilton, J. A. 1985. "Avoiding Methodological and Policy-Making Biases in Gender-Related Research." *US Department of Health and Human Services, Women's Health: Report of the Public Health Service Task Force on Women's Health Issues* 2: 54–64.

Hamilton, L. C. 2008. "Who Cares About Polar Regions? Results from a Survey of US Public Opinion." *Arctic, Antarctic, and Alpine Research* 40 (4): 671–78.

Hamilton, L. C. 2011. "Education, Politics and Opinions About Climate Change Evidence for Interaction Effects." *Climatic Change* 104 (2): 231–42.

Hamilton, L. C., and B. D. Keim. 2009. "Regional Variation in Perceptions About Climate Change." *International Journal of Climatology* 29 (15): 2348–52.

Harris, L. 1970. *The Public's View of Environmental Problems in the State of Oregon.* New York: Louis Harris and Associates.

Harry, J., R. Gale, and J. Hendee. 1969. "Conservation: An Upper- Middle Class Social Movement." *Journal of Leisure Research* 1: 246–54.

Howell, S. E., and S. B. Laska. 1992. "The Changing Face of the Environmental Coalition: A Research Note." *Environment and Behavior* 24 (1): 134–44.

Hunter, L. M., and L. Rinner. 2004. "The Association Between Environmental Perspective and Knowledge and Concern with Species Diversity." *Society and Natural Resources* 17 (6): 517–32.

Inglehart, R. 1990a. "Post-Materialism in an Environment of Insecurity." *American Political Science Review* 75 (4): 880–900.

Inglehart, R. 1990b. *Culture Shift in Advanced Industrial Society.* Princeton University Press.

Inglehart, R. 1997. *Modernization and Postmodernization. Cultural, Economic, and Political Change in 43 Societies.* Princeton, NJ: Princeton University Press.

Jahn, D. 1998. "Environmental Performance and Policy Regimes: Explaining Variations in 18 OECD-Countries." *Policy Sciences* 31: 107–31.

Jensen, C. B., and J. Spoon. 2011. "Testing the 'Party Matters' Thesis: Explaining Progress Towards Kyoto Protocol Targets." *Political Studies* 59 (1): 99–115.

Jones, R. E., and R. E. Dunlap. 1992. "The Social Bases of Environmental Concern: Have They Changed Over Time?" *Rural Sociology* 57 (1): 28–47.

Kallis, G. 2011. "In Defence of Degrowth." *Ecological Economics* 70 (5): 873–80.

Kamieniecki, S. 1995. "Political Parties and Environmental Policy." In *Environmental Politics and Policy: Theories and Evidence,* ed. J. P. Lester. Durham NC: Duke University Press.

Kanagy, C. L., C. R. Humphrey, and G. Firebaugh. 1994. "Surging Environmentalism: Changing Public Opinion or Changing Publics?" *Social Science Quarterly* 1 (5): 804–19.

Karlsen, R. 2009. "Campaign Communication and the Internet: Party Strategy in the 2005 Norwegian Election Campaign." *Journal of Elections, Public Opinion and Parties* 19 (2): 183–202.

Karvonen, L. 2010. *The Personalisation of Politics: A Study of Parliamentary Democracies.* Colchester: ECPR Press.

Kenski, H. C., and M. C. Kenski. 1980. "Partnership, Ideology, and Constituency Differences in Environmental Issues in the US House of Representatives, 1973–1978." *Policy Studies Journal* 9 (3): 325–48.

Kidd, Q., and A. Lee. 1997. "Postmaterialist Values and the Environment: A Critique and Reappraisal." *Social Science Quarterly* 1: 1–15.

King, R. F., and A. Borchardt. 1994. "Red and Green: Air Pollution Levels and Left Party Power in OECD Countries." *Environment and Planning C: Government and Policy* 12 (2): 225–41.

Kitschelt, H. 1998. "Organization and Strategy of Belgian and West German Ecology Parties: A New Dynamic of Party Politics in Western Europe?" *Comparative Politics* 20 (2): 127–54.

Klineberg, S. L., M. McKeever, and B. Rothenbach. 1998. "Demographic Predictors of Environmental Concern: It Does Make a Difference How It's Measured." *Social Science Quarterly* 79 (4): 734–53.

Klingemann, H., R. I. Hofferbert, and I. Budge. 1994. Parties, Policies, and Democracy. Boulder CO: Westview Press.
Konisky, D. M., J. Milyo, and L. E. Richardson. 2008. "Environmental Policy Attitudes: Issues, Geographical Scale, and Political Trust." *Social Science Quarterly* 89 (5): 1066–85.

Lake, L. M. 1983. "The Environmental Mandate: Activists and the Electorate." Political Science Quarterly 98 (2): 215–33.
Larsson, A. O., and B. Kalsnes. 2014. "'Of Course We are on Facebook': Use and Non-Use of Social Media Among Swedish and Norwegian Politicians." *European Journal of Communication* 29 (6): 1–16.

Laver, M., ed. 2003. *Estimating the Policy Position of Political Actors.* London: Routledge.

Laver, M., and W. B. Hunt. 1992. *Policy and Party Competition.* London: Routledge.

Malka, A., J. A. Krosnick, and G. Langer.

2009. "The Association of Knowledge with Concern About Global Warming: Trusted Information Sources Shape Public Thinking." *Risk Analysis* 29 (5): 633–47.

Malkis, A., and H. G. Grasmick. 1977. "Support for the Ideology of the Environmental Movement: Tests of Alternative Hypotheses." *Western Sociological Review* 8 (1): 25–47.

Malthus, T. R. 1878. *An Essay on the Principle of Population: Or, a View of Its Past and Present Effects on Human Happiness, with an Inquiry into Our Prospects Respecting the Future Removal or Mitigation of the Evils Which It Occasions.* London: Reeves and Turner.

Mancini, P., and M. Mazzoni. 2014. "Politici e social network: un trampolino per i media mainstream. Un Sistema ibrido (tutto) italiano." In *La politica in 140 caratteri*, ed. S. Bentivegna. Milano: FrancoAngeli.

Marchetti, R., and D. Ceccobelli. 2016. "Twitter and Television in a Hybrid Media System. The 2013 Italian Election Campaign." *Journalism Practice* 10 (5): 626–44.

Mazmanian, D., and P. Sabatier. 1981. "Liberalism, Environmentalism, and Partisanship in Public Policy-Making. The California Coastal Commissions." *Environment and Behavior* 13 (3): 361–84.

McAllister, I. 2007. "The Personalization of Politics." In *The Oxford Handbook of Political Behavior*, eds. R. Dalton and H. Klingeman. Oxford: Oxford University Press.

McCombs, M. E., and D. L. Shaw. 1972. "The Agenda-Setting Function of Mass Media." *Public Opinion Quarterly* 36 (2): 176–87.

McCright, A. M. 2010. "The Effects of Gender on Climate Change Knowledge and Concern in the American Public." *Population and Environment* 32 (1): 66–87.

McEvoy, J. 1972. "The American Concern with the Environment." In *Social Behavior, Natural Resources and the Environment*, ed. W. R. Burch. New York: Harper & Row.

Meadows, D. H., D. L. Meadows, J. Randers, and W. W. Behrens. 1972. *The Limits to Growth*. New York: Universe Books.

Mill, J. S. 1882. "Principles of Political Economy." *Proceedings of the American Academy of Science* 1881: 417.

Mitchell, R. C. 1980. "Public Opinion on Environmental Issues." In *Environmental Quality: The Eleventh Annual Report of the Council on Environmental Quality*. Washington, DC: Council on Environmental Quality.

Mitchell, R. C. 1990. "Public Opinion and the Green Lobby: Poised for the 1990s?" In *Environmental Policy in the 1990s: Toward a New Agenda*, eds. N. J. Vig and M. E. Kraft. Washington, DC: CQ Press.

Mohai, P. 1992. "Men, Women, and the Environment: An Examination of the Gender Gap in Environmental Concern and Activism." *Society & Natural Resources* 5 (1): 1–19.

Mohai, P., and B. W. Twight. 1987. "Age

and Environmentalism: An Elaboration of the Buttel Model Using National Survey Evidence." *Social Science Quarterly* 68 (4): 798–815.

Murch, A. W. 1971. "Public Concern for Environmental Pollution." *The Public Opinion Quarterly* 35 (1): 100–106.

Murdock, S. H., and E. C. Schriner. 1977. "Social and Economic Determinants of the Level of Support for Environmental Protection and Economic Growth in a Rural Population." Paper presented at the Annual Meeting of the Rural Sociological Society. Madison, WI.

Neumayer, E. 2004. "The Environment, Left-Wing Political Orientation and Ecological Economics." *Ecological Economics* 51 (3): 167–75.

Nielsen, R. K., and C. Vaccari. 2013. "Do People 'Like' Politicians on Facebook? Not Really. Large-Scale Direct Candidate-to-Voter Online Communication as an Outlier Phenomenon." *International Journal of Communication* 7 (24): 2333–56.

Page, B. I., and C. C. Jones. 1979. "Reciprocal Effects of Policy Preferences, Party Loyalties and the Vote." *American Political Science Review* 73 (4): 1071–89.

Papacharissi, Z. 2002. "The Virtual Sphere: The Internet as a Public Sphere." *New Media & Society* 4 (1): 9–27.

Parmeggiani, B. 2015. "A relação entre representante e representados no Facebook: Um estudo de caso da fanpage de Dilma Rousseff." *Contemporânea* 12 (1): 78–90.

Passino, E. M., and J. W. Lounsbury. 1976. "Sex Differences in Opposition to and Support for Construction of a Proposed Nuclear Power Plant." *The Behavioral Basis of Design Book* 1: 1–5.

Pierce, J. C. 1977. "The Role of Preservationist Identification in the Belief Systems of Water Resource Group Leaders." *Polity* 9: 538–50.

Pierce, J. C., and N. P. Lovrich. 1980. "Belief Systems Concerning the Environment: The General Public, Attentive Publics, and State Legislators." *Political Behavior* 2 (3): 259–86.

Ritt, L. G., and J. M. Ostheimer. 1974. "Congressional Voting and Ecological Issues." *Environmental Affairs* 3: 459–72.

Roberts, M., W. Wanta, and T. H. D. Dzwo. 2002. "Agenda Setting and Issue Salience Online." *Communication Research* 29 (4): 452–65.

Rohrschneider, R. 1993. "New Party Versus Old Left Realignments: Environmental Attitudes, Party Policies, and Partisan Affiliations in Four West European Countries." *The Journal of Politics* 55 (3): 682–701.

Rüdig, W. 2012. "The Perennial Success of the German Greens." *Environmental Politics* 21 (1): 108–30.

Samuel-Azran, T., M. Yarchi, and G. Wolfsfeld. 2015. "Aristotelian Rhetoric and Facebook Success in Israel's 2013 Election Campaign." *Online Information Review* 39 (2): 149–62.

Schneider, F., G. Kallis, and J. Martinez-Alier. 2010. "Crisis or Opportunity? Economic Degrowth for Social Equity and Ecological Sustainability. Introduction to this Special Issue." *Journal of Cleaner Production* 18 (6): 511–18.

Schoenfeld, A. C., R. F. Meier, and R. J. Griffin. 1979. "Constructing a Social Problem: The Press and the Environment." *Social Problems* 27 (1): 38–61.

Scichilone, L. 2008. *L'Europa e la sfida ecologica: storia della politica ambientale europea (1969–1998)*. Bologna: Il Mulino.

Selden, T. M., and D. Song. 1994. "Environmental Quality and Development: Is There a Kuznets Curve for Air Pollution Emissions?" *Journal of Environmental Economics and Management* 27 (2): 147–62.

Shanahan, J., M. Morgan, and M. Stenbjerre. 1997. "Green or Brown? Television and the Cultivation of Environmental Concern." *Journal of Broadcasting & Electronic Media* 41 (3): 305–23.

Springer, J. F., and E. Costantini. 1974. *Public Opinion and the Environment: An Issue in Search of a Home*. New York: Praeger.

Steger, M. A. E., and S. L. Witt. 1989. "Gender Differences in Environmental Orientations: A Comparison of Publics and Activists in Canada and the US." *The Western Political Quarterly* 42 (4): 627–49.

Stern, P., T. Dietz, and L. Kalog. 1993. "Value Orientations, Gender, and Environmental Concern." *Environment and Behavior* 25: 322–48.

Sundquist, J. L. 1968. *Politics and Policy.* Washington DC: Brookings Institution.

Tognacci, L. N., R. H. Weigel, M. F. Wideen, and D. T. Vernon. 1972. "Environmental Quality: How Universal is Public Concern?." *Environment and Behavior* 4 (1): 73–86.

Torras, M., and J. K. Boyce. 1998. "Income, Inequality, and Pollution: A Reassessment of the Environmental Kuznets Curve." *Ecological Economics* 25 (2): 147–60.

Tranter, B. 2010. "Environmental Activists and Non-Active Environmentalists in Australia." *Environmental Politics* 19 (3): 413–29.

Trop, C., and L. L. Roos Jr. 1971. "Public Opinion and the Environment." In The Politics of Ecosuicide, ed. L. L. Ross Jr. New York: Holt, Rinehart and Winston.
Uyeki, E. S., and L. J. Holland. 2000. "Diffusion of Pro-Environment Attitudes?" *American Behavioral Scientist* 43 (4): 646–62.

Vaccari, C., and A. Valeriani. 2013. "Follow the Leader! Direct and Indirect Flows of Political Communication During the 2013 Italian General Election Campaign." *New Media & Society*, DOI: 10.1177/1461444813511038

Van Dijck, J., and T. Poell. 2013. "Understanding Social Media Logic." *Media and Communication* 1 (1): 2–14.

Van Liere, K. D., and R. E. Dunlap. 1980. "The Social Bases of Environmental Concern: A Review of Hypotheses, Explanations and Empirical Evidence." *Public Opinion Quarterly* 44 (2): 181–97.

Volkens, A., O. Lacewell, P. Lehmann, S.

Regel, H. Schultze, and A. Werner. 2012. "The Manifesto Document Collection." Manifesto Project (MRG/CMP/MARPOR).

Wanta, W., G. Golan, and L. Cheolhan. 2004. "Agenda Setting and International News: Media Influence on Public Perceptions of Foreign Nations." *Journalism & Mass Communication Quarterly* 81 (2): 364–77.

Weigel, R., and J. Weigel. 1978. "Environmental Concern the Development of a Measure." *Environment and Behavior* 10 (1): 3–15.

Williams, C. B., and J. Girish. 2012. "Social Networks in Political Campaigns: Facebook and the Congressional Elections of 2006 and 2008." *New Media & Society* 15 (1): 52–71.

Xiao, C., and R. E. Dunlap. 2007. "Validating a Comprehensive Model of Environmental Concern Cross-Nationally: A US-Canadian Comparison." *Social Science Quarterly* 88 (2): 471–93.

Zelezny, L. C., P. Chua, and C. Aldrich. 2000. "New Ways of Thinking About Environmentalism: Elaborating on Gender Differences in Environmentalism." *Journal of Social Issues* 56 (3): 443–57.

Zulianello, M. 2014. "Analyzing Party Competition Through the Comparative Manifesto Data: Some Theoretical and Methodological Considerations." *Quality & Quantity* 48 (3): 1723–37.

State and Regional Administrative Coordination in Spain: A Case Study of the Spanish Sectoral Conferences on Environmental, Health, and Educational Policies (2001–2012)

Jaione Mondragón Ruiz de Lezana, Alberto de la Peña Varona, Arantxa Elizondo Lopetegi, Juan Luis Mokoroa Arizkorreta, Francisco Juaristi Larrinaga[A]

Since 1978 Spain represents an example of a particular territorial model, intermediate between the unitarian and federal cases. In such an institutional framework, the coordination of sectoral policies has been ensured by inter-governmental bodies like the Sectoral Conferences, which are meant to integrate regional partners in the shared rule of the central State. By the same token, these Conferences should be a way to establish horizontal coordination for the Autonomous Regions in a context, such as the Spanish case, where no other tools for inter-territorial power sharing were designed. In this article, the main conclusions of a research project funded by the Spanish Instituto Nacional de Administración Pública (INAP) are presented. This project was devoted to analyzing the workings, dynamics, and results of the Sectoral Conferences as well as their role as shared government instruments. In other words, an empirical analysis was made of the coordination effectiveness of such bodies, taking their working dynamics as a reference. This means that, apart from the formal analysis, attention was paid to some elements that are sometimes out of reach of a normative framework and that have a close relationship to human factors, leadership, ideology or the very nature of the topics discussed.

Keywords*: intergovernmental relations; inter-territorial coordination; Spanish territorial organization; shared-government; sectoral conferences*

Introduction

Over the past few decades an inexorable advance has been observed of a new form of governing in which interdependence, collaboration, and cooperation among the elements of the state are crucial in the decision-making processes and public administration. This article aims to study the formal mechanisms of inter-governmental relations among the Autonomous Regions and the central government of Spain, more specifically those that are carried out by means of the so-called Sectoral Conferences. It focuses

[A] University of the Basque Country, Spain

doi: 10.18278/epa.2.2.6

firstly on institutional aspects, particularly the workings, dynamics, and results of these conferences; secondly, it explores the influence of the Spanish party system on the role the conferences play as co-governmental bodies; and finally, it takes into account the ideological and cultural background of the members of these conferences.[F] The aim is to analyze the extent to which these conferences act as an effective tool for inter-governmental relations among the elements that constitute the Spanish regional model of territorial organization.[G]

The concept of inter-governmental relations, according to Wright (1997, 8–9), includes two dimensions: the first is the connections that are established among different territorial levels of government, and the second dimension is relationships among governmental bodies at the same territorial level. This study examines certain institutions of vertical and multilateral collaboration in Spain, the Sectoral Conferences (SCs), given that these are the means most extensively used for shared government or collaboration among authorities (Colino and Parrado 2009, 25), despite the fact that they display a series of characteristics that reduce their potential as genuine instruments for channeling inter-governmental cooperation (Ruiz González 2013, 11).

Our research project covers the 2001–12 period because this was the time when most activity was registered in these co-governmental institutions. Three of the most long-standing conferences are dealt with: Environment, Health, and Education. With the compiled data and information, an in-depth diagnosis of the Sectoral Conferences is carried out, looking at the different aspects that could explain their real workings.

Inter-governmental Relations in the State of the Autonomous Communities

The State of the Art

Consideration of the system of inter-governmental relations as an object of study in Spain is relatively recent. It is worth pointing out that there are many studies on the essential elements of the political-administrative system tackled from a legal-public perspective.[H] However, more recently there has been a rise in other kinds of approach, less concerned with searching for the ideal model and more focused on the performance of the institutions, on ensuring levels of efficiency and effectiveness that are acceptable in public policy (Dente 1985) and on an interest in the appropriate operation of each policy

---

[F] The article includes part of the analysis carried out in the study "The Sectoral Conferences (2001–2012): Working dynamics and the values and perceptions of the political and technical agents", funded by the INAP in 2014, and whose focus was the Sectoral Conferences on Education, Health and the Environment.

[G] In this article we refer to the particular Spanish territorial model as the "State of the Autonomous Communities" or the "State of the Autonomous Regions" ("Estado Autonómico" in Spanish). We use both expressions interchangeably to describe an institutional framework that is intermediate between the federal and unitary states.

[H] As stated in Arbos et al. (2009), German cooperative federalism inspired the dominant doctrine of Spanish public law in the study of the State of the Autonomous Communities.

or program (Padioleau 1989).

In the field of Spanish Politics and Administration, there have been a considerable number of publications regarding the analysis of inter-governmental relations since the 1990s. The Canadian experience (Arbos et al. 2009) has acted as a framework of analysis, given the more structured workings of its parties and the cultural and linguistic diversity there. The configuration of the inter-governmental relations system in Spain has been variable and has gone through different stages with several actors playing distinct roles and strategies (Bañón and Tamayo 1997). This evolution has not been free of obstacles that have stood in the way of effectively dealing with complexity and interdependence. Of these obstacles, as identified by Mendoza, it is possible to highlight the great importance in the political culture of State-Autonomous Regions rivalry, an administrative culture reluctant to "lose" competences and a clear lack of traditional mechanisms of the bureaucratic kind to respond to the needs of a decentralized and plural administrative context (Mendoza 1990).

The work carried out by Agranoff (1993) on inter-governmental relations and the State of the Autonomous Regions provides another interesting study, dealing with the transfer of competences, funding, political strength, bureaucratic structures, and the creation of programs for political action. From another perspective, Goma and Subirats analyzed the style of formulation of public policies in Spain within the framework of territorial complexity and multi-level governance, as key elements of policy style. This analysis demonstrated how territorial complexity involves referring to two simultaneous dynamics: Europeanization and territorialization,

both understood as displacements of the processes of government, toward the European Union and the sub-national level (Goma and Subirats 1998). Later, Subirats and Gallego (2002) tackled the study of the nominalization of the Autonomous Regions within the Spanish system of inter-governmental relations using different indicators such as the legislative production of the Autonomous Regions, the profile of the political elites, and the organizational structures and human resources of the regional authorities, in an analysis of regional performance. There have also been other contemporary studies that are interesting for our purposes, such as those by Máiz, Beramendi, and Grau (2002); López Nieto (2006); Garcia Morales, Montilla, and Arbós (2006); Ramos, Alda, and Cicuéndez (2006); Ridaura (2009); Sevilla, Vidal, and Elias (2009) and Saniger Martinez and Escribano Zafra (2010). All of them take a broad perspective on the phenomenon of intergovernmental relations in the Spanish case, worrying about consolidation and institutionalization of inter-territorial relations. Particularly relevant to our topic are some of them that deal with specific Sectoral Conferences like those written by Colino (2002) and Alda and Ramos (2004).

The studies by Arbós et al. (2009) and Colino (2012) are two of the analyses that have gone into greatest depth as regards the real workings of the instruments of cooperation in the State of the Autonomous Regions. Those contributions and the work of León and Ferrín (2012) represent a fundamental starting point for the present research. Their findings and conclusions, particularly with respect to the operation of the Spanish Sectoral Conferences, have led us to tackle the matter through an analysis of the real workings of these bodies, based on the selection of three of them (Education,

Health, and the Environment). However, we have tried to operate in a complementary way: thus, while the work by León and Ferrín focuses on the formal arrangements reached by the Sectoral Conferences, we pay attention to the participants´ interventions, thus trying to capture the weight of partisan rivalries in their real praxis: in other words, whether party discipline plays a role at the time of explaining attendance, agenda-settings, dynamics, and interaction among participants.[1]

Multilateral Relations in the State of the Autonomous Communities

As mentioned above, our intention with this analysis is to test the extent to which the Sectoral Conferences have fulfilled the functions that were first planned for them by law. In this respect, we would like to stress three independent variables that, in accordance with our theoretical basis, have a strong influence on the way the conferences have been carried out in practice. All of them are related to contextual political and historical conditions that have set limitations on the way these organizations perform and how the actors play their roles within them: the broad institutional framework for territorial organization, the party system and the cultural background of political and administrative elites.

As regards the institutional framework, we should keep in mind the fact that the decentralization process in Spain—regardless of its achievements— is marked above all by the retention of historical nationalities within the State, holding them together (Linz 1997, 35–9). Thus, at the level of the central state architecture, one of the aspects that sets

conditions for interterritorial cooperation is the absence of major federalist institutions for shared government (Máiz, Beramendi, and Grau 2002, 388). The example most commonly cited when this aspect is analyzed is the insufficient territorial nature of the Senate, which can only partially be considered a chamber for representing the Autonomous Regions, as it is subordinate in the legislative process and subjected to inter-party relations. But this is not the only feature of the Spanish polity that shows such a lack of shared government: as noted by some authors, Spanish intergovernmental structures tend to be vertical, lacking horizontal-multilateral intergovernmental arrangements and mechanisms. In this sense, even the Sectoral Conferences show an incomplete institutionalization as they do not produce legally binding agreements (Bolleyer 2006, 398).

Bearing in mind this institutional design, it is to be expected that, in some comparative studies, such as that by Marks, Hooghe, and Schakel (2008), the Spanish case should appear as a territorial model that is still far from federalism. Although in terms of self-government the Spanish case puts its Autonomous Regions on the same level as territorial bodies characteristic of federal models, the other side of decentralization— that of *shared government*—remains at a level of development similar to that of the cases commonly considered as exemplifying centralized states. In other words, the State of the Autonomous Regions is characterized by conceding important powers to the territorial bodies without allowing these to take part in communal decision-making.

As far as the party system is concerned, we assume that the way federal

---

[1] For a more detailed use of data, the reader may consult a previous publication by this research group (Mondragon et al. 2015).

institutions work is frequently determined by the internal organization and interactive relations of political parties (Riker 1964).[J] This is particularly the case for Spain, where territorial matters have been resolved through inter-party competition rather than within inter-governmental institutions (Méndez Lago 2004, 50). Therefore, it is not strange that party competition has been one of the most influential factors for explaining the work of sectoral conferences and the probability of reaching formal agreements in their meetings (León and Ferrín 2012, 75).

As far as the party system is concerned, the most general assumption is that the Spanish case represents an example of that Sartorian category of the "limited multi-party system", as just a small number of *significant* parties have been present in the lower chamber for most of the democratic period (Oñate and Ocaña 2005). In this sense, the formation of governments and parliamentary majorities have always been in the hands of the two major state-wide parties (the social democratic Socialist Party, PSOE, and the conservative Popular Party, PP, see appendix 2) with the occasional support of smaller organizations, such as the Catalan and Basque moderate nationalist parties. It is also noteworthy that in those cases when the nationalists' support has been needed, eventual agreements have included concessions of a territorial nature (Heller 2002; Máiz, Beramendi, and Grau 2002, 393), reproducing the idea that a bilateral relationship is needed for central state governability (Máiz, Beramendi, and Grau 2002, 420). In any case, support from those party organizations for a federalist aspiration has been rather weak: only within

the social democrats can a few voices be heard claiming that federalism is the best way to tackle historical territorial conflicts in Spain. However, this is not the case for the conservatives or the bulk of the Socialist Party, who considers decentralization to be a rather problematic issue, still under review and subject to the evolution of political circumstances, as the recent economic crisis has showed. Moreover, the Basque and Catalan nationalists show a certain unwillingness for symmetrical decentralization, and they have tended to feel unenthusiastic about cooperating with other regional actors of the State, especially from the beginning of the process of standardizing powers begun in 1992 (Aja 2014, 56).

Lastly, if the cultural background of political and administrative elites is analyzed, it is also possible to indicate a historical absence of that "federal thinking" that Elazar considers an essential component of power sharing (Elazar 1991, 192–97). Put in other words, Spanish administrative elites tend to show a hierarchical administrative culture that is not at all disposed to cede competences or seek cooperative mechanisms; it is the reflection of a political culture that has not yet managed to normalize the coexistence of a diversity of territorial interests and in which a resistance to the decentralization of power lives on (Mendoza 1990, 266–67; Moreno 1997, 102–5). Consequently, a bureaucratic model predominates that is inflexible and excessively tied, in operational terms, to the strict delimitation of competences and specialization. Given this situation, these authorities are unable to meet the needs of a new political-administrative context

---

[J] Such a relationship between the territorial and partisan variables might well be bidirectional in some cases, where the territorial institutional framework results in particular party structures where sub-national organisation tends to prevail (Simeon, 1980).

that requires a high degree of complexity and interdependence in terms of political-administrative action. As a result, multi-level relations marked by conflict have predominated since the beginning of the State of the Autonomous Communities.[K]

Hypothesis

Given the political context that has been described thus far, it would be expected that the Sectoral Conferences should suffer all the reluctance of the different political actors with respect to a territorial model that even today has a precarious ideological-political basis. In this regard, the starting point is one which includes a relatively small number of actors committed to cooperative federalism and an institutional framework that has not favored the reversion of this trend. We propose that this inevitably has an influence on organizations such as the Sectoral Conferences, which are institutions intended to facilitate shared government, that is to say, the participation of the territorial bodies in the State's communal decisions.

Against that background, a hypothesis is proposed that will be tested later on by means of analysis: the Sectoral Conferences in Spain represent a party-oriented activity, rather than fulfilling the normative commitment of implementing co-decisions. Thus, although designed for coordinating and making possible inter-governmental relations, the Sectoral Conferences reproduce government/opposition dialectics, leaving the formal objectives of the institution in a subordinate position. In this context, representatives of those regions with a strong identity, such as the Basque Country and Catalonia, prefer bilateral frameworks over coordination and bargaining in multilateral forums.

Origins and Evolution of the Spanish Sectoral Conferences

At the beginning of the 1980s, the first Sectoral Conferences were set up at the request of the different territorial actors. Law 12/83 of 14 October on the *Proceso Autonómico* ("Regional Process") and later the *Acuerdos Autonómicos* ("Regional Agreements") of 1992 involved the recognition of the Sectoral Conferences, giving them institutional status as the essential instrument for the development of cooperative action among the State and the Autonomous Regions. Later, Law 30/1992 on the *Régimen Jurídico de las Administraciones Públicas y del Procedimiento Administrativo Común* ("Legal Framework of the Public Authorities and the Common Administrative Procedure") recognized the Sectoral Conferences as organs of cooperation among the State and Autonomous Regions (art. 5), set up as formalized mechanisms of vertical, multilateral cooperation of a sectoral and political nature (Ruiz González 2012, 293).

The current situation is one of different rates of development and rhythms among the 44 Sectoral Conferences and other assimilated bodies, according to Ministry of Finance and Public Administration (MINHAP) figures (2014).

[K] According to Agranoff (1993, 91–2), this panorama particularly characterises the first stage (1975–85) of the development of the autonomous communities, and the Sectoral Conferences, our subject of study, were designed particularly for this. What is being looked at here is the extent to which the conferences have, over the years, acted to correct this initial situation.

However, it is possible to point to a number of shared aspects: they all have a sectoral criterion; although the number of meetings varies over the years, an increasing trend is noticeable (Graph 1); all of them develop supporting bodies (sectoral commissions) which are responsible for facilitating the work of plenary sessions; most of them have procedural regulations; they tend to adopt consensus as the most common form of decision-making; and they include representation of the Autonomous Regions at the EU with a specific conference (Sectoral Conference for EU Matters), which does not share in the sectoral approach of the others.

on Education, Health, and the Environment. This is for three reasons: the three were among the oldest ones as they were created between 1986 and 1989; secondly, all of them were distinguished by their regular activity from 2001 to 2012 (Aja 2014, 729; García Morales 2008); and, thirdly, the three deal with policies of considerable prominence with substantial portions of public spending and territorial projection which sometimes implies a high level of political and ideological confrontation. In this sense, this argument could be further justified bearing in mind another question: both Education and Health Conferences tend to deal with what has been called "high politics," while the Environmental

Graph 1. Number of meetings of the Sectoral Conferences per year (1981–2014)

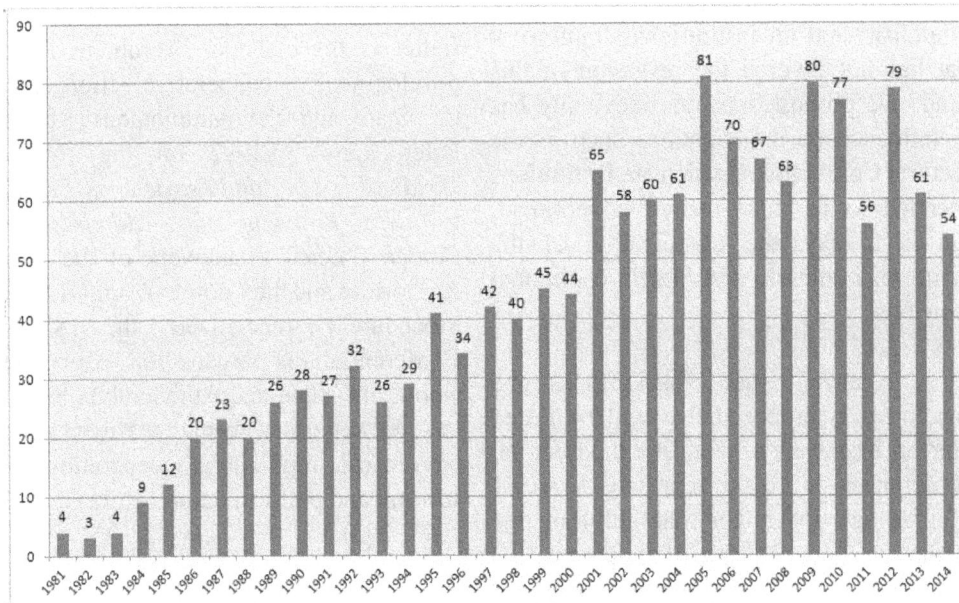

Source: Elaborated by the authors using MINHAP data (2014).

To test the elaborated hypothesis, we focused our study on the years 2001–12, as this is the period during which the greatest number of Sectoral Conference meetings took place. Furthermore, not all the Sectoral Conferences were analyzed. The research included just three: the Sectoral Conferences

Conference represents that kind of rather technical policies that are often hidden from broad public attention in the sense indicated by Lazar (2006, 25). Thus, we think that our three-conference sample should neutralize different possible objections regarding their consolidation, regularity and the very nature of the policies dealt with (which could be argued as significant drivers for explaining different patterns of interterritorial relations).

This study combines qualitative and quantitative techniques in order to describe the workings, dynamics, and results of these three conferences. The research was based, firstly, on in-depth interviews with participants in the Sectoral Conferences (basically regional government ministers and central government personnel who participated in these three conferences between 2001 and 2012, as can be seen in Appendix 1). Secondly, we analyzed the contents of the agendas and minutes of the Sectoral Conference meetings during this period. On this point, different aspects related to the workings of the conferences, such as the duration and venue of meetings, those attending, and the items on the agenda, were noted. These agenda items were the main unit recorded in our analysis. They were classified according to the actor making the proposal, the subject matter dealt with in them, whether they propose consent or dissent, and the number of people who take the floor to talk about the subject, with a classification of whether these interventions are critical or affirmative in nature. Lastly, an analysis was made of the laws that cover the Sectoral Conferences, the regulations of the three conferences studied and the reports on Sectoral Conference activity that appear on the website of the Ministry of Finance and Public Administration's General Directorship for the Coordination of Competences with the Autonomous Regions and Local Government.

Working Dynamics of the Sectoral Conferences

Each Sectoral Conference works very differently, depending on the sectoral policy and, particularly, the framework of competences. However, all of them show a number of common characteristics with respect to their performance that will be described throughout this section, taking into account their formal rules, the dynamic of their meetings, and the information provided by our interviewees.

Composition of and Attendance at the Sectoral Conferences

The regulations of the Sectoral Conferences establish that the conferences' plenary sessions are constituted by the holder of the pertinent ministry, acting as chairman thereof, and with the corresponding regional ministers representing the Autonomous Regions. The possibility that regional ministers' participation can be delegated to a lower-ranking member of the regional government, such as a vice-minister, as well as to another minister from the same regional government, is only allowed for in the regulations of the Education Conference. However, drawing on the available data, it was a practice that was done to a greater or lesser extent at the other conferences. However, with the reform of the regulations of the Interterritorial Health Council and the Environment Conference, the possibility of delegation is not included in the first of these, and at the Environment Conference it is permitted to delegate to people with the rank of regional minister, belonging either to the regional government of their region, or to the Sectoral Conference. This gives them a more political character.

Table 1 includes the attendance data for the three conferences analyzed according to the rank of their participants. In the cases of the Health and Environment Conferences, a differentiation is made of the periods when different regulations are in force. Given the overall comparative figures for the three conferences, it can be observed that the highest percentages of attendance occur at the time when delegative practices are most permissive. In fact, failure to attend reaches its highest levels after the approval of regulatory modifications, with the last period analyzed of the Environment Conference showing 33.3% non-attendance. In turn, progress toward the goal that justified the change in the regulations does not appear to be reflected fully in the results obtained. The impact of these measures had conflicting effects. While the percentage of attendance by regional ministers increased at the Health Council plenary sessions (from 82.5% to

In the evaluation made by interviewees, it can be observed that non-attendance or delegation to people below the rank of regional minister is presented as a way of showing disagreement with the homogenizing model that the Conference, in their opinion, represents. In this sense, the words of a nationalist representative of the Basque Government are highly illustrative:

…my position in this regard was not to attend the Education Conference, unless it was something very important, really important politically. (…) So, we wanted to maintain, if we could, the bilateral relationship with the minister of the moment, rather than go to a conference where attention would be spread among 17 Autonomous Regions. (Interview 1)

From his perspective, bilateralism should be the way to manage territorial interests between the central administration and those communities, like the Basque Country, Catalonia, and Galicia, that have a strong identity profile. For those actors,

Table 1. Education Sectoral Conference, Environment Sectoral Conference and Interterritorial Health Conference (2001-2012). Attendance by rank.

	Regional Minister		Other		Non-attendance		Total	
	N	%	N	%	N	%	N	%
Education (32)	443	81.4	93	17.1	8	1.5	544	100.0
Health (a) (7)	104	82.5	18	14.3	4	3.2	126	100.0
Health (b) (40)	668	87.9	0	0.0	92	12.1	760	100.0
Environment (a) (21)	301	75.6	61	15.4	36	9.0	398	100.0
Environment (b) (6)	58	50.9	18	15.8	38	33.3	114	100.0

Source: drawn up by the authors.

Health (a): Period before the change of the Regulations. (15/04/2002-23/07/2003). Health (b): Period after the change of the Regulations. (3/12/2003-20/12/2012). Environment (a): Period before the change of the Regulations. (01/02/2001-06/09/2007). Environment (b): Period after the change of the Regulations. (07/06/2010-15/10/2012). The numbers in brackets indicate the number of plenary sessions held under each set of regulations.

87.9%) at the Environment Conference this figure decreased significantly (from 75.6% to 50.9%).

the Sectoral Conferences reflected a rather futile attempt by the central elites to dilute their particularities in the melting pot of the Spanish State. Similar interpretations appear over and over again in the interviews with nationalist delegates of the Catalan and Basque governments.

Nonetheless, non-attendance is also used as an instrument to express occasional disagreement with the ministry, discrepancy between the government and the opposition, and to stage party confrontations.

We even held an Interterritorial Council in Barcelona that was not attended by the PP. (…), but before, with Ana Pastor (PP Health Minister), for a time the PSOE didn't attend. (Interview 5)

It is clear, then, that these tactics largely respond to the influence of party politics in the conferences' daily routine, an aspect that is repeated in the other analytical dimensions considered here.

Agenda and Decision-Making. A Central Coordination Model

As noted by Warhurst, central co-ordination becomes an essential feature when analyzing intergovernmental relations (Warhurst 1987, 273). In this sense, the initiative of creating some Sectoral Conferences arose from the respective ministries; this is the case, for example, with the Interterritorial Council on the National Health System and the Education Sectoral Conference, two of the three conferences analyzed here (Arbós et al. 2009, 143). However, independently of the circumstances of their creation, the ministry takes the lead from the moment the conference's meetings are convened and their agendas drawn up. All the people interviewed pointed out that, in accordance with the regulations upon which the different Sectoral Conferences are based, it is the ministry that convenes meetings and sets agendas. Specifically, it is each ministry's secretary of state who, in the name of the pertinent minister, calls the Autonomous Regions to the meeting.

Regarding the matters to be dealt with at the meetings, most of those interviewed point out that the agendas are essentially determined by the preparatory commissions, although the ministers have the last word and they can set or alter the agenda, including subjects that may not have been dealt with at the commission stage.

In any case, although it is true that the regulations include the possibility that representatives of the Autonomous Regions can add items to the agenda (except in the case of the Health Conference, which does not include this possibility), this does not commonly happen, as was indicated by one of our interviewees. In this context, matters of interest to representatives of the Autonomous Regions are usually relegated to the "any other business" item, with its connotation of less important issues.

The possibility exists, and the Autonomous Regions can include matters on the agenda after it has been received. This is stated in the regulations: they have a set period during which they can propose issues, but this does not happen frequently. The most common thing is for the ministry to take the initiative....The Autonomous Regions make use of the 'any other business' section of the Sectoral Conference to discuss their specific concerns regarding a certain matter, and then the ministry takes note of these concerns and arranges a later meeting. But to include an item formally at the Sectoral Conference is very rare. No, it doesn't happen. (Interview 7)

Table 2: Agenda Items per Proponent (Environment SC).

	J. Matas (PP)	E. Rodrí- guez (PP)	C. Narbo- na (PSOE)	E. Espino- sa (PSOE)	R. Aguilar (PSOE)	M. Arias (PP)	Total
Central Minister	39	6	139	35	13	25	257
Regions	6	1	9	2	3	2	23
Total	45	7	148	37	16	27	280

Source: Elaborated by the authors

Table 3: Agendas Items per Proponent (Education SC).

	P. del Cas- tillo (PP)	M.J. San Se- gundo(PSOE)	M. Cabrera (PSOE)	A. Gabilon- do (PSOE)	J. I. Wert (PP)	Total
Central Minister	18	12	15	34	18	97
Regions	4	0	3	3	4	14
Total	22	12	18	37	22	111

Source: Elaborated by the authors

Graph 2. Agendas Items per Proponent (Education SC).

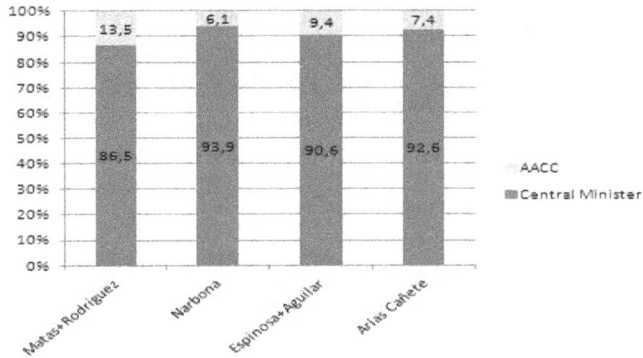

Graph 3. Items on the agenda of the Education SC meetings, by minister

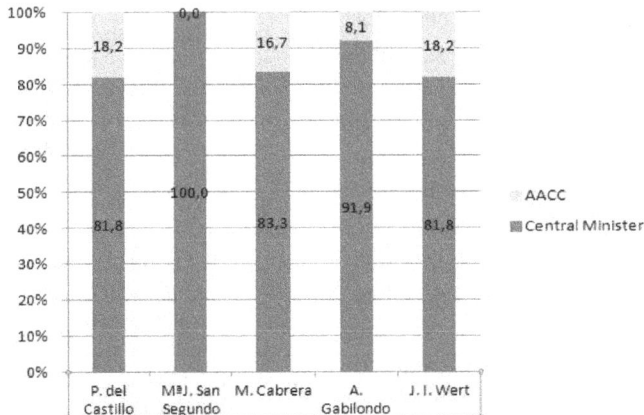

These views coincide with the data taken from the analysis of the Sectoral Conference meeting agendas. Looking at the data concerning the items on the agenda of the Environment and Education Sectoral Conference meetings during the 2001–12 period, it can be seen that the percentages of items put forward by the ministry are 91.8% and 87.4%, respectively (Tables 2 and 3).

Even considering the periods when people belonging to different parties are at the head of the ministry, it can be seen that the pattern hardly varies (Graphs 2 and 3). This shows how exceptional it is for regional actors to propose items for discussion, whichever party is in government.

In short, when drawing up meeting agendas, a clearly centralist vision rules. According to this vision, the government practically controls the matters to be discussed at meetings, applying a top-down way of thinking that does not involve the principle of horizontality that should be at least partially employed by a body intended for co-government and cooperative federalism.

(…) the problem in terms of leadership is, of course, that everyone's personality is very important, but what is even more important is the fact that normally the capacity to propose matters lies with the ministry. (…) So the leadership is an almost absolute leadership by the ministry. This is not so much due to the personality of whichever minister it is, but because really there has been a series of issues related to the Sectoral Conference in which the only capacity for initiative came from the minister in office. (Interview 11)

Once the agenda is set, the decision-making process undertaken at the Sectoral Conferences further illustrates the central importance of the ministers and their privileged position over regional representatives. In accordance with the rules regulating the operation of these conferences, agreements are adopted with the assent of conference members and, in the absence of this, by the favorable vote of the State's administration and the majority of the Autonomous Regions. According to the operational dynamic reported by the interviewees, the issues are presented by the minister, they are debated and, if there are no major discrepancies, the minutes show that they have been approved. In fact, most of the regional ministers interviewed did not remember having voted at the Sectoral Conferences. In most cases, the ministry presents its proposals and the representatives of the Autonomous Regions give their opinion, but there is no vote. Most often, those participating at the conferences assent to what the minister has announced. The conferences seek consent at all times and when there are controversial matters, there is an attempt to resolve disagreements at the commission stage, that is to say, at the Sectoral Conference's preparatory meeting; when this is not possible, consensus is reached at the conference itself. That is to say, even when a controversial matter is dealt with, the most common thing is that it is approved consensually, by a majority of representatives at the conferences.

In short, and as shown in the last quote by the person interviewed, the practice at these conferences legitimizes an institutional leadership of a vertical nature, in which the central administration, acting through the pertinent ministry, acquires a privileged position.

The Dynamics of Conference Meetings

Another of the aspects covered in our analysis was the meeting dynamics, a matter that touches directly on the interactions among the individuals who attend these meetings and which might possibly have some influence on the institution's performance.

In this respect, our informants state that the human factor, particularly with regard to the personal profile of the Sectoral Conference's chair, seems to have an effect on the way in which the meetings take place, on the atmosphere during them and, possibly, on the fact that the Sectoral Conferences discuss fewer or more issues.

(…) here again there is a part played by the human factor, the personality, the character of the person in charge at the Sectoral Conference, that is to say, the person responsible, the minister. If you are willing to enter into dialogue and you go along in order to listen, even to disagree, to see whether you can integrate that point of view, then that is worth a lot. (Interview 2)

Another indicator considered here is relevant at this point: the duration of the Sectoral Conference meetings. Looking, for example, at the duration of the Environment Sectoral Conference sessions, a certain influence of the minister's personality can be seen: specifically during the mandate of Cristina Narbona, reputedly the most conservationist-minded minister in charge of the department during the period analyzed, the duration of meetings was considerably longer (Graph 4). Furthermore, during her time as minister, this was the only period when the physical venue of the conference changed and meetings took place in different Spanish cities. That is to say, the process, in terms of duration, matters dealt with and the overall approach of the conference underwent a change that disappeared when new ministers, some of them from the same political party (Elena Espinosa and Rosa Aguilar), chaired the conference.

The authors consider that changes in this indicator can be considered as evidence of the effect of the human factor on how meetings are run, but that this effect is neutralized by the processes, in terms of the institutionalization of the conference, whose internal regulations dictate how decisions are taken and the very form of understanding these decisions, meaning that any changes are limited.

In further reference to the meeting dynamics, our interviewees describe how, depending on the nature of the matters dealt with, the alignment of the participants, according to which parties they belong to, is more explicit. In other words, the more political prominence the items on the agenda have, the clearer it is that Sectoral Conference participants adhere to the government-opposition dynamic.

(…) at that time the Socialist Party was in government, and, furthermore, the party was practically in a majority in the Autonomous Regions as well. However, in general, the Popular Party acted as a block, that is to say, normally when there was a matter that they opposed, they would oppose it together. It was not an operational process. There, they did not represent the Madrid Region or the Valencia Region; they went to present a series of political objections, not territorial ones. Yet the same happened with the PSOE; the PSOE regional representatives supported, often indiscriminately, ministerial proposals, whether or not these proposals agreed with their own ideas or the interests of their regions. (Interview 9)

Interaction Between Ministers and Regional Representatives

In terms of the workings of the Sectoral Conferences, perhaps the sphere where the importance of political party is clearest is in the relations of the different administrative levels or, to put it another way, in the interaction between regional representatives and the central administration. In this regard, the extent of the party conformity of participants in a body designed for inter-authority cooperation is striking. For example, when preparing Sectoral Conference sessions, it often happened that regional representatives belonging to a single party held prior meetings in order to establish common positions. Obviously, in these situations, political-ideological and electoral criteria take priority when deciding on discourses and strategies.

They would bring together all the Socialist regional ministers… the Popular Party did the same with people from that party… so discussion blocks were pre-established, a thing that was not very healthy because many of these matters should not have such a political character and should involve technical discussion, but it was politicised… Party discipline won out over conversations that should have been more and more technical in nature. (Interview 14)

Before the Sectoral Conference meeting there was a discussion that was not only technical, but also political. The ministry wanted its proposals to get the go-ahead, and so it notified the Autonomous Regions beforehand, particularly (…) those Autonomous Regions of the same party, in order to have the support of the commissions, of the conferences, of the regional government departments themselves. (Interview 11)

This way of working was taken even further at the Education Sectoral Conference meetings of January 27 and February 25, 2010, during the last Socialist legislature. At these meetings the regional ministers belonging to the PP established not only a common position, but also a spokesperson, respectively the Valencian and Galician representatives. However, the high point of this party allegiance of Sectoral Conference participants had happened previously, on June 2, 2005, also at the Education Sectoral Conference. This was when the Organic Law on Education, proposed by the Socialist central government, was discussed: the regional PP representatives left the meeting halfway through in order to express their disagreement with the documentation sent.

Furthermore, the partisan factor is clearly visible if we analyze the responses that take a critical viewpoint given by representatives of the Autonomous Regions. Tables 4 and 5 show agenda items from the Education and Environment SCs during the period analyzed, on which the different Autonomous Regions intervened. Specifically, we calculated not the total number of interventions by the regional representatives, which would be much greater, but the number of agenda items which register at least one intervention by them. Furthermore, we registered as "critical" those interventions on agenda items which demonstrate an open criticism of the intentions of the proposing agent—almost always, as has been noted, the ministry—whether over procedural matters or because of the content of the intervention.

As can be seen here, there are more and less active Autonomous Regions:

Catalonia and Asturias have a greater mean number of items (9.6 and 9.2, respectively) in Education and Aragon and Castille-Leon have more in the Environment (14.2 and 13.0). We believe that this, in itself, is an interesting piece of data, since it shows that in three out of four cases, the regions most likely to intervene do not have a national identity profile

In any case, the information displayed on Tables 4 and 5 is particularly interesting when the critical interventions of the Autonomous Regions are analyzed: noting the mean values and comparing them with the figures for general interventions, a series of percentage values is obtained that shows which

Table 4: Number of Agenda Items with Interventions by the Autonomous Regions (Education SC) (*).

Regions	P. del Castillo		Mª J. San Segundo		M. Cabrera		A. Gabilondo		J. I. Wert		Mean	
	Int.	Crit.	Int.	Crit.	Int.	Crit.	Int.	Crit.	Int.	Crit.	Int.	Crit.
Andalusia	13	8	5	0	7	1	9	0	11	8	9.0	3.4
Aragón	7	6	6	1	4	0	8	0	9	0	6.8	1.4
Asturias	12	8	5	0	6	1	10	1	13	8	9.2	3.6
Baleares	5	5	4	2	5	0	5	0	8	0	5.4	1.4
Canarias	9	3	5	1	6	1	9	0	8	4	7.4	1.8
Cantabria	4	0	4	0	3	0	7	0	5	0	4.6	0.0
Castilla-Mancha	11	6	5	1	4	0	9	0	11	0	8.0	1.4
Castilla León	5	1	5	2	6	2	13	4	8	1	7.4	2.0
Catalonia	6	3	6	3	10	1	14	0	12	9	9.6	3.2
Extremadura	9	6	5	0	4	0	6	0	7	0	6.2	1.2
Galicia	3	0	2	1	3	0	13	6	9	0	6.0	1.4
Madrid	5	0	6	5	9	2	9	4	9	0	7.6	2.2
Murcia	8	0	5	3	3	0	8	3	8	0	6.4	1.2
Navarre	6	0	5	1	3	1	10	1	10	0	6.8	0.6
Basque Country	4	3	6	2	5	0	7	0	13	10	7.0	3.0
La Rioja	6	0	4	4	7	1	8	2	9	0	6.8	1.4
Valencia	6	0	5	4	6	3	10	5	7	0	6.8	2.4
Ceuta	0	0	0	0	0	0	0	0	0	0	0.0	0.0
Melilla	0	0	0	0	0	0	0	0	0	0	0.0	0.0
TOTAL	119	49	83	30	91	13	155	26	157	40	121	31.6

Source: Elaborated by the authors.

(*) The numbers of agenda items with critical interventions are shaded in grey.

other than the Spanish one, which seems to indicate that the SCs are not forums that reproduce the differences resulting from the center-periphery cleavage that is characteristic of the Spanish political system. However, this could also be a result of the data regarding attendance given above.

regional representatives play more or less critical roles. In this regard, it can be seen that regions such as Cantabria have a very low profile in terms of objections made (none of its interventions at the Education SC during 2001–12 is critical and only during the mandate of Cristina Narbona in the Environment did it refute some agenda items), while other regions show clearer opposition (see, for example, the case of Andalusia in Education or La Rioja in the Environment).

Relating the partisan factor with the positions taken by the regional actors it can be seen that certain significant patterns are revealed. For example, Graphs 5 and 6 show the percentage of critical regional interventions at the Environment SC during the mandates of Jaume Matas (PP) and Cristina Narbona (PSOE) in order to reveal which Autonomous Regions react to ministerial proposals critically. It is therefore striking to see how, during the legislature of Matas, all the regions with

a proportion of critical interventions above 20% are governed by political parties other than the one in office in the central government: Andalusia, Asturias and Extremadura by the Socialist Party, Catalonia by CiU and the Basque Country by the PNV-EA-EB coalition. Furthermore, during the next legislature, when a Socialist minister, Cristina Narbona, chaired the Sectoral Conference, the five most critical regions (Balearics, Madrid, Navarre, Basque Country, and Valencia), whose interventions are critical on more than 40% of occasions, were all governed by parties other than the PSOE.

So it can be seen that the tone

Table 5: Number of Agenda Items with Interventions by the Autonomous Regions (Environment SC) (*).

Region	J.Matas Int	J.Matas Cr.	E.Rodríg. Int	E.Rodríg. Cr.	C.Narbo. Int	C.Narbo. Cr.	E.Espin. Int	E.Espin. Cr.	R.Aguilar Int	R.Aguilar Cr.	M. Arias Int	M. Arias Cr.	Mean Int	Mean Cr.
Andalusia	17	7	1	1	30	8	3	0	3	0	3	0	9.5	2.7
Aragón	15	1	2	1	63	19	2	0	1	0	2	0	14.2	3.5
Asturias	18	5	4	1	32	6	2	0	1	0	5	0	10.3	2.0
Baleares	11	1	3	1	50	27	3	2	1	0	0	0	11.3	5.2
Canarias	2	0	2	0	31	11	4	1	0	0	2	0	6.8	2.0
Cantabria	11	2	2	0	33	8	5	0	0	0	5	0	9.3	1.7
Castille-Mancha	12	2	2	0	23	4	1	0	3	1	2	0	7.2	1.2
Castille León	12	1	3	0	50	18	6	1	1	0	6	0	13.0	3.3
Cataluña	8	2	1	0	56	15	5	1	2	0	2	0	12.3	3.0
Extremadura	13	3	2	1	30	3	10	0	1	0	1	0	9.5	1.2
Galicia	8	0	2	0	21	7	7	0	1	0	3	0	7.0	1.2
Madrid	15	3	2	0	41	21	0	0	5	2	5	0	11.3	4.3
Murcia	5	0	3	0	18	6	0	0	2	0	0	0	4.7	1.0
Navarre	8	1	1	0	29	12	5	0	2	1	0	0	7.5	2.3
Basque Country	12	5	3	0	37	16	0	0	1	0	3	1	9.3	3.7
La Rioja	10	0	3	0	52	19	5	3	2	1	4	0	12.7	3.8
Valencia	8	1	2	0	25	14	1	0	4	1	3	0	7.2	2.7
Ceuta	3	0	2	0	6	2	0	0	0	0	0	0	1.8	0.3
Melilla	1	0	2	0	6	0	1	0	0	0	0	0	1.7	0.0
TOTAL	189	34	42	5	633	216	60	8	30	6	46	1	167	45.0

Source: Elaborated by the authors.

(*) The numbers of agenda items with critical interventions are shaded in grey.

Graph 5. Percentage of critical interventions by regions (Environment SC. Matas' ministry.)

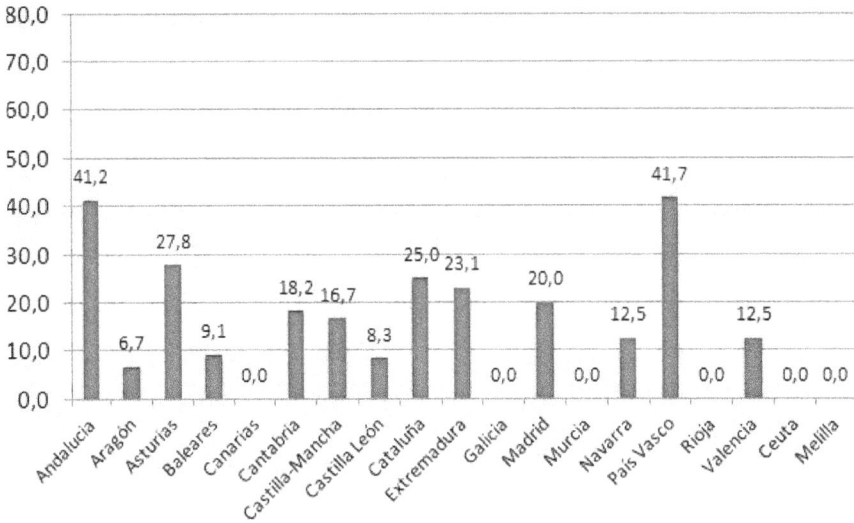

Graph 6. Percentage of critical interventions by regions (Environment SC. Narbona's ministry).

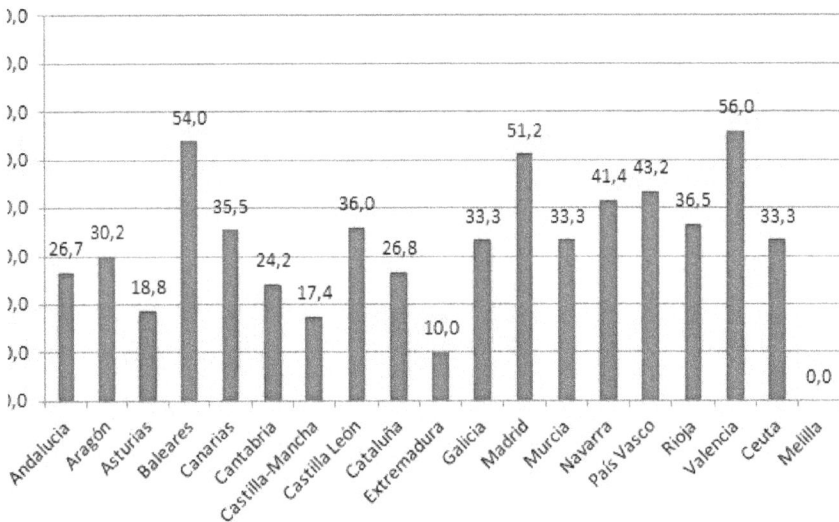

of interventions at the Environment Sectoral Conference is strongly marked by the partisan viewpoint of its members. However, this feature is not exclusive to the Environment SC, but is a trend that is even clearer in the case of the Education SC, perhaps because the matters for discussion have a much greater political-electoral saliency.

If the data are analyzed for the legislatures of Angel Gabilondo (PSOE) and José Ignacio Wert (PP), it can be seen that critical interventions are almost exclusively made by regions where parties other than the ruling party are in government. During Angel Gabilondo's mandate, the regions of Castile-Leon, Galicia, Madrid, Murcia, La Rioja, and Valencia—which made the greatest proportion of critical interventions—were governed by the PP; in the case of Navarre, which took up a slightly less strident opposition, this region was governed at this time by a conservative coalition (UPN-CDN). Only one Autonomous Region governed by a progressive coalition intervened critically: Asturias, which did so on 10% of the occasions when it took the floor (at that time it had a government made up of the PSOE and the United Left (IU).

Likewise, during the years when the José Ignacio Wert was head of the department, the regions of Andalusia, Asturias, Canarias, Catalonia, and the Basque Country practically monopolized the critical interventions during meetings. All of them were, at that time, governed by parties other than the PP. In some cases, the criticism raised by these regions is particularly noticeable when the regional governing parties did not undergo a change between the time of Gabilondo's ministry (the previous legislature) and Wert's. This is the case, for example, with Andalusia and the Basque Country, both

governed during both legislatures by the Socialist Party: during the period when Gabilondo was minister, they did not intervene critically, but when Wert was minister they expressed their opposition on more than 70% of the occasions.

In short, the debates during both Sectoral Conferences seem to be guided, above all, by the government-opposition dialectic, so that the ministry's plans tend to be contested by regions with the opposite political tendency, and deferred to by regional representatives of the same party. We believe that, together with the other patterns analyzed in previous sections, this shows the influence of the partisan factor on the dynamic of these institutions' meetings. In principle, and looking just at the design of the SCs, it would be important to have a much more multilateral debate, given both that territorial interests are very varied in kind, and also that the requirements of inter-authority coordination are exceedingly technical in nature. However, this complexity is reduced by practical considerations, with a recreation, to

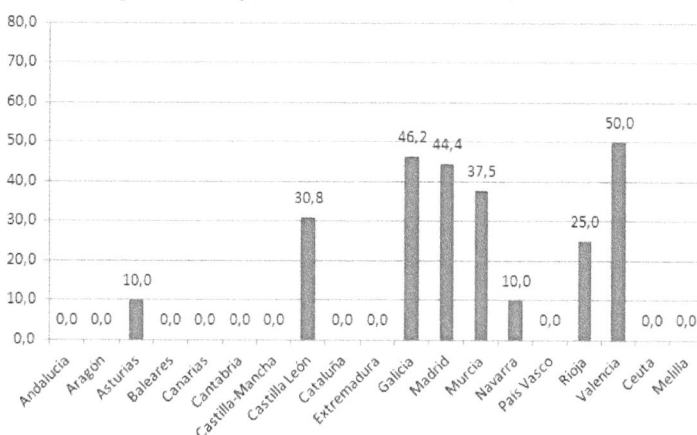

Graph 7. Percentage of critical interventions by region (Education SC. Angel Gabilondo's ministry)

a certain extent, of a government-opposition dialectic in which the proposal and decisions presented by the central government are not evaluated so much with regard to their territorial projection, as depending on their political-electoral implications. In this regard, the SCs act as a kind of parliamentary chamber of territorial representation, but one mainly guided by partisan interests, no matter whether the nature of sectoral policies are more ideological (Education) or technical (Environment).

Conclusions

The Sectoral Conferences appear in the Spanish political-administrative system as a formal instrument to channel relationships between the State and the Autonomous Regions. At first sight, their study shows a diverse world, with different origins and rates of development. However, when the working dynamics are analyzed in terms of composition and attendance, agenda organization, and the dynamics of meetings, it is possible to

appreciate a series of shared, although not identical, aspects.

In this regard, we consider that the hypothesis of the influence of party politics on the workings of the Sectoral Conferences is proved by the data: the very attendance at the meetings and interaction among their participants show a strong partisan influence on the daily routine of this institution. As seen above, the agenda is controlled by the governing party which counts on the support of allied regional representatives, establishing a top-down hierarchy in a theoretically more horizontal institution. In this regard, both the Socialists and the conservatives of the PP have played a very similar role when in power, regardless of their different projects for Spain's territorial organization. By the same token, and from the sub-national perspective, the reaction against the central government's proposals seems to be driven by their opposing role in parliamentary politics rather than by regional interests alone. For instance, attending the meetings has

Graph 8. Percentage of critical interventions by regions (Education SC-J.I. Wert's ministry)

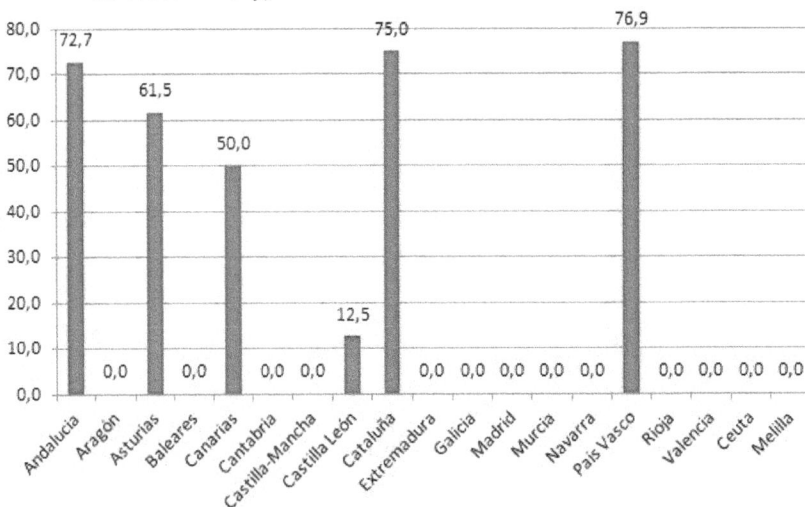

sometimes not been considered as an obligation by the sub-national delegates, but as a way to show conformity or protest. This logic has perhaps reached its highest peak at those moments when the regional representatives have explicitly followed party directives at meetings, both before the sessions (with unofficial meetings to set positions and strategies) and during them (leaving the meetings as a way to protest against governmental initiatives). Furthermore, it has been seen how, even at moments of relative calm, the very nature of sub-national delegates' interventions has been decisively conditioned by partisan relations: critical interventions at meetings, particularly, were almost monopolized by those delegates belonging to opposition parties. This state of affairs reinforces the strategy previously followed by some peripheral nationalist governments, namely those of Catalonia and the Basque Country, which have traditionally sought bilateral relations with the central administration. In their view, such federalist institutions deserve no credit, and the behavior of Catalan and Basque delegates is, in general, to be explained by this broad ideological critique.

In this context of a relative lack of federalist values, an alternative hypothesis could have been put forward, emphasizing the importance of the human factor to explain variations in the conferences' dynamics. In fact, a certain influence of personal profile has been identified, in the way that meetings proceeded with certain ministers that tried to give a different character to the Sectoral Conferences under their mandates. For instance, the Environment Minister Cristina Narbona managed to establish more serious

and thorough sessions that were held in different cities around the country. However, the impact of this personal factor has proven to be rather limited because of the normative consolidation of conferences. In other words, the very fact that they are determined by a law and specific regulations establishes clear ways to arrive at decisions that are absolutely independent of the will of particular subjects. Regulations therefore leave little room for other kinds of proceedings.

In short, the history of the Sectoral Conferences is symptomatic of the main problems with the Spanish territorial model. The relative absence of actors who are decidedly committed to interterritorial cooperation empties these institutions of content, furthering the lack of shared government that is characteristic of the Spanish regional model. This shared government should, it must not be forgotten, go hand in hand with decentralization when it comes to advancing toward a properly federal model.

References

Agranoff, Robert. 1993. "Las Relaciones Intergubernamentales y el Estado de las Autonomías." *Política y Sociedad* 13: 87–105.

Aja, Eliseo. 2014. *Estado autonómico y reforma federal*. Madrid: Alianza.

Alda, Mercedes, and J. Antonio Ramos. 2004. "El marco de las relaciones intergubernamentales de la política de medio ambiente en el Estado Autonómico." *Gestión y Análisis de Políticas Públicas* 28: 87–104.

Arbós, Xabier et al. 2009. *Las relaciones intergubernamentales en el Estado autonómico. La posición de los actores*. Barcelona: Institut d´Estudis Autonómics, Generalitat de Catalunya.

Bañón, Rafael, and Manuel Tamayo. 1997. "Las relaciones Intergubernamentales en España: el nuevo papel de la administración central en el modelo de relaciones intergubernamentales." *Papeles de trabajo de Gobierno y Administración*. Madrid: Instituto Universitario Ortega y Gasset.

Bolleyer, Nicholas. 2006. "Intergovernmental Arrangements in Spanish and Swiss Federalism: the Impact of Power-Concentrating and Power-Sharing Executives on Intergovernmental Institutionalization." *Regional and Federal Studies* 16 (4): 385–408.

Colino, César. 2002. "Diseño institucional y eficacia de las políticas. El federalismo y la política medioambiental." In *Análisis de Políticas Públicas en España: enfoques y casos*, eds. Mireia Grau and Araceli Mateos. Valencia: Tirant lo Blanch, 305–52.

Colino, César. 2012. "Las relaciones intergubernamentales." *In Las administraciones públicas en España*, eds. J. Antonio Olmeda, Salvador Parrado, and César Colino. Valencia: Tirant Lo Blanch, 215–52.

Colino, César, and Salvador Parrado. 2009. "Análisis de la práctica y la dinámica de los procesos formales e informales de las relaciones intergubernamentales." In *Las relaciones intergubernamentales en el Estado autonómico. La posición de los actores*, eds. Xabier Arbós et al. Barcelona: Institut d´Estudis Autonómics, Generalitat de Catalunya, 135–240.

Dente, Bruno. 1985. *Governare la frammentazione*. Bologna: Il Mulino.

Elazar, Daniel J. 1991. *Exploring federalism*. Tuscaloosa, AL: University of Alabama Press.

García Morales, Mª. Jesús. 2008. "Las Relaciones de colaboración con las Comunidades Autónomas." In *Informe Comunidades Autónomas 2007*, dir. Joaquín Tornos. Barcelona, Institut de Dret Públic, 70–110. http://idpbarcelona.net/docs/ public/iccaa/2006/convenios_2006. pdf (accessed September 14, 2016).

Garcia Morales, Mª. Jesús, J. Antonio Montilla, and Xabier Arbós. 2006. *Las relaciones intergubernamentales en el Estado autonómico*. Madrid: Centro de Estudios Políticos y Constitucionales.

Goma, Ricard, and Joan Subirats. 1998. *Políticas públicas en España*. Barcelona: Ariel.

Heller, William B. 2002. "Regional Parties and National Politics in Europe. Spain's Estado de las autonomías, 1993 to 2000." *Comparative Political Studies* 35 (6): 657–85.

Lazar, Harvey. 2006. "The Intergovernmental Dimensions of the Social Union: A Sectoral Analysis." *Canadian Public Administration* 49 (1): 23–45.

León, Sandra, and Mónica Ferrín. 2012.

"¿Qué factores promueven o dificultan la cooperación intergubernamental en el Estado Autonómico?" In *La práctica de la cooperación intergubernamental en España. 1st ed.,* eds. César Colino, Sandra León, and Mónica Ferrín. Madrid: Centro de Estudios Políticos y Constitucionales, 55–78.

Linz, Juan J. 1997. *Democracy, Multinationalism, and Federalism. Estudios/Working Papers Instituto Juan March e Investigaciones 103.* Madrid: Centro de Estudios Avanzados en Ciencias Sociales.

López Nieto, Lourdes, ed. 2006. Relaciones intergubernamentales en la España democrática: interdependencia, autonomía, conflicto. Madrid: Dykinson.

Máiz, Ramón, Pablo Beramendi, and Mireia Grau. 2002. "La federalización del Estado de las Autonomías: evolución y déficit institucionales." In *Veinte años de autonomías en España: leyes, políticas públicas, instituciones y opinión pública, coord.* Joan Subirats, and Raquel Gallego. Madrid: Centro de Investigaciones Sociológicas, 379–424.

Marks, Gary, Liesbet Hooghe, and Arjan H. Schakel. 2008. "Measuring Regional Authority." *Regional & Federal Studies* 18 (2): 111–21.

Méndez Lago, Mónica. 2004. *Federalismo y partidos politicos: los casos de Canadá y España,* Working Paper 232. Barcelona: Institut de Ciències Polítiques i Socials.

Mendoza, Xavier. 1990. "Técnicas gerenciales y modernización de la administración pública en España." *Documentación Administrativa 223*: 261–90.

Ministry of Finance and Public Administrations (MINHAP)-Gobierno de España. 2014. *Informe sobre la actividad de las Conferencias Sectoriales durante el año 2014.* http://www.seap.minhap.gob.es/dms/es/web/publicaciones/centro_de_publicaciones_de_la_sgt/Periodicas/parrafo/Conferencias_sectoriales_2014/INFORME-CONFERENCIAS-SECTORIALES-2014-AA/INFORME%20CONFERENCIAS%20SECTORIALES%202014%20AA.pdf (accessed September 14, 2016).

Mondragón, Jaione, Arantxa Elizondo, Alberto de La Peña, Patxi Juaristi, and J. Luis Mokoroa. 2015. *Análisis de las conferencias sectoriales (20012012): valores y percepciones de los agentes políticos y técnicos y dinámica de funcionamiento.* Madrid: Instituto Nacional de Administración Pública.

Moreno, Luis. 1997. *La federalización de España. Poder político y territorio.* Madrid: Siglo XXI.

Oñate, Pablo, and Francisco A. Ocaña. 2005. "Las elecciones generales de marzo de 2004 y los sistemas de partidos en España: ¿Tanto cambio electoral?", *Revista española de ciencia política* 13: 159–82.

Padioleau, Jean G. 1989. El Estado en concreto. México: Fondo de Cultura Económica.

Ramos, J. Antonio, Mercedes Alda, and Ruth Cicuéndez. 2006. "La dimensión institucionalizada de las Relaciones Intergubernamentales en el Estado autonómico." In *Relaciones Intergubernamentales en la España democrática: interdependencia, autonomía, conflicto y cooperación, coord.* Lourdes Lopez Nieto. Madrid: Dykinson, 281–94.

Ridaura, Mª. Josefa. 2009. *Relaciones intergubernamentales Estado-Comunidades Autónomas.* Valencia: Tirant Lo Blanch.

Riker, William H. 1964. *Federalism: Origin, Operation, Significance.* Boston: Little, Brown and Co.

Ruiz González, J. Gabriel. 2012. "La cooperación intergubernamental en el Estado autonómico: Situación y perspectivas." *Revista d'Estudis Autonòmics i Federals* 15: 288–327.

Ruiz González, J. Gabriel. 2013. *Logros y retos de las Conferencias Intergubernamentales en España.* GIGAPP Estudios Working Paper. Madrid: GIGAPP. http://www.gigapp. org/administrator/components/com_ jresearch/files/publications/WP-2013-30. pdf (accessed September 14, 2016).

Saniger Martinez, Nieves, and Escribano J. Miguel Escribano Zafra. 2010. "La necesaria reforma de los mecanismos de cooperación en el sistema de relaciones intergubernamentales del Estado de las autonomías y el nuevo papel del gobierno local." *In La administración pública entre dos siglos. ed. Manuel Arenilla.* Madrid: Instituto Nacional de Administración Pública, 457–90.

Sevilla, Jordi, J. María Vidal, and Cristina Elias. 2009. Vertebrando España. *El Estado autonómico.* Madrid: Biblioteca Nueva.

Simeon, Richard. 1980. "Intergovernmental Relations and the Challenges of Canadian Federalism." *Canadian Public Administration* 23 (2), 14-32.

Subirats, Joan, and Raquel Gallego, eds. 2002. Veinte años de autonomías en España. *Leyes, políticas públicas, instituciones y opinión pública.* Madrid: Centro de Investigaciones Sociológicas.

Warhurst, John. 1987. "Managing Intergovernmental Relations." In *Federalism and the Role of the State*, eds. Herman Bakvis and William M. Chandler. Toronto: University of Toronto Press, 259–76.

Wright, Deil S. 1997. *Para entender las relaciones intergubernamentales.* México: Fondo de Cultura Económica.

Appendix 1. Technical Data of the In-Depth Interviews

Interview	Field	Autonomous Region/Ministry	Political Party	Position	Interview date
01	Education	País Vasco	EA	Regional minister	19-05-2014
02	Education	País Vasco	PSE	Regional minister	10-06-2014
03	Education	Madrid	PP	Regional minister	22-04-2014
04	Education	Cataluña	PSC	Regional minister	25-04-2014
05	Health	Cataluña	PSC	Regional minister	08-05-2014
06	Environment	Ministry of Agriculture, Food and the Environment	–	Secretary of the Environment Commission	22-06-2014
7	Environment	Ministry of Agriculture, Food and the Environment	–	Secretary of the Environment Sectoral Conference	16-05-2014
08	Health	Cataluña	CDC	Regional minister	17-06-2014
09	Environment	Cataluña	ICV	Regional minister	20-06-2014
10	Environment	País Vasco	EA	Regional minister	26-06-2014
11	Environment	Madrid	PP	Regional minister	16-05-2014
12	Education	Cataluña	PSC	Director General	18-07-2014
13	Regional Cooperation	Ministry of Finance and Public Administration	–	Assistant Director General of Regional Cooperation	12-10-2014
14	Health	País Vasco	PSE	Regional minister	24-07-2014
15	Regional Cooperation	Ministry of Finance and Public Administration	–	Assistant Deputy Director General of Regional Cooperation	12-10-2014
16	Environment	País Vasco	EA	Vice-minister	22-05-2014

Appendix 2. Initials of the Spanish Political Parties

CDC	Convergencia Democrática de Catalunya
CiU	Convergencia i Unió
EA	Eusko Alkartasuna
EB	Ezker Batua
ICV	Iniciativa per Catalunya-Els Verds
IU	Izquierda Unida
PNV	Partido Nacionalista Vasco
PP	Partido Popular
PSC	Partit dels Socialistes de Catalunya
PSE	Partido Socialista de Euskadi
PSOE	Partido Socialista Obrero Español
UPN-CDN	Unión del Pueblo Navarro-Convergecia Democrática de Navarra

Demographic Change and Migration in the European Care Sector
Introduction to the Special Focus

Uwe Hunger[A] and Marlene Neumann[B]

Demographic change affects all European societies. Although there are national and regional differences, almost all European societies are increasingly aging and shrinking. As a result, many European economies are already affected by a serious labor shortage in certain branches. Several demographic outlooks forecast that this trend might strengthen in the next years and decades with far-reaching consequences for economic development, labor markets, welfare systems, and numerous other policy fields. One sector that has to face these challenges particularly is the healthcare sector. Demographic change affects this sector in two ways: On the one hand, aging societies lead to a growing demand for healthcare and elderly care and, on the other hand, the young skilled healthcare workers in Europe cannot cope with this growing demand. As a result, an expanded recruitment of healthcare workers from abroad is seen as a prime solution for that labor shortage.

The contributions of the following special issue aim to conduce to the debate on the consequences of healthcare migration for both receiving and sending countries. The included papers will analyze the structural differences in healthcare systems of different European countries and present how these differences affect the strategies to meet the possible labor market shortage. In this regard, the papers will also broaden the perspective on the consequences of demographic change in Europe especially for foreign countries, such as Poland and Greece, sending healthcare workers. The papers will illustrate how demographic change, labor shortage, and foreign recruitment lead to a transnationalization of the healthcare sector in Europe and beyond. The first two contributions of this series deal with the consequences of labor migration in the healthcare and elderly care system in Germany. *Marlene Neumann and Uwe Hunger* (Neumann and Hunger 2016) analyze a special form of circular migration of Polish care workers in the German elderly-care sector and its consequences for the German labor market and the migrants. The second contribution in this special issue by *Andreas Gkolfinopoulos* (Gkolfinopoulos 2016) focuses on the migration of Greek physicians to Germany and its effects on the German and Greek healthcare systems. Both papers illustrate how different sectors tend to address various challenges with different strategies and solutions, depending on the specific

[A] Institute for Political Science, University of Muenster, Germany
[B] Welcome Center Heilbronn-Franken, Germany

doi: 10.18278/epa.2.2.7

constellations of political opportunity structures, sector condi-tions, actors, and forms of collaboration.

References

Gkolfinopoulos, Andreas. 2016. "The Migration of Greek Physicians to Germany: Motivations, Factors and the Role of National Health Sectors." *European Policy Analysis* 2 (2).

Neumann, Marlene, and Uwe Hunger. 2016. "Circular Migration of Live-ins in Germany—Reinforcing the Segmentation of the Labor Market?" *European Policy Analysis* 2 (2).

European Policy Analysis - Volume 2, Number 2 - Winter 2016

Circular Migration of *Live-ins* in Germany— Reinforcing the Segmentation of the Labor Market?

Marlene Neumann[A] and Uwe Hunger[B]

In past years, circular migration has been used as a theoretical idea in political discussions, and also on the standard of the European Union. Within these discussions, the types of circular mobility already in existence within the EU are often ignored. This article explores the circularity of so-called live-ins in Germany: those who stay with the people they take care of and are usually migrant workers. The focus is on how the circularity is organized and what implications it has for the migrants. What are the practical consequences of the legal framework for live-ins? How does this subsector relate to the elderly care sector in Germany?

This article is built on the results of a two-year study with more than 35 interviews conducted in the elderly care sector showing that the employment of live-ins takes place in a semi-legal sphere, which marginalizes the employees and limits their labor rights. The results further suggest that the circularity fosters a segmentation of the labor market because the limited time of the stays prevents live-ins from becoming accustomed and integrating into local hierarchies, which constitutes a necessary step toward claiming their full rights. The study shows how this type of employment is built on circularity with great implications for the actual living and working situations. On the political level, however, the term circular migration is not used in this case, which is why it is important to engage in a discussion on consequences of live-in arrangements in the European Union, regulations favoring this type of employment and how labor rights can be assured.

On the other hand, the study has also indicated that while migration plays hardly any role in the elderly care sector, the whole subsector of live-ins would not exist without migration. The legal framework—together with societal changes and structures such as emancipation, demographic change and the elderly care sector itself with its inherent financial shortage—lead to a gap that is covered by live-in arrangements.

Keywords: *Circular Migration, Care Sector Germany,* Live-ins

[A]Welcome Center Heilbronn-Franken, Germany
[B]Institute for Political Science, University of Muenster, Germany

doi: 10.18278/epa.2.2.9

Introduction

The European Network for Migration [EMN] published a paper (EMN 2011), which explains the potential benefits from a circulation of migrants between the country of origin and the receiving society. According to them it can lead to a so-called "triple win" scenario, in which all involved parties benefit. First, sending countries benefit, because money earned by migrants boosts local economies in the form of remittances. Second, the receiving countries benefit from circular migration, as it helps to meet labor shortages and increase economic growth. Third, the proponents also predict that migrants themselves benefit from repeated mobility, as they can increase their personal skills during their stay(s) abroad. This helps them to improve their socio-economic status in their country of origin. Rother (2013) has criticized this "triple win" idea suggesting that it is being used as a sort of "mantra" in policy-making, which has been repeated so many times that it became acknowledged truth while actually not having much to do with the already existing practices and possibilities for circularity. In the case of policy-making in the European Union [EU], circular migration is seen as a process, which requires a high level of regulation and management. Wickramasekara criticizes this definition as belonging to the "definitions which attempt to describe desirable or good practice circular migration programs rather than those that exist today" (Wickramasekara 2011, 11). Vertovec (2007) further suspects that within more managed and regulated circular programs

there is less social mobility as they lead to "people returning year after year to the same job rather than trying to negotiate their way into better jobs and localities like unregulated circular migrants might do" (pp. 6).

In academia there is no common definition scholars have agreed on, but a trend can be observed in which circular migration is defined as unregulated and free movement across borders (Triandafyllidou 2013). This definition is more in line with what Wickramasekara (2011) calls spontaneous circular migration. While circular migration has been a topic in policy debates in the EU and academic literature, there has been little focus on how this circularity works in practice in Germany (Schneider and Parusel 2011).

This article aims at closing this gap of knowledge about already existing patterns of circular migration by exploring the employment of *live-ins* in the German elderly care sector. *Live-ins* are employees, mainly from Eastern European countries, who work in informal care and live with the person they are taking care of (Schilliger 2013). While in the USA this profession is usually referred to *as home health care workers*, recent European studies also quoted in this paper used the term *live-ins*. The tasks include domestic work and care work, however, there is no clear description of duties and in some cases care work such as having a walk with the person in need of care is counted as free time (Schilliger 2013). Tießler-Marenda (2014) states that estimations of the numbers of live-ins in Germany revolve around 150,000–200,000. In many cases *live-ins* are employed in line with the principle of the freedom to provide services in the EU, which makes it possible for foreign agencies to send their employees to other member states and offer services there. The competitive advantage within this legal arrangement is that the working conditions from the country of origin apply and only basic German employment rights are effective which are listed in article two of the Law on Posted Workers (Arbeitnehmerentsendegesetz [AEntG] 2009). One example of these basic rights is the Act on Working Hours (Arbeitszeitgesetz [ArbZG] 2012) which limits the possible working hours per day to 8–10 hours. Another basic regulation in Germany, which took effect on the 1st of January 2015 is the general minimum wage of 8.50 € per hour, which also applies to *live-ins* (Mindestlohngesetz [MiLoG] 2015). However, in many cases these basic regulations are surpassed because of difficulties in law enforcement, uncertainties about the content of the work and the protection of private homes, which make a control of the working conditions of live-ins nearly impossible (sueddeutsche.de 2014; Tießler-Marenda 2014).

When exploring the example of *live-ins* it becomes apparent that the freedom to provide services within the EU enables this circular migration of informal care workers. But even though this circularity is promoted by EU regulations, when speaking of circular migration, there is no mention of live-ins and their circular movements. This reflects the criticism about the political discussion and its detachment from the actual phenomenon. The aim of this article is to close this research gap by exploring the circular migration of *live-ins* and answering the following questions. What is the impact of the circularity on the employment situation and working conditions? How does it relate to the statement of Vertovec (2007) about social mobility? Is it an example of managed migration like it is suggested in EU debates or are movements spontaneous like the academic definitions propose? How does the employment fit into the context of the elderly care sector in Germany and demographic change?

Methods

To answer these research questions, this article is based on a research study on the consequences of demographic change for regional development, especially in the elderly care sector. In order to understand the situation of the circularity of *live-ins*, a total of over 35 interviews were conducted with migrants, placement agencies in Germany, families who hired a live-in via an agency like that, elderly care institutions, agencies organizing recruitment programs for nurses in elderly care, employers unions, the Federal Employment Agency, care unions, employee unions, and educational centers, etc. The interviews were semi-structured and conducted in German language. Several interview guides were used depending on the interviewee and the relevant topics. These guides systematically pursued certain topics while leaving enough space for the interviewee's own ideas outside these guidelines. In order to analyze the data, the interviews were transcribed and analyzed through a developed relevant codes system according to Mayring

(2010), which would help to structure the transcriptions and answer the research questions. Subsequently, the content of the interviews and interesting quotes were summarized according to the codes. This summary in the form of a table facilitated the analysis, as all statements made during the interviews concerning one topic were listed in a clearly arranged manner.

Results

Live-ins and Circular Migration

In cases of the *live-ins*, the legal grounds of the arrangements are often built on circularity. The live-ins are employed by the agency in their countries of origin and can only work in Germany for a limited amount of time. In order for the placements to take place within the jurisdiction of the freedom of services the temporary nature of the assignment has to be established from the beginning and workers have to keep the center of their lives in their countries of origin, meaning that they still have to be registered there (IHK Berlin 2013). This impossibility to relocate the center of life to Germany further enhances the circularity as they keep their personal lives in their home countries. This separation of the private and the professional in two spatial spheres is also reflected in the following statement of one informant.

Yes, we were looking forward to the new one and of course also said goodbye to the old one with tears in our eyes, but okay, well, they also still have their private lives. (Family member who employed a *live-in*)

When one interviewee was asked why some could not stay longer she explained that most of the *live-ins* had family at home and that they wanted to go back to see them. What is intriguing about the circularity of *live-ins* is that even though the profession is built on the re-entry of migrants, the term circular migration is not mentioned in policy debates around the topic. When we talked to a representative of the Federal Employment Agency, we were told that there is no mention of live-ins in the context of circular migration. In their experience, in the EU policy documents, circular migration is used only in the context of the migration of "skilled" workers.

Organization of Live-in Employment

In the case of live-ins there are several actors who have an influence on the employment situation; the person they take care of and their families (among which there might also be conflicting interests), the agency in Germany and the legal employer, the agency in the sending countries. As many actors are involved, organizational issues are complex. The following part aims at exploring these complexities and tries to give some insight into how each employer impacts the employment situation of *live-ins*.

The length of stays of the *live-ins* varied in general, but in practice in the two care settings, none of the *live-ins* stayed longer than 3 months, while some even only stayed for 14 days. These shorter stays took place especially in the transition period in the beginning. The representatives of the agencies both portrayed the length of the respective stays as more flexible than they actually were in the two cases and one even explained that they could stay up to 2 years. However, they both admitted that the usual scenario is that there is a sort of rotating system forming where two or three live-ins share one family and switch after 6 or 8 weeks.

The head of one agency in Germany explained the procedure of the employment of a *live-in* as follows: first, the live-in receives the profile of a potential family for employment. If they approve, their own profile will be sent to that family and if these again approve as well, the *live-ins* are usually sent there for 6 weeks to 2 months.

But that does not mean that it will really work like that. That means that when after a week they do not get along, then we better get them back and get someone new before they club each other to death. Because of that, those are just guiding length. It could be the other way around just as well, that she only wanted to come for six weeks, but then feels good there and they all get along so well that I get a call from the family and the agency abroad gets a call from the live-in, I would like to stay longer. Then we make that possible of course, why should we separate people that get along well? But that is why you cannot say that there is a special rotation system in place, because it is totally different in each case. (Head of a German agency for *live-ins*)

She further explained that *live-ins* also decide for themselves if they want to go back to work in Germany immediately, they might also take their vacation time or they work in their own country for a while. The agencies abroad are also active in the care business in their home countries and the *live-ins* have the possibility to work in their countries[c] of origin.

There are of course some who say this is too difficult for me, I want to go home, well, then we just send a new one. (Head of German agency for *live-ins*)

This statement also shows that there is no shortage of labor in this subsector, at least that is the way it was portrayed by this informant. Apparently there are enough potential employees in the pool of the agency abroad to easily replace *live-ins* in Germany. One of the family employers also clarified that the length often depended on different circumstances, for example if the mother (the person in need of care) had to go to the hospital, if the live-ins already had their next assignment by the agency or sometimes there was an event in their country of origin, which they wanted to go back to.

The establishment of a rotation system with the same *live-ins* depended on the families and the live-ins themselves. When both contacted the agencies and expressed the wish to repeat employment with a certain family, the two agencies interviewed said that they would make that possible. The agreement had to be mutual though, if either the live-in or the family did not wish for a repetition, it would not be organized.

They often agree to that among themselves, when they feel comfortable the ladies also like to come back. So, both have to want that, the client just as the lady or the gentleman. We do not push

---

[c] In order to legally post workers in Germany, foreign agencies have to be active in the labour markets of the countries of origin as well (Lorenz 2010).

anybody to go there. When the ladies want to, then that is fine of course, we will plan it like that, then it will be easier also for all involved parties. But if they do not want to, the client can beg as he pleases, then we will not send her of course. (Head of a German agency for *live-ins*)

The families also explained that they approached the *live-ins* they liked personally and asked them if they would want to come back. In one case, after one live-in had come back another time, she did not want to come back again because she preferred to be employed in Berlin. In another case, the family itself recommended the *live-in* not to come back because the work had become heavier due to the increasing illness of the mother of the family. As the *live-in* had back problems herself, the family recommended her not to come back as the work would have been too hard for her.

When we asked one of the heads of the agencies placing *live-ins* with families in Germany about the rotation system and who organizes it, she replied that this is mainly organized by the agencies abroad.

No, that is organized by the agencies in the foreign countries, because they have nationwide, often also in Austria and Switzerland, placed their ladies and I cannot do that from here with my pool [pool= available live-ins], but we are in the pool of that agency. I am just placing them here. (Head of a German agency for *live-ins*)

The cases described here were arrangements where the *live-ins* were legally employed by the agency abroad and could work in Germany in the frame of the freedom to provide services in the EU. Another possible way to hire live-ins

would be if families directly employed the EU citizens, which would then be in the frame of the freedom of movement for workers. One such institution, a church-based organization, which offers support and matching for families who want to employ live-ins themselves has also been interviewed. The informant explained that the costs are double the price in comparison to hiring live-ins in the frame of the law on posted workers.

When one of the families who employed a live-in via an agency was asked about the possibility to directly employ the live-in she explained that she offered this possibility to one care worker staying with her. The employee declined, however, with the explanation that she needed the agency in case something would happen with the mother of the family. In this case she would need a new employment quickly and this could only be provided by the agency in her country of origin. The head of one of the agencies also explained that the contracts prevent the live-ins from switching to direct employment because they would get a contract penalty. She admitted, however, that she could not control if employees terminate their contracts with the agencies in their home countries and then move to Germany to directly work for one of the families.

Direct employment of a 24-hour live-in worker in Germany is of course not possible anymore, that should not be forgotten. That is not the same service anymore and when it is the same that is not legal anymore. That is often underestimated. Then the customs comes ringing at your door sooner than you know. An employment in Germany is only possible with 8 hours, 10 hours a day, and you have to keep a certain resting time per day and so on. And that is not the service you get with the Law on Posted Workers. As soon as the employer hires them himself then he cannot have them there 24 hours at your service, that does not work, than they have to have normal working hours, normal free time. It really only works if you do it with the Law on Posted Workers and they are employed in their country of origin. (Head of a German agency for *live-ins*)

This statement is interesting because what she described is also illegal in Germany. As has been mentioned before, basic working rights apply for all workers in Germany, also those who are employed by foreign agencies. Intriguingly, the informant uses the Law on Posted Workers (AEntG 2009) as the legal foundation for the precarious working conditions, a law aimed at protecting basic working rights of posted workers in Germany. One regulation which does applies is the Act on Working Hours (ArbZG 2012) which limits the possible hours per day to 8–10 hours. In a 24-hour care setting, which the agency described, these basic rules are broken. This shows that there are uncertainties about valid laws even within the agencies who place *live-ins* in German families. The circularity of live-ins is thus founded on a partially wrongful interpretation of valid laws and takes place within a legal grey area, also due to the inability of the state to control working conditions. This shows the precary of the situation of *live-ins*, as controls in other sectors contracting a high share of posted workers, such as the construction industry, is realized more easily.

The interviews indicate that there is a high degree of organization involved in the employment of *live-ins*, which also points to a high degree of controllability. One of the reasons for this increased controllability is because of the nature of the business. The employees never know how long they can keep a position because the person they are taking care of might die, which results in the loss of the position. This is why they highly depend on the agencies to get a new position soon afterwards. Families and *live-ins* themselves have a limited influence on the rotating system, as they can only navigate within the set boundaries. But beyond that, they both depend on the agency and are bound to them because they have the information necessary for the employment to take place.

Consequences of Circularity

Now that the organization of circularity has become clear, what are the consequences of this circularity on the situation of *live-ins*? What advantages does circularity have for the employers? One advantage of the recruitment of live-ins for the receiving country is that this recruitment fills positions, which would otherwise stay empty. The profession of live-ins is what Piore (1979) calls an immigrant job, a result of the bifurcation of the labor market with an increasing number of lower paid jobs, which are unattractive for natives.

In the case of *live-ins* it can be argued, that the demand for their labor also derives from other processes in society such as emancipation. One informant pointed out, that because of emancipation in Germany, this kind of caring and domestic work has become unattractive for women as they have a wider range of professions to choose from. The informant explained that this process of emancipation is not that evolved yet in Eastern European sending countries, so the women are still willing to do such jobs and to devote themselves to the more traditional female tasks.

*The Eastern European employees are more used to live in big families still where you help each other, also with the work that we do not do anymore, even not for money, for them it is normal, it is part of everyday life. Also to service which we in Germany cannot do anymore. [...] And that can still come from Eastern Europe, because they are one generation behind when it comes to that. [...] Yes, that is really like three generations ago there, really, where everybody lives in the same village and where you meet regularly and I do not know if you still have that here, maybe in the villages, but that is also crumbling slowly. And in the city it is not like that already for a long time. (*Head of a German agency for *live-ins)*

With this statement the informant does not only link the debate around live-ins to wider questions of emancipation but she also seems to "ethnitized" this kind of work, as she generalizes that Eastern European employees are better suited for the tasks the jobs entail. What is further interesting about linking the employment of *live-ins* to processes of emancipation in their country of origin is that it suggests these processes mutually influence the other. If the informant says that they are "one generation behind" when it comes to emancipation, how will the employment of *live-ins* develop once emancipatory processes evolve? Will this lead to a lower willingness of Eastern European women to take on these jobs? These questions raise doubts on the sustainability of relying on informal care workers from abroad for supplying the local demands for care.

Other interviews confirmed that the rise of female employment has led to a restructuring of the households. Formerly female tasks such as caring for relatives are increasingly unoccupied as women have their own careers outside the traditional roles at home. At the same time, the political approach in elderly care has been following the idea of "outpatient care before inpatient care" ("ambulant vor stationär"). The head of several elderly homes pointed out that while societal changes led to household care being outdated, politics still proposed it as the solution for the increasing demands in elderly care. As full professional care at home is very expensive and family structures changed, live-ins fill those gaps that cannot be covered by outpatient care or families.

The interviews have also indicated that contrary to the situation in elderly care homes there is no shortage of labor when it comes to *live-ins*. To explain this development only with the willingness of live-ins to fill these positions would be oversimplifying the situation, however. There might be societal structures in the sending countries, which inhibit women to reach other positions. It could also be that because of the lack of job opportunities in the sending countries in general, the *live-ins* are forced to take these jobs in order to make a living. Even though this limitation to the lack of emancipation should be handled with caution as other factors play a role, it still shows what kinds of skills are asked of the workers filling the position as live-ins in Germany.

It is further interesting to consider how the head of a German *live-in* agency explained what qualifications are asked of the *live-ins*. He clarified that many did have other qualifications, but that he did not care for those.

I act according to the references that they had themselves, because those are closer and linked to the work, than any papers saying what someone has done so far, there are differences. I do not care if a paper is provided that she is an examined nurse, but she does not know how to organize the main daily routine. (Head of a German agency for live-ins)

This is in line with the previous statement on how in the informant's explanation Eastern European women are more caring and more willing to do this kind of work compared to German women. What is expected of the *live-ins* is not called "qualified" work necessarily, in the way the agencies portray the tasks. It is domestic work and includes "traditional women's tasks". In this way one could argue that it is not only the case that processes of emancipation influence live-in employment but also vice versa. Some of the mainly female workers have higher qualifications, sometimes related to the sector, sometimes on other fields. During *live-in* employments, these other qualifications are unused which constitutes an inability for the *live-ins* to build a career and a consequent loss of human capital.

In the earlier part on circular migration in practice, the differentiation between private and professional lives of live-ins has already been explained, but what are the implications of this spatial separation of private and professional lives? The head of an agency in Germany explained, that in the frame of the freedom to provide services within the EU, an around-the-clock service was possible. This shows that in these arrangements the live-ins do not have time for their private lives while they are employed in Germany. Knowing this, the question arises whether the separation into private and professional spheres is not the basis of this intense 24-hours care arrangement. Because of limitations in time, *live-ins* are prevented from building a private life while they stay with families in Germany. In order to have private lives, they have to go back to their countries of origin, which results in this rotation system built on the circularity of the employees.

Live-ins as a Sub Sector Within Elderly Care in Germany

The interviews with elderly homes and outpatient care institutions indicated that while the subsector of *live-ins* is mainly occupied by migrants, migration does only play a marginal role in other care intuitions of the sector.

One informant explained difficulties in recruitment and the frustrations on the side of the employers.

That is really not an easy task, not an easy area, and to be honest, many of the German employers are frustrated by now, they get 40 people from somewhere and five or seven stay in the end. (Press officer of an employer's association)

One of the main reasons why the recruitment costs are high and linked to a high risk for elderly care homes and outpatient care is that the training of nurses and their subsequent tasks are organized very differently in other countries. While in Germany there are two separate vocational trainings for nurses in the health care system and nurses in elderly care, in most other countries nurses have an academic training. This leads to differences in the content of work, which carries a potential for disappointment on the side of the nurses when taking on a job in Germany. Additionally the recognition of the foreign qualification is a lengthy process and especially the high language requirements are an obstacle. Another reason why nurses from abroad might not stay on is because of the relatively unattractive working conditions in Germany, which is expressed in the following statement of a staff manager in an elderly home:

I could imagine that something like that happens, it is not a secret. I mean, we are the exception, with the working conditions, which are changing a lot, getting worse in Germany. [...] The nurses that we recruit, we should not forget that, all have an academic qualification and by moving here they changed their environment. But they are neither stupid nor blind, they will inform themselves here and they will find out that there are countries, in which working conditions are better than here, like Switzerland or Scandinavia. And then they will think, I did it once, if they cannot maybe do it again and leave. [...] And it is already in the foreign press, the information has spread, that the working conditions in Germany in the care sector are not the best. (Staff manager of an elderly home)

This indicates that the shortages of qualified staff in the elderly care sector will not easily be covered with the recruitment of staff from abroad if working conditions do not improve. This study has shown, however, that because of a lack of representation in the form of labor unions or other employee organizations, the position of nurses is weakened in comparison to those of doctors for example. In elderly care there are additionally different financial structures and the care insurance is not intended to cover all occurring costs, but it is only meant as a partial insurance. The other part of the costs for elderly care are covered by the individual. Increasing wages and financially restructuring the sector is thus more complicated. Additionally, many interviewees mentioned the increasing pressures in elderly care with those in need of care getting older and having more sicknesses simultaneously (multi morbidity, e.g. dementia in combination with physical inabilities). This means that taking care of them is more taxing for care workers leading to even more demanding working conditions.

Discussion and Conclusion

When it comes to *live-ins*, the analysis has shown that only the separation of private and professional lives in two different spheres makes it possible to work under such intense circumstances. Because of the 24-hour care arrangements live-ins are isolated in German households and have no local personal networks. If they would stay for a longer period of time, they would eventually want to establish a life outside the homes of the families they live with, which is prevented by the circularity. This isolation has further impact on the situation of the live-ins. The circularity of live-ins is mainly due to the impossibility for them to settle in Germany, which creates a self-perpetuating circularity. Piore (1979) explained, that once migrants settle, they understand local hierarchies and will eventually strive for an improvement of their position. This is what leads to conflicts with natives, as they start to compete for similar positions. Circular migration in the case of *live-ins* is an example on how circularity can inhibit this social mobility. The isolation during their stays in Germany further impedes any demands for an improvement of working conditions. *Live-ins* with their up to 24 hours on-call duties have not only relatively bad working conditions compared to the average jobs in Germany, their working conditions are often against valid German legislation. Interaction with local people would probably mean that they learn more about common working rights and conditions. *Live-ins* would most likely claim their rights and strive for an improvement of their situation. The circularity and the limitation of the stays help these arrangements to work, because it helps to keep live-ins uninformed about their rights and keeps their point of reference when it comes to social hierarchies their home countries. With this in mind, it is doubtful whether the circular migration of live-ins really leads to a triple-win scenario in which all involved parties benefit, including the migrants themselves.

What has also been shown in the interviews is that the tasks of the live-ins are portrayed more like domestic work, rather than care work. This links this profession to the plea of the International Domestic Workers Federation (IDWF 2014) to acknowledge private households as workplace and thus domestic work as equal to any other work. Schilliger (2013) also describes, that in the work situations of live-ins many tasks such as having a walk with the person they take care of, are not generally seen as part of the work but as free time. This is again also related to a demand voiced in one of the workshops of the conference "Germany in the Elderly Care Crisis – Perspectives and Problems of Care Migration" (Heinrich-

Böll Stiftung 2014). In order for the general acknowledgement of live-ins and their profession, an official description of the occupation including the tasks should be drawn. Like this it would become clearer, which tasks constitute a part of the job and what having "free" time really means. *Live-ins* and the way their work is portrayed, is also related to the general undervaluation of tasks traditionally assigned to women. In this way it could be argued that foreign recruitment in this field, with these tasks does just as Piore (1979) predicted, circumvent the general revaluation of this work in German society.

During fieldwork, it became clear that the legal grounds for the employment were not clearly established, even within the agencies placing live-ins in German families. This shows that there is a grey area in which the rights of the workers are likely to be cast aside. This is in line with what Castles (2006) was worried about, when he compared "guest worker" recruitment with circular migration and explained that they are similar in the likelihood that workers rights are breached. Both Lutz and Palenga-Möllenbeck (2011) and Schilliger (2013) also compare the situations of the live-ins with those of the former "guest workers", as responsibilities for social security are shifted to the sending countries and the individual. Apart from this similarity, there is a difference between the two, however, which can be highlighted when looking at structures of circularity. Many of the former "guest workers" did settle in Germany, subsequently started to understand local hierarchies and strive for an improvement of their position. What this analysis has shown is that additionally to the restrictive rights, the circularity of live-ins also prevents this acclimatization to local hierarchies from happening, keeping them from claiming their rights and improving their situation.

In her conclusion, Schilliger (2013) explains that there is a deregulated market developing, "a precarious, gendered and ethnitized labour market" (2013, 156). Schilliger's (2013) results also show that only because of the circularity this sort of work can be done by the live-ins because after 3 month they are exhausted by the hard work and they recover again in their home countries. Another aspect Schilliger (2013) points to is the description of the work and that even though some of the live-ins are highly qualified, what is asked of them are traditionally female tasks. This way of framing the work could also be seen in the results of this study. Even though some of the live-ins had higher qualifications, those did not matter in this situation as they were mainly doing domestic tasks. Informants pointed out, that these domestic tasks do not only "come naturally" to the *live-ins* because they are mainly women, but also because they are Eastern European women, who are "less emancipated" than German women. This sort of framing should be paid particular attention to because employers, especially the agencies in Germany, can strategically frame the work in this way to avoid seeing it like "real" work, which should follow the basic laws any other work applies to.

While the subsector of *live-ins* is based on migration, in elderly homes and outpatient care migration only plays a marginal role. Recruiting nurses has proven to be risky and not as effective, partly also due to unattractive working conditions. While in one of the interviews, live-in arrangements have been portrayed as a temporary phenomenon and as no alternative to professional care, there is an undeniable gap in services. The emancipation in Germany and changes in traditional family structures increase the shortage of labor in this sector. While the shortage of labor in elderly care homes and outpatient care will most likely not be covered by the recruitment of nurses from abroad, the gap in "in-house care" giving rise to the subsector of live-ins will likely remain or even grow in size.

Even though it is not called circular migration this analysis has shown that the profession is built on the circular movements of the live-ins. Interestingly enough, at first glance the circularity of *live-ins* fits well into the definitions of circular migration as "spontaneous" and unregulated movement. This points to a dichotomy in the definitions between state run "programs" and the spontaneous circular migration. The circularity in the case of live-ins, however, has been proven as not fitting in either of the two definitions. Even though it might not seem like managed circular migration at first sight, because the "managers" of the movement are no state officials, the placement of live-ins is a highly managed process. The possibility of live-ins to influence their situation themselves is still limited as they depend on the agencies abroad. The first reason for this dependency is that as a precondition for the freedom to provide services to apply, the *live-ins* have to be employed by an agency in the sending countries. The second reason for the dependency on the agencies is that they possess the information to find new employers in Germany and can replace *live-ins* within days, after a former client has passed away. This high level of management also leads to what Vertovec (2007) suspected would happen in circular programs, the low social mobility among migrants.

This study indicates that the dichotomy between regulated and spontaneous definitions of circular migration might not do justice to those circular movements, which are highly regulated and navigate within the set of given rules, but without direct state involvement.

This study examined the circularity of live-ins in Germany and what consequences this type of mobility has on the employment situation and the working conditions of the labor migrants. The freedom to provide services within the EU enables the temporary placement of informal carers and has given rise to an employment model, which is based on circular movements and the repeated employment of workers in other EU countries. The circularity is supported by the legal framework but also by the separation of private and professional lives in two geographical spheres. The system is built in such a way, that in order for *live-ins* to have free time, they have to go back to their countries of origin. This change between private and professional time supports the circularity and enables the extraordinary working conditions. While the live-ins are employed in Germany, they provide around-the-clock care and when they are exhausted and need time for themselves they go to their home countries. Without this distinction in two spheres and the circularity, the

employees would probably demand more free time and better working conditions for their placements in Germany.

The results of this study have further shown that this type of migration enables a segmentation of the labor market because circularity inhibits social mobility and the possibilities to integrate into local labor markets. Their positions meet local labor shortages in the elderly care sector in receiving societies, because as Piore explained, they take on jobs, which are not interesting for the native population. The interviews of this study have also pointed to a higher degree of emancipation in Germany which in turn increases the shortage of labor in this sector because of the ability of woman to choose from a wider range of opportunities apart from the traditional role of the carer of the family.

The results further indicate that agencies in the sending countries have an influential position in this setting. One reason for this dependence is because they are the legal employer and live-ins are bound to them by contract. Furthermore, the agencies possess the information, which is needed for the placement and last but not least, the whole legal grounds of the placement is based on the foreign employment by the agencies. Even though the 24-hour care arrangements are illegal, the grey area is utilized to offer a service, which would not be possible if the *live-ins* were employed in Germany. This increases the dependability of *live-ins* on the agencies abroad.

Another interesting insight of the analysis is that existing definitions of circular migration do not fully capture the phenomenon. In order to understand circular migration and the management of it, the term management itself should be opened up. The way it has been used in EU documents, it mainly refers to the state as being the managing actor. This case has shown, however, that there are other factors playing a role when managing circular migration such as favorable legal regulations (the freedom to provide services within the EU) and none-state actors such as recruitment agencies. To fully understand circularity among migrants, these factors should be included into an analysis and an oversimplified dichotomy between state led circularity and free circularity should be avoided. The portrayal of spontaneous circular migration on the one hand and state managed migration on the other hand creates the illusion that circular migration either happens freely or managed by the state.

To sum up, the analysis has shown that circular migration does take place and can hinder social mobility just not necessarily in the shape one would expect when following policy debates. Piore's (1979) theory, although he did not include circular migration as part of his study, can give interesting insights into the phenomenon, as the circularity prevents eventual aspirations to improve the situation on the side of the migrants. The results of this study stress a discussion around two topics. Firstly, if for providing care for the elderly, Germany relies on foreign recruitment, it is an absolute necessity to ensure working rights of those employed in the sector. The tasks of the profession of *live-ins* have to be officially registered and this information has to be provided to the employee.

Secondly, a long overdue discussion on the value of elderly care in our society should be conducted. Live-in employment with its grey area and breached workers rights is a symptom for wider processes in society, such as the undervaluation of traditionally female jobs, the "ethnitization" of whole sectors in the economy and the future of the local elderly care sector. With the impacts of demographic change increasing not only in Germany, but also in Eastern European sending countries, addressing these questions is of vital importance for a fair and sustainable development of our societies.

References

Arbeitnehmerentsendegesetz (AEntG). 2009. "Gesetz über zwingende Arbeitsbedingungen für grenzüberschreitend entsandte und für regelmäßig im Inland beschäftigte Arbeitnehmer und Arbeitnehmerinnen (Arbeitnehmer-Entsendegesetz)." http://www.gesetze-im-internet.de/bundesrecht/aentg_2009/gesamt.pdf.

Arbeitszeitgesetz (ArbZG). 2012. "Arbeitszeitgesetz." http://www.gesetze-im-internet.de/bundesrecht/arbzg/gesamt.pdf.

Castles, S. 2006. "Guestworkers in Europe: A Resurrection?" *International Migration Review* 40 (4): 741–66.
Castles, S. 2006. "Guestworkers in Europe: A Resurrection?" *International Migration Review* 40 (4): 741–66.

EMN. 2011. "EMN Inform - Temporäre und zirkuläre Migration: Welche politischen, praktischen und künftigen Optionen bieten sich den EU-Mitgliedsstaaten?" http://www.bamf.de/SharedDocs/Anlagen/DE/Publikationen/EMN/SyntheseberichteEMN-Inform/emn-inform-temporaere-und-zirkulaere-migration.

Heinrich-Böll Stiftung. 2014. "Pflegenotstand und Care Migration." http://www.boell.de/de/2014/03/20/pflegenotstand-care-migration (accessed April 25, 2014).

International Domestic Workers Federation (IDWF). 2014. "Who we are." http://www.idwn.info/about.php.

IHK Berlin. 2013. "Auslandsentsendung von Arbeitnehmern." http://www.ihk-berlin.de/linkableblob/bihk24/recht_und_steuern/downloads/816106/.21./data/Auslandsentsendung-data.pdf.

Lorenz, F. 2010. *Arbeitnehmerfreizügigkeit und Dienstleistungsfreiheit in der Europäischen Union: rechtliche Rahmenbedingungen und politischer Handlungsbedarf ; Expertise im Auftrag des Gesprächskreises Migration und Integration der Friedrich-Ebert-Stiftung.* Bonn: Friedrich-Ebert-Stiftung, Abt. Wirtschafts- und Sozialpolitik. http://library.fes.de/pdf-files/wiso/07445.pdf.

Lutz, H., and E. Palenga-Möllenbeck. 2011. "Das Care-Chain-Konzept auf dem Prüfstand. Eine Fallstudie der transnationalen Care-Arrangements polnischer und ukrainischer Migrantinnen." *GENDER – Zeitschrift für Geschlecht, Kultur und Gesellschaft* 3 (1). http://www.budrich-journals.de/index.php/gender/article/view/4968.

Mayring, P. 2010. Qualitative Inhaltsanalyse Grundlagen und Techniken. Weinheim: Beltz.

Mindestlohngesetz (MiLoG). 2015. "Gesetz zur Regelung eines allgemeinen Mindestlohns." http://www.gesetze-im-internet.de/milog/.

Piore, M. J. 1979. *Birds of Passage: Migrant Labor and Industrial Societies.* Cambridge, NY: Cambridge University Press.

Rother, S. 2013. "A Tale of Two Tactics-Civil Society and Competing Visions of Global Migration Governance from Below." In *Disciplining the Transnational Mobility of People.* Geiger, M., Pécoud, A. (Eds.) New York: Palgrave Macmillan.

Schilliger, S. 2013. "Transnationale Care-Arbeit: osteuropäische Pendelmigrantinnen in Privathaushalten von Pflegebedürftigen." In *Who cares? Pflege und Solidarität in der alternden Gesellschaft.* Schweizerisches Rotes Kreuz (Eds.) Zürich: Seismo-Verlag.

Schneider, J., and B. Parusel. 2011. *Zirkuläre und temporäre Migration-Empirische Erkenntnisse, politische Praxis und zukünftige Optionen in Deutschland.* Working Paper 35 (EMN).

sueddeutsche.de. 2014. "Wenn die Pflege zuhause zu teuer wird. sueddeutsche.de." Dezember. http://www.sueddeutsche.de/wirtschaft/folgen-des-mindestlohns-wenn-pflege-zuhause-zu-teuer-wird-1.2264455-3.

Tießler-Marenda, E. 2014. "Pflege und Migration in Europa." http://www.boell.de/de/2014/02/26/pflege-und-migration-europa (accessed April 10, 2014).

Triandafyllidou, A. ed. 2013. *Circular Migration Between Europe and Its Neighbourhood: Choice or Necessity?* Oxford: Oxford University Press.

Vertovec, S. 2007. "Is Circular Migration the Way Forward in Global Policy?" *Around the Globe* 3 (2): 38.

Wickramasekara, P. 2011. *Circular Migration: A Triple Win or a Dead End? International Labour Organisation, Geneva*

The Migration of Greek Physicians to Germany: Motivations, Factors and the Role of National Health Sectors

Andreas Gkolfinopoulos[A]

Even before the outbreak of the Eurozone crisis, a migration trend of Greek physicians into the German health system was well underway. With particular focus on Greek physicians who are practicing medical specialization training, this article investigates the subjective motivations for their decision to emigrate with the help of six semi-structured qualitative interviews. This article also intends to explain this migration case by considering the role played by the political framework according to an institutional approach, based on the approach of Robyn Iredale and the research findings of Kirsten Hoesch. This is mainly achieved by comparing the German and Greek health sectors, focusing on the key actors in control of the structure's development. Finally, this article aims to demonstrate that the subjective motivations of the interviewees are related to employment considerations and conditions in Greece and Germany, as consequences pertaining to the structures of both health systems and the relevant political framework - the main actors of the health sectors, the state in Greece, as well as the physicians' associations in Germany.

Keywords: Greek health sector, German health sector, financial crisis, physicians' migration, push and pull factors

Introduction

Undoubtedly, the multidimensional effects of the financial crisis, which have been weighing upon Greece at least since 2009, affect the country at the social, political, and economical levels. Focusing on the effects of the crisis at a social level, one must note the remarkable emigration trend among young people aged 25-39, which reached 223,000 emigrants in the years 2008-13 (Bank of Greece 2016, 74). One can be certain that a large number of highly skilled people left the country along with this population mass (Triandafyllidou and Gropas 2014; Lamprianidis 2015; Gkolfinopoulos 2016), though the number cannot be properly assessed due to lack of statistical data. Lamprianidis estimates the number of highly skilled Greek employees abroad at about 190,000 (2015). However, not every highly skilled person faces the same conditions in the labor market. It is clear, as the results of the Political Economy of Migration in an Integrating Europe (PEMINT) project demonstrate, that each vocational sector presents different circumstances for a case of highly

[A] University of Siegen, Germany

doi: 10.18278/epa.2.2.8

skilled migration and therefore needs to be examined according to its specific vocational arena (Bommes et al. 2004). Separate from other financial sectors with fairly different structures are the migration cases within welfare sectors, where the involvement of the state is still transparent.

Physicians in Greece, as a vocational group of highly skilled persons, have also followed the emigration trend described here. It is notable that according to the Greek Medical Association, almost 15,000 physicians have left the county in the last several years (IS Athens 2016). Germany appears to be a highly attractive country for these physician migrants. In 2015, the Athenian Medical Association alone issued 83 certificates for physicians who had moved to Germany (Mpouloutza 2015). At the same time, Greek physicians form the second-largest group of foreign physicians in the German health sector according to the German Medical Association, numbering 3,017 physicians with Greek nationality in 2015 (Bundesärztekammer 2015a). Moreover, there is also a remarkable situation regarding the medical graduates in Greece who intend to undergo their medical specialization training. According to research performed by the Medical School of Democritus University on the perceptions of Greek medical students toward the medical profession, 38 of a total of 111 interviewed medical students would like to undertake their medical specialization training in the German health system (Labiris et al. 2014, 205). Therefore this article will deal at this point with the plausible question of why so many Greek physicians, and specifically Greek medical graduates, prefer the German health system for undergoing their medical specialization training.

Furthermore, the large demand of health professionals in OECD countries is thought to be a phenomenon stemming from demographic issues—namely, an aging population—which in turn sets the stage for migration (Raghuram and Kofman 2002, 2075; Bach 2003, 9). Based on shortages, some OECD countries have recruited personnel mostly from less developed countries, e.g. the US from overseas countries (Pond and McPake 2006, 1450). England (Clark, Clark, and Stewart 2007, 3) and France (Bach 2003, 7) followed the same pattern by recruiting medical staff from former colonies. In Germany, according to the European Commission, the shortages of physicians in the German health sector are expected to reach 45,000 in 2020 and 165,000 in 2030 (European Commission 2012, 6). However, it is interesting that the case of the present article refers not only to two OECD countries and members of the EU, but also to countries both facing demographic problems with ageing populations. In Greece, 20.9% of the total population was over 65 years old in 2015, while in Germany the equivalent was 21.0% (EUROSTAT 2015). Parallel to that, Greece, with 6.3 practicing physicians per 1,000 people, had the biggest ratio of practicing physicians among the OECD countries during 2013, whereas the same ratio for Germany (4.0 practicing physicians) was above the OECD average (3.3 practicing physicians), but remarkably under the Greek ratio (OECD 2015).

There is an apparent oversupply of physicians in Greece, which is not a new phenomenon, having existed since the 1980s (Kalamatianou, 1993, 293). But in fact, there is a remarkable disparity in physician density in Greece. Attiki, the metropolitan area around Athens, for example, provides 7.15 practicing physicians per 1,000 people according to the OECD figures, followed by Northern Greece with 4.99 practicing physicians per 1,000 inhabitants (OECD 2009). Nowadays, many hospitals in other regions of Greece are facing shortages in health personnel, according to the Greek Chamber of Health Personnel in the Public Health System (POEDIN 2016).

After 2009, the health sector in Greece, as with the entire Greek public sector, has been at the center of reform policies undertaken by the Greek government following the directives of the so-called Troika, formed by the International Monetary Fund (IMF), the European Union (EU), and the European Central Bank (ECB). Therefore, the phenomenon of physician migration from Greece could be plausibly associated with these reform policies and accompanying aspects of the financial crisis, such as unemployment and recession.

It is obvious that the political factor plays a key role in this case, since the government is responsible for shaping the health policy and directing the national health sector. Consequently, it will also be interesting in the context of the present article to investigate how the structures and current developments in the public health sectors of both countries influence this case of migration—as well as the subjective reasons for emigration expressed by the Greek physicians in Germany interviewed—in order to assess the role of the political framework in each country. Kirsten Hoesch has proved that the structural characteristics of a country's health sectors play a vital role in a migration case, especially in the case of the German health sector (Hoesch 2009; 2012). This second basic research question and Hoesch's argument emphasize the notion of focusing on both health sectors

and on the key actors responsible for the health policy and also for the regulation of the corresponding labor markets.

Hypotheses and Theoretical Framework. At the micro-level, the present article will try to lay out the subjective reasons for the migration of Greek physicians from Greece to Germany, as they have been expressed during interviews with six Greek physicians undergoing their medical specialization training in the German health sector. Taking into consideration the better economic situation of the German health sector (which translates into better salaries for a physician), as well as the many vacancies resulting from shortages of physicians in the German health sector, it is assumed that these factors, which intend economic maximization according to neoclassical economic theories, would be the main reasons for the migration. According to representatives of neoclassical economics, migration occurs due to estimation of personal income maximization, and therefore the migrant concentrates on the income differentiation between countries, on personal qualifications, on the employment rates in the destination country (Todaro 1969), but also on the employee's age and on the relevant costs of migration according to Sjaastad (1962). Later, Pissarides and Wadsworth integrated the factor of employment rates in the home country in this model (Pissarides and Wadsworth 1989).

Generally, neoclassical economic approaches focus on the classic "push and pull" argument, concerning the differences in wage levels between the health sectors of the countries in the case of physicians, and on the role of the national labor markets as primary mechanisms of migration flows. Therefore, an analytic focus on the national labor markets and specifically on the health sectors of both countries is significant, in order to illuminate this migration case.

Furthermore, and in connection with the arguments of Hoesch, I assume that the different types of health sectors in these countries (a mixed model of Beveridge and Bismarckian system in Greece and the traditional Bismarckian model in Germany) directly affect and shape the migration case of the Greek physicians who undertake their medical specialization training in Germany. In particular, the political developments in Greece during the last several years, which negatively affected[1] the Greek public health sector, such as the role of the key actors in health sector workforce planning in Greece and in Germany, is expected also to influence this migration case decisively.

Reasonably, Iredale's approach about the role of professional bodies in the migration of health professionals should also be considered in context with the second research question, as well as with the second hypothesis. According to Iredale, professional bodies and associations can play a key role in regulating entry into a health sector for foreign health workers, since this mandate is no longer controlled solely by government players (2001). Of course, a precondition for this is the overcoming of national boundaries for foreign health personnel. This can happen through resident and work permits, which are basically being granted by state actors. However, the professional bodies are likely to be responsible for the recognition of qualifications and the issuing of professional licenses, in this way regulating the labor market in health sectors for foreign

physicians. For example, if the professional bodies of medical professions possess sufficient power through the mentioned responsibilities, and if at the same time the proportion of migrants in the labor market is also significant, they try to define well-established criteria for the recognition of the foreign qualifications (Iredale 2001). Additionally, as Hoesch stated, "while professional actors quite often justify restrictive admission policies with the aim to preserve high-quality standards, it is obvious that other interests—mainly keeping away too much competition—are also driving forces" (2012, 6). Apart from the power of professional bodies, the role of transnational or supranational agreements—e.g. the law framework of the EU for free movement, free establishment, and provision of services—is also crucial for the issue of recognizing qualifications, such as those regulating resident and work permits (Iredale 2001, 11).

Consequently, the analysis of the health sectors of both countries should not only highlight their main characteristics and structures, but also emphasize the role of gatekeepers of the health sector's labor market and illuminate the key actors within them. It is also necessary that the present article will focus on the form of labor markets and inequities between them, which have resulted from decision-making and interaction of the relevant political players and the key actors in the health sectors.

Material and Methods. The present article bases its findings on three main sources of data, both quantitative and qualitative, which will be presented in the following.

---

[1] See the section "Overview of the Greek health system".

Firstly, the article takes stock, on the one hand, of the annual statistical data of the German medical association regarding the health sector workforce, but also the statistical data provided by the Greek statistical authority concerning the number of physicians in the Greek health sector, on the other. These data will provide information about the migration of Greek physicians to the German health sector in numbers, and they will contribute to discovering the needs for assessing the looming shortages or oversupply in physicians within the health sectors of both countries.

Secondly, concerning the section on the health sectors, the article takes the existing literature into consideration, which focuses on the analysis of health sectors in Greece and in Germany. The article will focus more on the literature that explains the role of the key actors in the German health sector by the migration of health workers (Hoesch 2009; 2012), and the structures and main reforms in the Greek health sector in the context of the loan agreements with Troika and the economic adjustment program (Economou et al. 2014).

Thirdly, the data about the migration motives of Greek physicians who migrated for specialization training in the German health sectors originate from an analysis of semi-structured interviews. The semi-structured interviews with three female and three male Greek physicians took place in Germany between June 2014 and August 2015. All the interviewees are persons who came to Germany after 2010 and were between 28 and 35 years old at the time of

the interviews. These data will explain the subjective factors crucial in the decision to leave Greece in the first place (push factor), as well as those subjective factors that were decisive for choosing the German health sector as the favored working environment for undergoing medical specialization training (pull factors). The interview findings will be presented thematically and according to these two categories with the help of quotations from the interviewees.

The presentation of the findings will also follow this sequence, beginning with the statistical data on the workforce of physicians in both countries, and continuing with the analysis of both health sectors, in regard to their organization and the key actors responsible for planning the workforce of the health sectors. Last but not least, the subjective motivations for the migration from Greece to Germany according to the interviews will be presented in the last part of the findings in order to draw the final conclusions of this article.

Some Empirical Findings About the Physicians' Manpower in Both Health Systems

The remarkably high density of physicians in Greece is being translated into 68,807 physicians in total numbers during 2014. Those practicing in Attica represent 48.5%, indicating that this high density and the alleged oversupply of physicians does not affect the entire country, but primarily the metropolitan region of Athens. Table 1 presents the growth in numbers of physicians in the Greek health sector from 2002 to 2014. It is remarkable that their percentage development between 2002 and 2010 was 37.6%. The total number of

---

[2] Taking into account the protection of the personal data of interviewees, it was deemed necessary to use code names to assure the participants' anonymity.

the physicians in Greece appears to have stabilized between 2010 and 2011, and after this period began to decrease. Although it is hard to pinpoint the exact reasons for this decrease, it can be assumed that some discouraging facts engendered this trend, such as the measure for limited hiring in the public sector,[3] the presence of an overage of physicians, multiple retirements, and emigration.

The migration of Greek physicians into the German health system can be verified by their increase in total numbers since 2003, according to data from the German Medical Association, as shown in Table 2. It can be observed that from 2008 to 2013, the change in percentage over the previous years has always been more than 8.2%, while the increase was most noticeable between the years 2011 and 2013.

Furthermore, while the significant increase after 2008 coincides with the outbreak of the financial crisis, the deceleration of this increase in the numbers of Greek physicians after 2014 is an unexpected significant development. Additionally, the increase of Greek physicians in the years before the financial crisis cannot be underestimated. This fact supports the view that the reasons for medical migration from Greece to Germany require further research and cannot be exclusively reduced to the effects of the financial crisis.

The presence of Greek physicians in the German health sector arouses interest because they formed the second biggest group of foreign physicians in Germany in 2015. Furthermore, it appears that EU institutions play a very important role in this phenomenon of migration to Germany,

Table 1

Physicians in Greece in Numbers (2002–14)

	Total Number	Change Over the Previous Year in Percent
2002	50,347	—
2003	52,226	3.7
2004	53,943	3.3
2005	55,556	2.3
2006	59,599	7.3
2007	62,207	4.4
2008	67,795	9.0
2009	69,030	1.8
2010	69,265	0.03
2011	69,435	0.02
2012	69,125	-0.04
2013	68,886	-0.03
2014	68,807	-0.01

Source: Greek Statistical Authority, physicians and dentists, 2014 (in Greek).

---

[3] See the section "Overview of the Greek Health System."

Table 2

Greek Physicians in the German Health System in Numbers (2003–15)

	Total Number	Change Over the Previous Year in Percent
2003	1,162	7.3
2004	1,265	8.8
2005	1,357	7.2
2006	1,453	7.1
2007	1,554	7.0
2008	1,708	9.9
2009	1,863	9.1
2010	2,016	8.2
2011	2,224	10.3
2012	2,556	14.9
2013	2,847	11.4
2014	3,011	5.8
2015	3,017	0.2

Source: Bundesärztekammer (2003–2015).

Table 3

Foreign Physicians in the German Health Sector During 2015

	Origin Country	Total Number
1.	Romania	4,062
2.	Greece	3,017
3.	Austria	2,573
4.	Russia	2,149
5.	Syria	2,149
6.	Poland	1,987
7.	Hungary	1,666
8.	Syria	1,156
9.	Bulgaria	1,554
10.	Iran	1,295

Source: Bundesärztekammer (2015a).

as six EU countries represent the main sources for the filling of medical vacancies in the German health sector, as the Table 3 demonstrates.

Despite the significant migration of foreign physicians into the German health sector, this sector faces a notable trend of physicians' emigration due to economic reasons, as well as reasons related to physician working conditions (Kopetsch 2008, A-716). During 2015, the main destinations for physicians emigrating from the German health sector were the neighboring countries of Switzerland (629 physicians) and Austria (264 physicians). Table 4 shows the top five destination countries for emigrated physicians from Germany. As expected, the US and British health sectors also prove decidedly

Table 4

Emigration of Physicians from Germany in 2015

	Destination Country	Total Number	With German Nationality
1.	Switzerland	629	516
2.	Austria	264	89
3.	United States	104	83
4.	Greece	86	7
5.	United Kingdom	62	45
Total		2,143	1,251

Source: Bundesärztekammer (2015b)

attractive due to high salaries. However, the presence of Greece in this list is certainly also noteworthy. Nevertheless, of the 86 physicians that migrated to Greece, just seven of them held German citizenship; thus it appears a large portion of Greek physicians in the German health sector return to their home country after a number of years, or after completing medical specialization training.

The Health Sectors as Dynamic Fields for the Migration of Physicians

As already explained in the theoretical part of this article, the health sectors of both countries must be analyzed. In the following, the German health system, which is structured according to framework of the Bismarck model, will be presented first, followed by the Greek health system, the organization of which has characteristics typical of both the Bismarck model and of the Beveridge model.

Overview of the German Health System

Since 1883, when the Imperial Chancellor and Prussian Prime Minister, Otto von Bismarck, introduced a national system of social programs and health insurance, the German health sector has possessed characteristics of the so-called Bismarckian system, mainly based economically on the social security contributions of employers and employees. Since its establishment, the German health system has kept its corporatist elements, such as the participation of some privileged central interest groups in the formulation and implementation of the health policy (Bandelow 2004, 49).

Finance, Organization. In accordance with the structuring of the German state, the health sector in Germany has also adopted federal elements. This means that the coordination and management of the health sector is diffused, but clearly allocated to different levels. While the government legislates and sets the strategies for health care policy, mainly through the Ministry of Health (MoH), the federal states are responsible for the strategy and funding of hospital care services. Meanwhile, other self-ruling actors—on the one hand, the statutory health insurance companies as the main payers of health services in Germany, on the other, basically the resident physicians through their regional association of Social Health Insurance (SHI) Physicians (KVen)—are authorized to inform health policy, regulate quality standards for patients in the German health sector, and additionally to allocate funding into health services of the statutory health insurance (GKV).

Although the federal government of Germany appears theoretically to be the main policymaker and therefore the main actor of the German health sector, the fact that the health services in Germany are basically financed by social security contributions, bypasses the possibility of direct state interference in financial terms (Hoesch 2012, 9). However, the statutory health insurance (GKV) receives extra financing sources besides social security contributions, such as grants through taxation from the federal states and federal government.

Today, the basis of the German health sector—the statutory health

(GKV-*Spitzenverband*). In comparison to years prior, the number of health insurance companies in Germany has been reduced, mainly due to the implementation of an act to strengthen competition in SHI (GKV-*Wettbewerbstärkungsgestz*), which basically standardized a universal contribution rate, introduced the central reallocation pool (the so-called health fund), and allows each health insurance company to "match allocations and expenditures by either charging a supplementary community-rated premium from their insured or paying them back a certain amount" (Busse and Blümel 2014, 39). As a consequence of this implementation, many health insurance companies with additional contributions suffered heavy losses in membership (Schölkopf and Pressel 2014, 56). In Germany, insured persons have been able to choose their health insurance company freely and without limitation since 2009,

Figure 1: Health expenditure and financing in Germany (per capita, current prices in Euros) for the years 2009–14.

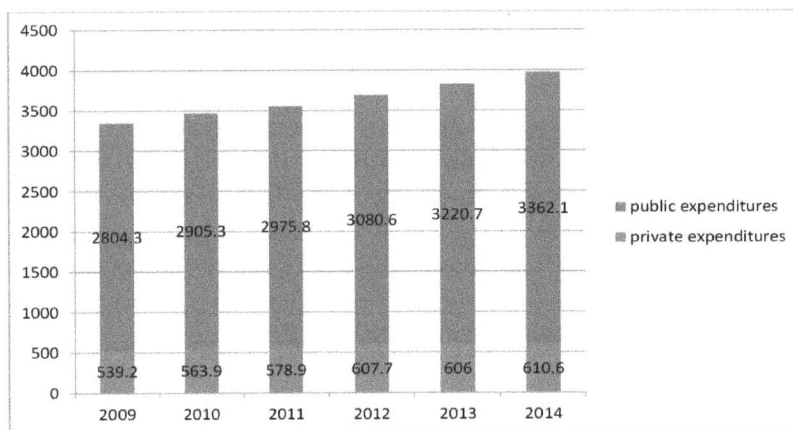

insurance (GKV) on which 90% of the German population is insured—is organized into 118 health insurance companies and has been represented within the system of joint self-ruling since 2009 by the federal association of insurance funds

but every employee with a monthly salary not exceeding the upper wage threshold (*Versicherungspflichtgrenze*) is obliged to be insured in the GKV.

This organization of the German health system described here guaranteed increasing health expenditures in Germany over the last several years, as the following Figure 1 demonstrates (OECD Health Statistics 2016). The majority of expenditures originate from public sources, although private expenditures are also on the rise, as the following table demonstrates.

Key Actors of the Health System in Germany. One very characteristic element of the German health system is the framing of the state actors, despite their central role in the health policy, by corporate elements and self-ruling organizations, as already explained. The most representative element is the dominant role of physician associations in Germany. First of all, the regional associations of SHI physicians distribute the remuneration from health insurance companies to their members. Apart from that, like the GKV organizations, the physician associations are able to influence legislation about health politics in preliminary stages (Wendt 2003, 110).

Furthermore, these groups of physicians have a privileged double function as recognized public bodies, especially as long as they participate in the federal joint committee (*Gemeinsamer Bundesausschuss*) through the association of SHI physicians, as well as through their federal associations into the federal association of insurance funds (GKV-*Spitzenverband*), but also as independent organizations, a practice which has secured strong influence in the formulation of health policies (Bandelow 2004, 52). This occurs due to their double representation and organization into self-ruling and corporatism—every licensed doctor is automatically a member of a chamber. At the same time, every SHI physician is also a member of his regional association of SHI physicians (KV). This fact endows these bodies with power, due not only to the numerous memberships of the physicians, but also financial security through the compulsory membership fees. (Hoesch 2012, 12).

The multidimensional and dominant role of physician associations can also be detected in the manpower configuration of the German health sector, especially regarding the current number of practicing physicians. In 1992, a reform concerning the introduction of a capped budget and a maximum number of doctors in the ambulant sector caused a strong reaction from physicians, who via lobbying had achieved a reduction in training capacities and access to medical schools in that same year by 22% (ibid., 13–14). According to Hoesch's research, this development and the reaction of the organized interest of physicians can be considered a very crucial moment for the current "looming shortages" because its effects on the number of practicing physicians in Germany were still felt 10-12 years later (ibid., 18).

One field where the role of an actor is also highly relevant to the case of medical graduates' migration is the issuing of professional licenses and the recognition of qualifications. Regarding the latter issue, Greek physicians in Germany have the privilege of facing fewer problems compared to their colleagues from non-EU countries, having the right to receive a full license while also having their qualifications automatically recognized. Seventeen medical chambers in Germany are responsible for recognition of specialist training, showing the connection of the physician associations in this field. Moreover, every federal state sets different norms and criteria about the issuing of professional licenses. Physician associations cannot be involved directly in these procedures, but they can indirectly influence the procedures of granting licences via lobbying and consultations (ibid.,19). This could explain the fact that the criteria for issuing licences to foreign medical graduates have become harder in some regions, like in North Rhine-Westphalia since 2010, where knowledge tests have been listed as requirements for the granting of a medical license.

Overview of the Greek Health System

The Greek health system was at the heart of great structural reforms in recent years. However, its main feature—centralization—has stayed intact. The following will concentrate on the organization and the financial funding of the Greek health system, while clarifying the identity of its key actors, whose actions impact the motives behind emigration from Greece.

Finance, Organization. In light of different typologies, the Greek health system cannot simply be classified into a definite category due to its unique characteristics (Wendt 2013, 203). Greece has a unified national health system (ESY), but its financing through public sources like taxation is also augmented by financing through contributions in social health insurance. This means that the Greek health system combines elements of both the Bismarck and the Beveridge systems.

Despite this mixed model, the state remains the main actor in the Greek health sector. Its dominant role is also evident in the Greek constitution, which defines the Greek state as responsible for the health of its citizens (Article 21 §3, The Constitution of Greece). State involvement in the health sector is materialized by different government institutions; for example through the Ministry of Finance, which defines the amount of monthly insurance fees; the Ministry of Labor, Social Insurance and Social Solidarity, which issues physician licenses; but mainly through the Ministry of Health, which implements and plans the health policy, organizes the health personnel in public units, and edits the lists for medical specialization training at public hospitals.

Until 2011, social health insurance in Greece included over 30 different health insurance companies, which provided health coverage and primary, secondary, and pharmaceutical care for almost 100% of the population. Nowadays, the social health insurance consists of just one unified social health company, known as EOPYY, which was established as a proposed reform measure by the Troika (Niakas 2013, 598). Although EOPYY is officially autonomous, it is in fact dependent upon the state, economically as well as administratively, because it is financed by it in the occurrence of deficits, and the government also appoints its directors.

During the period prior to the crisis, the health sector in Greece was facing several structural problems due to strong centralization in decision-making, which was also creating a lack of planning and coordination between the decision center and the health services. Additionally, some economic problems were also evident, like unequal and inefficient allocation of human and economic resources, high out-of-pocket payments, and phenomena of the black economy (Economou et al. 2014, 7–8). It was these kinds of malfunctions within the health sector that led to structural reforms and austerity measures, combined with the conclusion of the Troika government that health-related expenditures until 2009 were unacceptably high in correlation with the national GDP (Katelidou et al. 2016, 112). It is important to list these reforms not only because they kept the centralization of the Greek health sector stable, but also because they directly influenced the health sector's manpower. First of all, the salaries of health personnel had decreased by 12% in January 2010 and a further 8% in June 2010. Besides that, the horizontal cuts of the real wage of the health personnel, due to the tax increases, should also be taken into consideration. A "special salary system" was introduced for physicians, which contributed to a decrease in their salaries (Economou et al. 2014, 22). Furthermore, for the purpose of reducing general public expenditures, the measure for limited hiring in the entire public sector and therefore into the health sector was also introduced. According to this measure, for every five people retiring out of the system, only

one can enter employment. Additionally, a series of reductions in costs for hospital supplies was also implemented. These reductions refer not only to services like cleaning, catering, and security services, but also to cuts in hospital supplies, medical and technological staff, as well as pharmaceutical and chemical reagents. Austerity also affected the hospital sector, which was restructured by reducing the number of public hospital beds and also the number of clinics and specialist units (ibid., 19).

These measures were mainly intended to contribute to the fiscal consolidation of the Greek economy, but also to the fragmentation of the function and the financing of the health sector. Despite this, some malfunctions of the Greek health sector have remained intact, such as the black economy, corruption, and high out-of-pocket payments, which have been also increased from 2009 to 2012 (ibid.,14). The effects of these reforms on

Figure 2: Health expenditure and financing in Greece (per capita, current prices in Euros) for the years 2009–14.

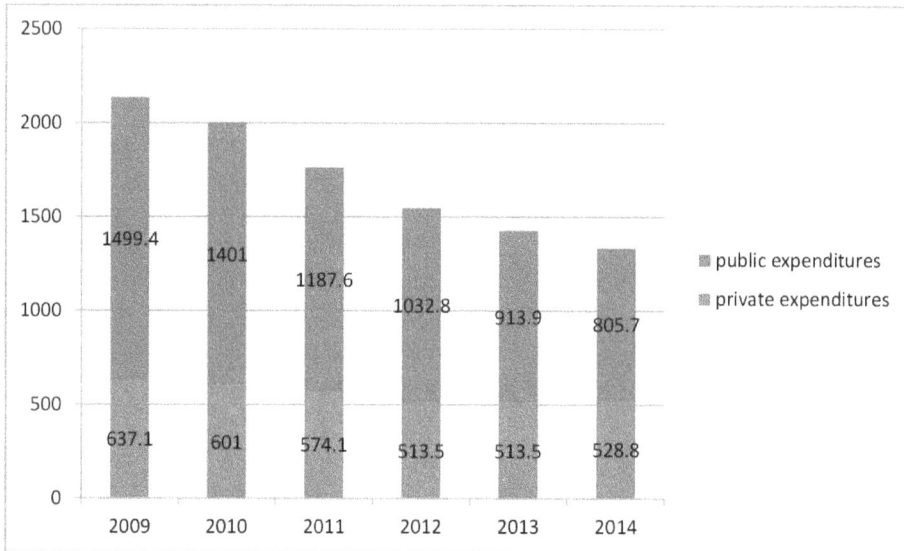

Greek health expenditures are illustrated in Figure 2 (OECD Health Statistics, 2016), which shows the health expenditures per capita and in current prices in Euros. The total reduction of health expenditures in Greece has been stable every year from 2009 to 2014, but the big reduction of public expenditures through these years (€-693.7 from 2009 to 2014) in comparison to the reduction of the private expenditures for the health (just €-108.3 for the same years) is remarkable.

Key Actors in the Health System of Greece. One goal of the reforms of the health sector during the crisis years in Greece was the decentralization of it. However, this goal has not been achieved and the state remains the dominant actor in the health care system, whichh is still characterized by strong centralization (Economou et al. 2014, 19). The state is the center of political decisions for the health system and controls the formation of its manpower, as already mentioned, through the Ministry of Health—which plans the personnel in public health services and edits the lists for the medical specialization trainings at the public hospitals—and also through the Ministry of Social Insurance and Social Solidarity, by issuing the physicians' licences. Even the issue of the number of medical students in Greek universities is the responsibility of the Ministry of Education, Research and Religious Affairs, which defines how many students can be enrolled in each medical school annually. These fields concern the manpower of the public health sector, and therefore they are important and relevant fields for the research of this migration case.

The dominance of the state in Greece provides no space for the physicians' bodies in the field of decision-making for the health sector. Although every physician in

Greece should be a member of his regional physician chamber, only the Panhellenic Medical Association and the Athenian Medical Association have a consultant role in the Ministry of Health (Economou 2010, 36). This fact forced the physicians' chambers to take on the role of veto-player in the Greek political field. The physicians' workforce has been the most important actor in blocking governmental reforms concerning the health sector in comparison to other medical health personnel by defending their interests (Mosialos and Allin 2005, 431).

Subjective Motivations Leading to Emigration from Greece

In the following passage the subjective motivations of the interviewed physicians that forced them to leave the country (push factors) will be presented as they were expressed during the interviews.

After graduation from a medical school in Greece, the interviewees, like every graduate of medical school, are supposed to complete their specialization training. This requirement appears to be a crucial factor in their decision to migrate, because at the same time the Greek public hospitals could not provide sufficient vacancies for medical specialization training. Therefore, the medical graduates, after their application for medical specialization training in the Greek health sector, would be registered and put on a waiting list. However, the waiting period varied from one hospital to another, depending on the number of applications received for the training and the existing medical personnel in specific medical specializations.[4] Almost all the interviewees stated that the main reason for the decision to leave Greece was the waiting time for medical specialist training, which also involves significant time unemployed. One physician[5] explained her motivations to leave Greece: "If I would have stayed in Greece, I would have been able to start with my medical specialization training in cardiology in 2013, although I took my degree in 2008. [. . .] I preferred to come to Germany and perform my specialist training here, instead of waiting for 6 years in Greece. The reason for my migration was mainly the long period of waiting." Consequently, in reference to the approach of Pissarides and Wadsworth, the unemployment situation for medical school graduates, due to the long waiting period for the specialization training in the Greek health sector, appears to be the main factor that led the interviewees to emigration from Greece.

Another decisive factor leading Greek physicians to emigration can be traced back to the unattractive working conditions in the Greek public hospitals. Although this factor is not relevant to economic motivations, it is nonetheless related to the current professional career of the interviewees, who are expecting well-structured working conditions in order to undergo qualitative specialization training. It can be argued that the dysfunctions in the Greek public hospitals have an impact on their decision to leave, especially as long as these dysfunctions are affecting the working environment. These factors were mentioned mostly by physicians who had their first work experiences during the financial crisis years

in Greek public hospitals. Another female physician[6] explained her main motivations for leaving Greece as such: "The working conditions forced me not to stay in Greece, and of course also the issue of the specialist training. I am talking mainly about the shortages in technology and in medical material. For example, at my hospital, there was no computed tomography." Besides that, another relevant factor mentioned during the interviews affected the shortages of medical personnel. Regarding this, one physician[7] emphasized the following: "Currently in Greece, I would not be able to learn something during a possible specialization training there, because, as I have experienced it, there is a huge trend in the migration of specialist physicians and big shortages of medical staff." These shortages contribute also to the worsening of training quality and they are causing overtime hours, making the working conditions in the Greek health sector for new physicians even more unattractive.

However, the low-income earnings of physicians in Greece in comparison to the high-income opportunities in the German health sector[8] obviously played a secondary role as a factor driving young physicians away from Greece. Just one physician[9] out of the six interviewees mentioned this aspect of motivation: "Certainly the income opportunities in Greece played a secondary role. The most important thing was the waiting period and the waiting list before the admission into

---

[4] However, the waiting time for specialization training nowadays has been strongly reduced and in some cases eliminated. It is assumed that the one factor for this development was the massive emigration of the medical graduates from Greece in order to undergo their specialization training. The waiting lists for specialist training remain mostly in some central hospitals in Athens and in some specific medical specializations, such as dermatology. The interviews conducted with the physicians in Germany for the purpose of the present article took place in 2014 and 2015. The most persons came to Germany in the period between 2010 and 2013 and they could not comment on these new developments in the Greek health sector, which I was able to confirm in the interviews conducted with medical graduates in Greece in 2015 and 2016.
[5] Interview W1.
[6] Interview W2.

the medical specialization training in a Greek hospital. Otherwise, unemployment means also no money, right? But I mean it was not an issue of income."

Furthermore, the physicians mentioned one more apparent secondary factor during the interviews: the experience with corruption phenomena in Greece. Except from experiences in the health sector, the interviewees had also personal experiences with corrupt civil servants, nepotism and clientelism in Greek society, as well as in different sectors (education, health, and public services).

Subjective Motivations Leading to Immigration to Germany

Having presented the main subjective motivations driving the medical graduates away from Greece, this section will give an overview of the subjective factors, which were decisive for the migration of the interviewees to Germany (pull factors).

As expected, in accordance with the main push factor of the Greek medical graduates about the limited employment opportunities in the Greek health sector, their motivations for choosing the German health sector are also connected to job-related factors. Those interviewed considered the German health sector to be a very stable labor market, which can guarantee them the opportunity of gaining admission into medical specialization training. For example, a physician,[10] who underwent her medical specialization

training spoke about her motivations to work in Germany: "I came to Germany because I knew that its health sector has shortages of specialist physicians and the issue to start with the training was going to be simple for me." Apart from the aspect relating to the available vacancies in the German health sector, one interviewee[11] expressed another opinion on this issue, which focuses on the system of employment in the German health system for a medical specialization training. "In Germany, you do not have a procedure of having exams in order to start your medical specialization training, like in France. In Germany and in Scandinavian countries, the director of a hospital can decide after one interview if he will employ you or not. So I think the issue of choosing the destination country was about the extent of the labor market, the system of employment for medical specialization training and having good knowledge of the language."

Obviously, the employment opportunities in the German health sector are presented as important factors by most of the interviewed Greek physicians. However, there are also other job-related factors concerning the training stage of the physicians. The quality of the specialization training in the German health sector, which includes highly technological equipment, has been positively evaluated by some, who mentioned this factor, too, as a reason for their decision to migrate. A similar argument is expressed in the following statement from a physician[12]: "The level of training in dermatology in Germany is much better than the training in Greece. While

---

[8] According to the interviewees a physician who undertakes specialist medical training in Greece gains net €1,027 monthly, while in Germany, although this depends on the hospital, the monthly wage is at least gross €4,100.
[9] Interview M1.
[10] Interview W3.
[11] Interview M2.

in Greece, the training in dermatology alone lasts three years; the same training in Germany lasts five years. Therefore, the dermatology training in Germany has a good level of quality, which includes also training in immunology. So I can say that I took this high level of training for my medical specialization training in Germany into consideration too."

Regarding the health sector in Germany, these two factors can be considered as the most important for the migrated Greek physicians in the German health sector. The income opportunities appear to play an unimportant role with respect to the pull factor of the German health sector, because none of the interviewed Greek physicians mentioned this factor as a subjective decisive motivation for migrating to Germany. However, other factors, which are indirectly connected to the health sector, appear to be very crucial for this case of migration, especially on the social level. The presence of the pioneer migrants from Greece in the German health sector has a significant impact, as it was stated by the majority of the interviewed physicians. These Greek physicians who first migrated play a key role in the migration of other colleagues, as they provided them important information about the labor market in Germany, the application procedure for training in a German hospital, and also the procedures of the recognition of qualifications or the issuing of a license. One physician[13] emphasized this point: "I had many friends here working in the German health sector. They could tell me a lot of things concerning the bureaucratic

issues, like how to obtain a license, to which hospitals I should apply and so on. I was very well informed about the situation here and this helped me a lot to make my decision to come to Germany." In other cases, prior experiences in Germany, such as the participation in the Erasmus program at a German medical university, contributed also to gaining access to collegial networks there.[14]

Furthermore, other pull factors, which are partly classic migration motivations of highly skilled migrants and do not have direct relevance with the health sector, were mentioned during the interviews, too. For example, the factor of gaining working experiences abroad is considered to be a quality addition to a curriculum vitae.[15] Quality of life in Germany is another factor that reinforces the motivation for a migrant.[16] Furthermore, possessing German language skills is a necessary requirement for better opportunities in the health sector labor market. For most of the interviewees, this skill, especially prior to their residence in Germany, was one additional motivation for choosing Germany as destination country.

Discussion and Conclusions

All in all, the present article intended to highlight and explain the current migration trends of Greek physicians undergoing their medical specialization training in Germany by focusing on the health structures of both countries and by also taking into consideration their subjective motivation for the decision to emigrate. Finally, this migration case can be presented as

---

[12] Interview M2.
[13] Interview W3
[14] The case of interveiw M1.
[15] The cases of interviews M1, M2, M3.
[16] The cases of interviews W1, W2, W3.

a consequence of the interactions of the main actors in the health structures of both countries, especially in the field of planning the physicians' workforce, in connection with the subjective motivations of the physicians.

Regarding the main factors for the migration of Greek physicians to Germany in the context of their medical specialization training, the obvious first point was the limited available vacancies or opportunities in the Greek health system. In parallel to this push factor, the most attractive pull factor for the interviewees was the simplicity of the procedure of finding a vacancy in the German health sector for the medical specialization training, i.e., the employment system in a hospital and the numerous available vacancies. Furthermore, these dominant subjective factors can only partially verify the statements of the neoclassical economic approaches. The interviewees seem to strongly take into consideration the employment opportunities mainly in the country of origin (approach of Pissarides and Wadsworth) and those in the destination country (approaches of Todaro, Sjaastad, Pissarides, and Wadsworth), but they do not really take into consideration the income differentiation between the two health sectors. Besides that, and in connection with the neoclassical economic approaches, their personal qualifications are obviously very important for choosing Germany as a destination country, focusing not only on their medical degrees, but also on their German language skills. Also, the existing collegial social networks between the interviewees with the pioneer migrants of this migration case are certainly a very important aspect of this migration

phenomenon, which is also likely going to play a key role in the perpetuation of this medical migration flow from Greece to Germany.

However, it appears that the phenomenon is developing new aspects over the years. First, the phenomenon cannot be directly linked with the financial crisis. The statistics indicate that the migration of Greek physicians to Germany was already beginning to be reinforced before the outbreak of the financial crisis. Furthermore, the interviewees confirmed that the waiting lists for medical specialization training in Greek hospitals, before the application of austerity measures in the national health system, were displaying extremely long waiting times[17] —a fact that cannot be verified at present, 6 years after the beginning of crisis. Nevertheless, two interviewees[18] with working experience in the Greek health sector who came to Germany after 2012, claimed that they suffered from severe shortages of both materials and specialist physicians. Of course this situation has an impact on the working conditions and quality of the medical specialization training period of a young physician. This factor is expected to be further an important push factor for the emigrated physicians, as a consequence of the implemented austerity measures in the Greek health sector during the financial crisis. Consequently, it can be stated that the migration of physicians from Greece is being basically driven by the poor conditions in the national health sector (unattractive labor market, working conditions, low technological level). Therefore, possible destinations for them would be states, which provide better

---

[17] In many cases the waiting time affected a time of over 8 years.
[18] Interviews with the codes W2 and M3.

working conditions in their welfare sectors, like Germany or USA.

Furthermore, by analyzing the structures and key actors of both health systems, it was possible to demonstrate a direct connection between the key actors, who affect the labor markets and contribute to the described inequities between both health systems, and this case of migration. Being heavily dependent on public funding, the Greek health sector is very centralized and the state is its dominant actor that concentrates all important, decision-making powers, and which also plans the development of the workforce in the health sector without considerable involvement of the physicians' organizations. Therefore, the state can be also considered the main culprit for the alleged oversupply of physicians in Greece linked with the remarkable physician density. However, the Greek health sector faces geographical disparities regarding the distribution of physicians, while at the same time the described problems with the waiting lists for medical specialization training in many Greek hospitals were also noticed. Especially important for this case is the fact that the state's responsibilities not only include the granting of the lists for the medical specialization trainings, but also regulating the number of new entrances in Greek medical schools on an annual basis. Regarding the huge problem with the waiting lists, it can be stated that there is a historical[19] disproportion, which continues to the present, between the outflows of the medical schools in Greece and the physicians' manpower needs of the health sector. In any case, bad planning for the workforce in the Greek health sector has already been defined as a problem

(Ifanti et al. 2014, 213). On the contrary, the Bismarckian German health system is characterized by its corporatist elements and the power of self-ruling groups, giving important privileges to the interest groups of physicians. Through these privileges the physicians' associations not only contributed to the so-called looming shortages in physicians, but they are also getting indirectly involved in important mandates about the present migration cases, such as by influencing the procedures for the licenses issuing through lobbying and consultation.

Nevertheless, the role of the EU, as an active supranational actor of this present case should be also considered as very important for this migration case between two member states. The most important contribution of the EU is of course the provision of the appropriate law framework for the facilitation of this migration case. According to article 45 of Treaty on the Functioning of the European Union (TFEU), Greek physicians are free as workers to move within the EU, and by virtue of the articles 26, 49 to 55, 56 to 62 of TFEU they have the freedom of establishment and the freedom to provide services in every member state. By virtue of the directive 2005/36/EU, which pertains also to physicians, qualifications, knowledge of languages and professional academic titles of them can be recognized within EU countries. In connection with the present migration case of Greek physicians in Germany, this legal framework of the EU completes the Ireadale's approach, which does not only emphasize the role of professional bodies in the welfare sectors as gatekeepers, but is also mentioning the

---

[19] Kalamatianou emphasizes that in 1989 the outflows alone of the medical school of Athens were able to refresh the physicians' workforce of ESY for the next years (1993, 182).

role of the transnational agreements for issues of recognition and for overcoming the national frontiers by the migration.

After the presentation of the article's conclusions, the need of further research on this topic seems to also be plausible. As it has already been mentioned, the phenomenon of the Greek physicians' migration to the German health sector with the intention of undergoing medical specialization training is still a work in progress. It would also be interesting if the same research did not focus exclusively on the physicians, who are practicing their medical specialization training, but also on physicians that are already specialized and have migrated to Germany, or on the potential migrants that are still in Greece and would like to migrate to Germany, for the purposes of examining and comparing their motivations with those of their migrated colleagues in the German health sector. Also, the comparison between migration cases of other physicians from EU countries in Germany with different health structures, like the Romanian case, would be of interest for migration studies and the research of health policy systems.

Other aspects concerning the effects of this phenomenon and the role of the EU are also worthy of further research. The EU was not only directly involved in this migration case through the provision of the legal framework, but also indirectly through its participation in the Troika, which also imposed austerity measures on the Greek health sector. While the German health sector gains medical personnel, the Greek health sector faces a loss of its trained physicians, indicating a case of brain drain. This migration case takes place in an area, which provides the possibility of free movement, establishment, and working activity, while every country is at the same time still responsible for funding and organizing its health sectors. This case of migration also highlights the dangers that arise within the EU regarding the distributions of physicians throughout the member states, due to unequal conditions of competition for health workers between richer and poorer health systems. This aspect should be considered a topic for the researchers, by especially focusing on the creation of possibilities for the financially weak national health sectors to transform the existing brain drain phenomena into brain gain within the EU.

Acknowledgments

The work presented in this article has been undertaken in the context of my extended research for my PhD thesis. I am grateful to Dr. Uwe Hunger for the constructive discussion and his valuable advice, but also to Dr. Leandros Fischer and to Sotirios Karampampas for their feedback and their ideas, which encourage me to write this article.

References

Bach, Stephen. 2003. "International Migration of Health Workers: Labour and Social Issues." *International Labour Office, Sectoral Activities Programme Working Paper No. 209*. Geneva: International Labour Office.

Bandelow, Nils C. 2004. "Akteure und Interessen in der Gesundheitspolitik: Vom Korporatismus zum Pluralismus?" *Politische Bildung* 37 (2): 49–63.

Bank of Greece. 2016. *Board's Report for the Year 2015*. [In Greek] Athens: Bank of Greece.

Bommes, Michael, Hoesch Kirsten, Hunger Uwe, and Kolb Holger. 2004. "Organisational Recruitment and Patterns of Migration. Interdependencies in an Integrating Europe." *IMIS-Beiträge Special Issue 25*. Osnabrück.

Bundesärztekammer. 2003–2015. *Ausländische Ärztinnen und Ärzte. Ärztestatistik der Vorjahre.* http://www.bundesaerztekammer.de/ueber-uns/aerztestatistik/aerztestatistik-der-vorjahre/ (accessed August 12, 2016).

Bundesärtzekammer. 2015a. *Ausländische Ärztinnen und Ärzte.* http://www.bundesaerztekammer.de/ueber-uns/aerztestatistik/aerztestatistik-2015/auslaendische-aerztinnen-und-aerzte/ (accessed August 12, 2016).

Bundesärztekammer. 2015b. *Abwanderung von Ärzten ins Ausland.* http://www.bundesaerztekammer.de/ueber-uns/aerztestatistik/aerztestatistik-2015/abwanderung-von-aerzten-ins-ausland/ (accessed August 12, 2016).

Busse, Reinhard, and Miriam Blümel. 2014. "Germany: Health System Review." *Health Systems in Transition* 16 (2): 1–296.

Clark, Darlene, Paul F. Clark, and James Stewart. 2007. "Migration and Recruitment of Healthcare Professionals: Causes, Consequences and Policy Responses." *Focus Migration, Policy Brief No. 7*. http://focus-migration.hwwi.de/The-Migration-and-Re.2496.0.html?&L=1 (accessed August 12, 2016).

Economou, Charalambos. 2010. "Greece: Health System Review." *Health Systems in Transition* 12 (7): 1–180.

Economou, Charalampos, Daphne Kaitelidou, Alexander Kentikelenis, Aris Sissouras, and Anna Maresso. 2014. *The Impact of the Financial Crisis on the Health System and Health in Greece.* Copenhagen: WHO Regional Office for Europe on behalf of the European Observatory on Health Systems and Policies.

European Commission. 2012. *Commission Staff Working Document on an Action Plan for the EU Health Workforce*, SWD (2012) 93. Strasbourg. European Commission.

EUROSTAT. 2015. "Proportion of Population Aged 65 and over % of Total Population." http://ec.europa.eu/eurostat/tgm/table.

Gkolfinopoulos, Andreas. 2016. "Kapital- und Brain-Drain in Griechenland: Ein Phänomen der Krise?" In *Griechenland im europäischen Kontext: Krise und Krisendiskurse*, eds. Agridopoulos Aristotelis and Papagiannopoulos Ilias. Wiesbaden: Springer VS, 159–75.

Greek Statistical Authority (EL.STAT.). 2014. "Physicians and Dentists" [In Greek]. http://www.statistics.gr/el/statistics/-/publication/SHE09/- (accessed August 12, 2016).

Hoesch, Kirsten. 2009. *Was bewegt Mediziner? Die Migration von Ärzten und Pflegepersonal nach Deutschland und Großbritannien.* Berlin: LIT Verlag.

Hoesch, Kirsten. 2012. "Migrant Britain, Sustainable Germany: Explaining Differences in the International Migration of Health Professionals." *Centre on Migration, Policy and Society*: WP-12–99.

Ifanti, Amalia, Andreas Argyriou, Foteini Kalofonou, and Haralabos Kalofonos. 2014. "Physicians' Brain Drain in Greece: A Perspective on the Reasons Why and How to Address It." *Health Policy* 117 (2014): 210–15.

Iredale, Robyn. 2001. "The Migration of Professionals: Theories and Typologies." *International Migration* 39 (5): 7–26.

IS Athens. 2016: "Visit of the Panhellenic Medical Association's Director Michail Vlastarakos in Messinia." [In Greek] http://www.isathens.gr/pis/6096-episkepsi-proedrou-pis-messinia.html (accessed August 12, 2016).

Kalamatianou, Aglaia. 1993. *The Outflow of Graduated Physicians from the Greek Universities and Their Employment in the National Health System. A Statistical Approach* [In Greek]. Athens: Papazisi.

Katelidou, Daphne, Maria Katharaki, Maria Kalogeropoulou, Charalambos Economou, Olga Siskou, Kyriakos Souliotis, Konstantinos Tsavalias, and

Lycourgos Liaropoulos. 2016. "The Impact of Economic Crisis to Hospital Sector and the Efficiency of Greek Public Hospitals." *European Journal of Business and Social Sciences* 4 (10): 111–25.

Kopetsch, Thomas. 2008. "Ärztewanderung, Das Ausland lockt." *Deutsches Ärzteblatt* 105 (14): A-716–A-719.

Labiris, Georgios, Vasileia Vamvakerou, Olympia Tsolakaki, Athanassios Giarmoukakis, Haris Sideroudi, and Vassilios Kozobolis. 2014. "Perceptions of Greek Medical Students regarding Medical Profession and the Specialty Selection Process during the Economic Crisis Years." *Health Policy* 117: 203–9.

Lamprianidis, Lois. 2015. "Outward Migration from Greece During the Crisis." *The Huffington Post* [In Greek] November 2015. http://www.huffingtonpost.gr/lois-labrianidis/-_2408_b_8520596.html (accessed August 12, 2016).

Mosialos, Elias, and Sara Allin. 2005. "Interest Groups and Health System Reform in Greece." *West European Politics* 28 (2), 420–44. doi:10.1080/01402380500060460.

Mpouloutza, Penny. 2015. "The Exodus of the Physicians." *I Kathimerini* [In Greek], June 26. http://www.kathimerini.gr/825077/article/epikairothta/ygeia/h-megalh-fygh-twn-giatrwn (accessed August 12, 2016).

Niakas, Dimitris. 2013. "Greek Economic Crisis and Health Care Reforms: Correcting the Wrong Prescription." International Journal of Health Services 43 (4): 597–602.

OECD. 2009. "Geographic Distribution of Doctors." *In Health at a Glance 2009. OECD Indicators.* OECD. DOI:10.1787/health_glance-2009-63-en.

OECD. 2015: *Health at a Glance 2015*. Paris: OECD.

OECD. 2016. "OECD Health Statistics" Online data-base: http://stats.oecd.org/index.aspx?DataSetCode=HEALTH_STAT.

Pissarides, Christopher, and Jonathan Wadsworth. 1989. "Unemployment and the Inter-Regional Mobility of Labour." The Economic Journal 99 (397): 739–55.

POEDIN. 2016. "Data About the Problems of Understaffing and Underfunding in the Hospitals Edited by General Council of POEDIN." [In Greek] *POEDIN* July 4. http://www.poedhn.gr/deltia-typoy/item/1734-stoixeia-pou-epimelithikan-gs-tis-poedin-sxetika-me-ta-provlimata-ypostelexosis-kai-ypoxrimatodotisis-pou-antimetopizoun-ta-nosokomeia (accessed August 12, 2016).

Pond, Bob, and Barbara McPake. 2006. "The Health Migration Crisis: The Role of Four Organisation for Economic Cooperation and Development Countries." *The Lancet* 367 (9520): 1448–55.

Raghuram, Parvati, and Eleonore Kofman. 2002. "The State, Skilled Labour Markets, and Immigration: The Case of Doctors in England." *Environment and Planning* 34: 2071–89. DOI:10.1068/a3541.

Schölkopf, Martin, and Holger Pressel. 2014. *Das Gesundheitswesen im internationalen Vergleich. Gesundheitssystemvergleich und europäische Gesundheitspolitik.* Berlin: Medizinische Wissenschaftliche Verlagsgesellschaft (2. Auflage 2014).

Sjaastad, Larry A. 1962. "The Costs and Returns of Human Migration." *Journal of Political Economy* 70 (5): 80–93.

Todaro, Michael. 1969. "A Model of Labor Migration and Urban Unemployment in Less Developed Countries." *The American Economic Review* 59 (1): 138-148.

Triandafyllidou, Anna, and Ruby Gropas. 2014. "Voting with Their Feet: Highly Skilled Emigrants from Southern Europe." *American Behavioral Scientist* 58 (12): 1614–33.

Wendt, Claus. 2003. *Krankenversicherung oder Gesundheitsversorgung? Gesundheitssysteme im Vergleich.* Opladen: Westdeutscher Verlag.

Wendt, Claus. 2013. "Methodische Grundlagen von Gesundheitssystemvergleichen." In *Gesundheitsökonomie: Lehrbuch für Mediziner und andere Gesundheitsberufe*, eds. Karl Lauterbach, Stephanie Stock, and Helmut Brunner. Bern: Verlag Hans Huber (3. Auflage 2013), 201–13.

Schubert, Klaus, Paloma de Villota, and Johanna Kuhlmann, eds. 2016. Challenges to European Welfare States. Wiesbaden: Springer International Publishing. ISBN: 9783319076805.

doi: 10.18278/epa.2.2.10

Johanna Kuhlmann, University of Braunschweig, Germany

What happened to European Welfare Systems after the financial crisis? This book provides the first comprehensive analysis of how European Welfare Systems have developed since 2007, thereby covering not only the financial crisis, but also multiple challenges such as the demographic change and the balance of risk prevention and opening up opportunities. Single-country studies (written by national experts) are complemented with comparative chapters. The core message is that, although European Welfare Systems are facing similar challenges, they are reacting to them in different ways, thus revealing that national diversity can still be considered one of the main characteristics of European Welfare Systems.

Benz, Arthur (in cooperation with Andrea Fischer-Hotzel, Dominic Heinz, Eike-Christian Hornig, Jörg Kemmerzell, Bettina Petersohn). 2016. Constitutional Policy in Multilevel Government. The Art of Keeping the Balance. Oxford: Oxford University Press. ISBN: 9780198786078. http://ukcatalogue.oup.com/product/9780198786078.do

Arthur Benz, University of Darmstadt, Germany

The book provides the first systematic comparative analysis of constitutional policy in federal and regionalized states. In its theoretical part, it explains why constitutional reform and evolution are relevant for maintaining or restoring the balance of power between central and regional governments. Moreover, it outlines a theoretical approach to constitutional policy which is applied to nine case studies on constitutional reform. Further chapters focus on the impact of amendment rules on constitutional negotiations and on constitutional evolution in cases of failed reform. A comparative analysis identifies conditions of a successful constitutional

doi: 10.18278/epa.2.2.11

policy and a robust federal or multilevel government. The book draws attention to an aspect so far underestimated in studies on federalism and multilevel governance. It addresses dynamics of these complex political systems from a new perspective. In view of disintegrative developments in the EU and a number of nation states, but also considering over-centralization and ineffective structures in many federations, the book deals with a topical subject and suggests ways of coping with these problems.

Böcher, Michael, and Max Krott. 2016. Science Makes the World Go Round. Successful Scientific Knowledge Transfer for the Environment. Cham: Springer. ISBN: 9783319340777.

Michael Böcher and Max Krott, Georg-August-University Göttingen, Germany

Our book starts with the observation that researchers in the environmental sciences are often frustrated because political actors do not follow their advice. The book describes a new political science-based approach for scientific knowledge transfer called RIU, for Research, Integration, and Utilization. This model sees the factors needed for knowledge transfer as being state-of-the-art research and the effective, political utilization to which it leads, and it highlights the importance of "integration," which, in this context, means the active bi-directional selection of those research results that are relevant for political practice. In addition, the model underscores the importance of special political allies who are powerful actors that support the application of scientific research results in society. The book demonstrates that scientific knowledge could drive the world—but only if powerful actors support science-based political solutions and enforce other actors to use them. The analytical power of RIU is demonstrated against the background of six Austrian case studies in which scientific research results successfully influenced political decisions. Moreover, in an outlook, we describe potential cases for future RIU analyses, like the role of the IPCC for climate policy, or for diversifying responsibility for "Responsible Research and Innovation (RRI)."

doi: 10.18278/epa.2.2.12

www.ingramcontent.com/pod-product-compliance
Lightning Source LLC
Chambersburg PA
CBHW081647270326
41933CB00018B/3372